D1708814

Survival

Diary of an American POW in World War II

4/11/00

Sam Higgins

Best Wishes

Sam. Higgins

Hellgate Press

Central Point, OR

Survival: Diary of an American POW in World War II
© 1999 Samuel G. Higgins
Published by Hellgate Press

HELLGATE PRESS
P.O. Box 3727
Central Point, Oregon 97502-0032

(541) 479-9464
(541) 476-1479 fax
info@psi-research.com e-mail

Editor: Kathy Marshbank
Book designer and compositor: Constance C. Dickinson
Typesetter: Jan Olsson
Managing editor: Constance C. Dickinson
Cover designer: Steven Burns

Higgins, Samuel, 1923–
    Survival : diary of an American POW in World War II / Samuel Higgins.
      p. cm. — (Hellgate memories World War II)
    ISBN 1-55571-514-1 (pbk.)
    1. Higgins, Samuel, 1923– 2. Stalag IXB. 3. World War, 1939–1945—Prisoners and prisons, German. 4. Prisoners of war—United States—Biography. 5. Prisoners of war—Germany—Biography. I. Title. II. Hellgate memories series
D805.G3 H485 1999
940.54'7243'092—dc21   99-047431

Hellgate Press is an imprint of Publishing Services, Inc., an Oregon corporation doing business as PSI Research.

Printed and bound in the United States of America
First Edition 10 9 8 7 6 5 4 3 2 1

 Printed on recycled paper when available.

When we've no power to fight along,
Not even strength to call our own,
Thanks be to God, for it is He,
Through His Son, gives Victory.

AUTHOR UNKNOWN

Written by Pfc. Samuel G. Higgins
inside the cover of his copy of
National Publishing Company's 1942 edition
New Testament

Contents

—— ⊷⊷⊷⊷ ——

Foreword

Sam's story is for veterans, not only of Company B, but of any other unit whose men were captured and spent many miserable months (some even years) in prisoner of war camps. I know it will bring back many memories. Some will be happy, some sad, some repressed and hidden deep in the heart and soul, many freely discussed over the years.

After five days on top of Falkenberg Mountain in the Vosges mountain range, in bitter sub-freezing temperatures, digging deep into two or more feet of snow in a futile effort to keep warm, no communication with battalion, no food, there was no relief in sight. It was a bitter pill for the men of Company B, 275th Infantry, to have to surrender to the Germans. But there was no choice. The company commander was badly wounded and remained unconscious until the bitter end. The weapons platoon commander was dead, a medic was also killed, as were a number of other men.

Company B had been undergoing rigorous training for eighteen months. From June of 1943 until August of 1944 at Camp Adair, Oregon, and then at

Fort Leonard Wood, Missouri, until we entrained for Boston, Massachusetts, and boarded the transport *West Point*. After those months of hard and very realistic training, we were confident that we would make a good showing against the Germans.

And we did, even though we were thrown into our first real-war battle against an elite German mountain division recently brought from Norway. The Germans were battle veterans. We were untested, mostly eighteen- to twenty-year-olds, not really knowing the big picture. The big picture was that we were right in the middle of the path of the Nordwind, a major offensive the Germans hoped would sweep through the Vosges Mountains, completely circumvent the American forces, and even reach Rotterdam on the coast.

But we were in the way. The first battalion, 275th Infantry stood fast, and the German offensive was stalled. Company B played its part too, keeping a large enemy force surrounding us until we finally had to surrender.

Sam's story picks up the tale, recounting more than three months of misery in a prisoner of war camp. I was more fortunate. I was imprisoned in what was supposed to be a hospital.

This is Sam's story, and I repeat what I said earlier: it will bring back many memories. I hope it will be read and appreciated by every Company B man, other prisoners of war, and all those who want to remember.

William C. Schmied
Major, U.S. Army, Ret.

Preface

In August 1965, a business associate visited Stalag IXB (Nine B), located in the mountains near Bad Orb, Germany. He sent me pictures of the prison camp where I was interned. His accompanying letter said, in part, "I have opened a Pandora's box for you ... I cannot but be a little frightened that I have hurt you again after so many years of healing." I had closed the box and for forty-eight years had refused to open it. Only at the insistence of family was this Pandora's box opened.

The German army began an offensive in the Belgium-Luxembourg area in mid-December 1944 that became known as the Battle of the Bulge because of the bulge they made in the American lines along the Ardennes front. It was one of the heaviest battles fought by the Allied forces — especially by the American army. On December 27 and 28, eight German divisions were pulled out of the northern sector in the Ardennes and transported south under the cover of darkness and silence for 100 miles to the border of northern Alsace which was then under the French flag.

The U.S. Seventh Army which occupied an 84 mile line in this sector of the front was spread thin, way too thin.

One of the German divisions that moved into the area opposite the U.S. Seventh Army was the 6th SS Mountain Division which was made up of 14,000 soldiers. These hardened veterans of battles in Finland were at home in the dense, tangled woods of the mountains of Alsace and the temperatures that hovered around minus-three degrees Fahrenheit. In the falling snow, the American soldiers stood out like brown bears, while the Germans seemed invisible in their long white cloaks.

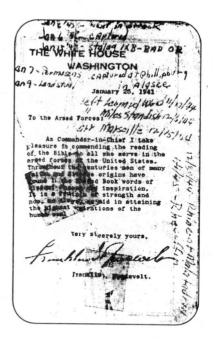

Just north of the village of Philipsbourg, France, were 800 soldiers of the 256th VG Division. Seven miles outside Philipsbourg in the village of Reichshoffen in a wire factory sat the 12 soldiers of the first squad, first platoon, B Company, 27th Infantry Regiment, 70th Division, United States Army. I was the Browning Automatic Rifleman (called a BAR) in that squad. Company B engaged the enemy on Falkenberg Ridge on the outskirts of Philipsbourg. We were overrun after one of the most intense battles of World War II, subsequently known as the Vosges Mountain Campaign. After fighting, surrounded, for 5 days in the mountains in sub-zero weather, I capitulated along with the other remaining members of Company B.

Subsequent to the harassment and a frightening interrogation, I walked thirty-six miles in three days through snow and ice in mountainous terrain with minimum clothing, to a box-car. I was confined in that 10-by-33-foot, sealed cattle car — referred to as a *forty et eight* — with 80 other POWs for the five-day trip to Bad Orb, Germany. I struggled five miles up a crooked mountain road to begin internment as a POW in the infamous Stalag IXB.

This book is historically true, based upon communications with former POW comrades and recall, while reading the short, pithy, daily entries I wrote in the margins of my New Testament. Those notes have triggered recollections of how, with quiet bravery and compassion for each other, several young American infantrymen endured loneliness, filth, and the shattering of pride and dignity as we sought to adapt to a marginal existence behind barbed wire.

Acknowledgments

⟶ ⟶ ⟵ ⟵

Many people encouraged me to reach back half a century and reconstruct the events of this book. There are a few I must mention.

Dr. Pamela Ball. She offered quiet encouragement and help in her ten-week writing course, How to Write a Novel from Life, at Florida State University.

Rodney Hosford. He busted my ego bubble with his incisive, candid edit of the original manuscript. His constant message of "describe, describe, ..." forced me to recall the events of the winter of 1944–45.

Lafayette Park Writers Group, Tallahassee, Florida. Every Thursday for five years the group contributed their expertise in fine tuning my rough drafts. The leader, Virginia Cooper, affectionately referred to as Teach, constantly said, "Write it, don't tell it." Laurie Hosford, in particular, offered constructive criticism of many small but significant details based upon her vast knowledge and experience in writing.

Bob O'Lary, computer guru of the Tally-Apply Users Group, calmed my frustrations with the computer.

Susan McNamara, editor and typist par excellence. She has a special place in my heart for her ability to take my cut-and-paste manuscript, edit and type it on a computer quickly and efficiently.

Pete House, Adjutant and Secretary of the 9A, 9B, 13B, and Berga Am Elster Association. His roster of 1,423 American soldiers interned in these prison camps and the history of Stalag IXBs conditions and facilities were invaluable in writing about my life as a POW.

Major Donald C. Pence, soldier, unsung hero and historian of the 70th Division, co-author of the book, *Ordeal in the Vosges*, the definitive source of the battles of the 275th Infantry. He constantly clarified my inquiries about the fate of B Company in the Vosges Mountain campaign.

Members of B Company, 275th Infantry, 70th Division, especially William C. Schmied, Company Commander. Some survived, some died in the battle of Falkenberg Heights, other in slave labor or prison camps. Their personal stories clarified my recall of the filth, starvation, and degradation as a prisoner of war.

My wonderful family tolerated my petulance and single-mindedness of purpose, offered encouragement, stayed out of the way, and did not delve into my prison camp experiences. Daughters Virginia and Marian taught me how to use my computer effectively and daughter Katherine answered a myriad of questions about Orthodox Judaism.

Gratitude for the quiet prodding of my wife, Bernice, cannot be adequately expressed in words. She has the innate ability to know when to listen, when to force me to relax, and when to say, "Just do it." She probably regrets suggesting five years ago that I enroll in a writing program to get "pumped up."

My sincere thanks to C. C. Dickinson, Senior Editor at Hellgate Press, who must have the eyes of a hawk. Her comprehensive editorial work spotted many inconsistencies. The precise and insightful suggestions she provided were invaluable. A yellow highlighter and small green sticky tags will always remind me of our collaborative adventure.

Missing in Action

WESTERN UNION

1201

A. N. WILLIAMS
PRESIDENT

The filing time shown in the date line on telegrams and day letters is STANDARD TIME at point of origin. Time of receipt is STANDARD TIME at point of destination

QA08

Q. WA33 44 GOVT=WASHINGTON DC 31 1133P

MRS LOUISE L PERRY=

208 KENAN AVE MOBILE ALA=

THE SECRETARY OF WAR DESIRES ME TO EXPRESS HIS DEEP REGRET
THAT YOUR NEPHEW PRIVATE FIRST CLASS SAMUEL G HIGGINS HAS
BEEN REPORTED MISSING IN ACTION SINCE EIGHT JANUARY IN
FRANCE IF FURTHER DETAILS OR OTHER INFORMATION ARE RECEIVED
YOU WILL BE PROMPTLY NOTIFIED=

J A ULIO THE ADJUTANT GENERAL..

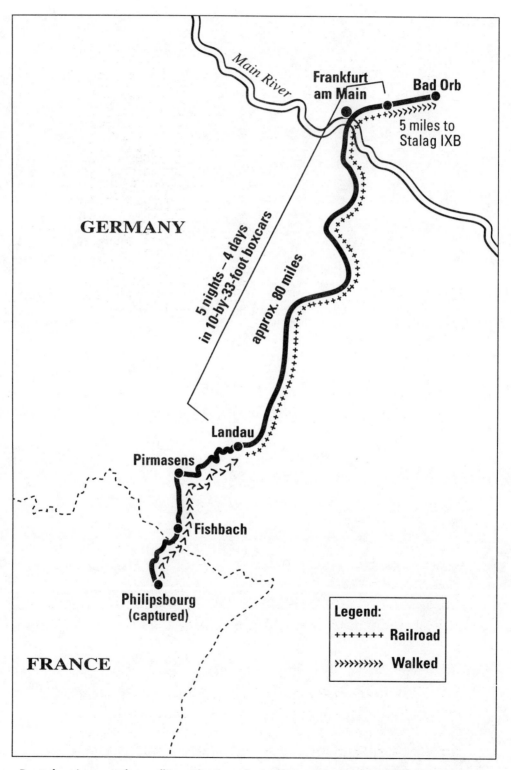

Route the prisoners took — walking, riding in cattle cars, then walking again — to the camp at Bad Orb

Chapter 1

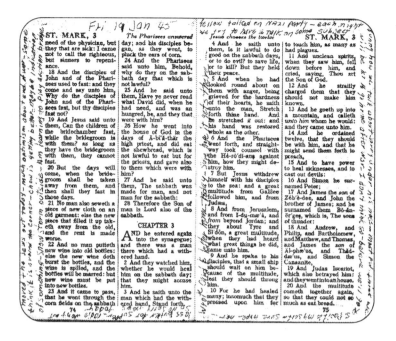

Week One

15 January–21 January 1945

·—·· ≡⧺≡ ··—·

Monday, 15 January

*Shaved for first time in three weeks — left goatee. We who live through this
should be better Christians and citizens; never should we complain again,
not after going through this. Men are trading watches for five cigarettes.
Men are smoking bark from trees; really hard-up for food.*

Tuesday, 16 January

*Father Hurley and Chaplain Neal talked to us. New camp — many other
prisoners besides Yanks; Yugo, Italians, French. Arranged ourselves in barracks; 240 men in a building 100' × 45'; two men to one straw mattress.
Two small stores. Eat in groups of six; one loaf of black bread to six men,
butter and weak tea.*

Wednesday, 17 January

Filled out Red Cross cards to notify family. Had tea for breakfast. Wrote first card home; couldn't say much. Everyone still has animal instincts in regards to food. It will be hard to get used to the morsels of food given. This is mighty depressing, there's nothing to do. Had pea soup for dinner; naturally, there was a big fuss on how to dish it out. Had accordion music — was very good. We are still pretty weak from so little food in such a long time. Everyone is still on edge and fussy. Now, 300 men in here; it's getting colder outside, and looks like a big storm is coming. Everyone thinks we'll be free by summer. I'm saying July at the latest. Sure hope it's soon!

Thursday, 18 January

Tea for break. Very cold and cloudy. Scraped our pockets for tobacco; used bark, dirt, crumbs in my pipe. Washed in cold H_2O (water), was rough. Had rice mush for dinner, best yet. Sun out for first time since we got here. Almost traded my pen for a razor, but didn't, not worth it. I sure lost weight, Bread, butter, meat & tea for supper, very small amounts. Are to take the Jews to another part of camp, not very democratic I'd say! A complaint is being made to Geneva about it. Sure is hard to just sit here all day, nothing to do; sure gets on my nerves. Traded my cig lighter for a razor and blade to Jerry. Wish I could wash my teeth.

Friday, 19 January

Moved the Jews out today. Much optimism about end of war; some think it is around the corner. The chow is getting better, maybe indicative of something. Learning to play auction bridge. Less butter for supper. Radio went out, so no Jerry news today. Fellow talked on Nazi party; each night, we try to have a talk on some subject. Funny how we talk about Jerry under his nose. Most POWs think we'll be the first to go home after the war. I don't think so; I believe we'll go to the South Pacific, myself — sure hope not. Wrote card and letter home today. Sure hope they get there.

Saturday, 20 January

My toes hurt like the deuce; so does my knee and back. Too bad we didn't get to an old POW camp. It's rough here. I'm awful homesick. Moved; seem to be feeding us better; might be an indication of something. POWs are really optimistic now, perhaps too much so. It is said that Red Cross packages are in Bad Orb. I'm very homesick; also miss my two brothers. Got 12.5 grams of bread more for supper; also had a little cheese. I never thought I'd live from day to day for a piece of bread and a little butter — it sure is hard to take. Too bad we had to get in this camp; never thought I'd live so much like an animal! My sweet tooth is worse than ever now, but my feet are beginning to thaw out at last.

Sunday, 21 January

Had a musical program last night; it was good and also passed the time away. Had mush for dinner; have meat for supper. Some say it is against international law the way we are being treated — I think so myself. Tried to get into church, but it was too crowded. I sure hope I can get home after this. I'm disgusted with the Army, and with this killing. After seeing how useless it was for Red to die, I'm ready to quit. We were really thrown away with regard to human life.

The train stops, the grayish-white light of day comes through the cracks of the boxcar. It's 15 January, 1945. Sharp, piercing, guttural shouts slice through the cracks in the boxcar. I shiver. My heart tightens with fear. I hate the German language and its harsh, incisive pitch. I hear shouts, accompanied by the stomping of boots on concrete; the jingle-jangle sounds of the equipment and other minutia that hang on the uniforms of soldiers.

Someone peeps out a crack in the side of the car and yells, "Hey, we're in a railroad station! I see civilians."

Another POW moans in a painful tone, "One of them can have my seat; I'm ready to get off. Hope he doesn't mind sitting in shit and piss."

POWs, frozen against the sides of the train, squirm to peek through the cracks. No one wants to give up his spot on the floor. If the train moves, the spot will quickly be filled by another body.

It is painful and impossible to move, with 80 men in an area 10 by 33 feet. We sit back-to-back, knees under chins, in three rows in the middle of the boxcar. Clothing is frozen to the floor, and, if we lean back, to the sides of the car. Cloth rips and ice cracks each time someone moves. We are nothing but crappy garments over bones, covered with loose-hanging skin. Not enough meat on all of us combined to fill one can of Campbell's soup. Cattle in such condition would be ignored at the Chicago stockyards.

I hear Germans talk in varying degrees of intensity. Inside the boxcar, it is silent. We lose interest after an initial look. Nothing can surprise any of us after five days of despicable, claustrophobic living. Just another day, each one a black hole of desperation.

Cattle car used to transport prisoners
On display at the Holocaust Memorial Museum and Educational Center in Maderia Beach, Florida

Gleason nudges me. "What time is it?"

I retrieve my watch from inside my shoe pac. "Looks like 0700."

I hear grunts and shouts as the Germans hit the frozen bolts with a blunt instrument. More guttural yelling; the doors slide open. Gray, misty fog enters the boxcar, accompanied by a sharp, cold breeze. I can see the peaks of mountains in the distance.

Fellman looks up and snaps, "Might have known it — mountains." He continues, "That air has a crisp, sharp, clean feeling. People pay big money to inhale this clear mountain air."

"They can have my place," I respond. "Mountain air doesn't excite me."

"Raust! Raust!" Nobody in the boxcar moves. The excrement, urine, putrid smells and frozen bodies create a sacrosanct bond. We're uncertain what awaits us on the outside. The guards grow impatient. They point guns in the door.

Damn I think, now what?

The Germans wave their arms and move their guns from side to side, screaming over and over, "Raust! Raust! Allus Raust! Schnell! Schnell!"

I know enough German to realize we'd better hustle or suffer brutal consequences. Still, we are slow to get up. It is painful. I'm stiff from sitting with my knees pulled under my chin for the past two days. Frozen uniforms crack. Finally, we stumble out of the boxcar, one by one. Some jump. I turn around and slowly lower myself to the ground.

The guards wave us across the tracks and onto a cement platform. I glance over my shoulder and quickly count five boxcars as I stumble across the tracks. Eighty men per boxcar — 400 prisoners of war. No wonder the German people laughed, jeered and hooted at the motley POWs. They thought the Fuhrer had captured the entire American army!

We line up five deep on the platform of the train station. The guards, 25 or so, wear steel helmets and carry rifles. Their uniforms are different colors; some black, others the conventional German gray. Some guards have patches over their eyes. A few guards look elderly, reminding me of my grandfather. Finally, snickers and comments like, "Hey, these guys aren't front line troops . . . they don't look too mean . . . some of them limp. Look at the different uniforms!"

A POW adds, "Yeah, but some have lightning bolts on their collars; others have SS on their sleeves. Better be careful, anyway."

Those of us from B Company, 275th Infantry, who were alive to be captured, go into what is referred to as "the shuffle." Pett, Gleason, Fellman, Cole, Smith and I get in the second row. Huckel, Strubinger, Zion and a few others get in the third row.

Pett made this suggestion the first time we had prisoner line-ups, "Always get in the middle row, in case the guards start to shoot." It became a natural movement to maneuver into the middle rank without drawing the attention of the guards. The intent is to give the impression of mass confusion by ignorant POWs. In some respects it is humorous, men stumble and bump into each other, face the wrong way, finally line up, but always in the middle rank. So far, the guards have never caught on to our slick maneuver. I guess misery has its moments of comic relief.

The guards recount once, twice, must have counted and recounted 15 times. Pett whispers, "They pick the dumbest guys to be guards. None of them can count past five."

Someone whispers we are in the village of Bad Orb. I note it is in a valley, surrounded by hills or small mountains, with stone buildings three or four stories high on each side of the street. Some of the buildings must be living quarters for residents, as I see housewives and small children looking out of the curtained windows. All of the buildings are built into or against the mountains, making it a walled city. It has openings at both ends for roads and railroad tracks. I wonder why. My curiosity is satisfied about a month later, when a German guard said the town was built with a wall around it about A.D. 1200 to protect the citizens from invaders.

I glance over my shoulder. "Hey, Huckel, how high are those mountains?"

"I'd say about 300 meters."

"Speak feet," I reply.

He sighs. "Won't you ever learn conversions, Higg? Oh, I'd say about 1,000 feet. Denver is over 5,000 feet, it's called the Mile-high City, so 1,000 feet isn't too high."

"Enough to give me a nosebleed."

Pett says, "And thin air, too; makes it hard to breathe."

Fellman jabs me in the side. "Here comes the big man. I bet he's a corporal, and I'll bet he'll speak to us in English. All German corporals speak English. That's why they get promoted."

A large German soldier with a bullhorn steps in front of the assembled POWs. "I am Corporal Gefreiter Weiss . . . ."

"See, I told you!" Fellman gleefully whispers.

". . . and I am the official interpreter for the camp in which you will be interned." He stands erect. His uniform has the formal look of a combat soldier, but his long overcoat has only the stripes of a corporal on the arms. The cap is soft and sits squarely on his head; black hair hangs over the top of his ears. He didn't have a combat helmet.

Corporal Weiss appears to be about five feet and eleven inches and weighs between 175 and 200 pounds. He wears glasses and has soft, sad eyes. There is a half-smile on his face, not cynical, not humorous, sort of nervous-like. His mustache runs the length of his lips, bushier and longer than that of the Fuhrer's. He looks friendly, but so do vipers. Time will tell. Can it, I wonder, be kindness before the kill? I've heard that purring, gooey type before.

Corporal Weiss speaks into the bullhorn with an accent that is clipped British and New England. He probably went to Harvard, or Oxford. "You have reached your final destination, at least, until spring. The location is a town about 350 meters up the mountains."

I say, "I think it's called Bad Orb."

Corporal Weiss jerks his head in my direction. I had spoken too loud. He scowls, but doesn't comment.

"What the hell is a meter? Why doesn't he speak in feet?" Strubinger snarls.

"About 1,000 feet," Pett answers.

The train whistle screams its shrill, ear-splitting sound, then lumberingly begins to move. The corporal pauses and drops the bullhorn to his side. Everyone turns to watch the boxcars rock along the track, rumble around a bend, and disappear.

I wonder about the frozen bodies in the cars. Damn! I didn't think to get anyone's dog tags. No one got them. Poor bastards! Missing in action. Forever.

Maybe that is better. Families will think they died in battle rather than cooped up in a boxcar like frozen beef. I can't recall any names, not even the body near me the past two days. I knew he was dead when he wouldn't take the helmet of crap and pass it toward the slit at the top of the car.

When the train disappears, the corporal continues. "As I was saying ... and, I might add, you have seen the last of the railroad cars."

No one cheers or claps.

"Liar," I hiss under my breath.

Our heads remain bowed toward the ground, the "prison look." All of us have learned since capture to never look a guard in the eye; always look despondent and beat-out, never happy or contented.

"You will walk a few kilometers up the mountain," Corporal Weiss intones, "to a camp named Stalag IXB. After you register, you will get hot showers and a hot meal. If you need medical attention, you will receive it. Upon assignment to a barracks, you will have many games for your enjoyment. Your length of stay depends upon your army, that is, when it surrenders. This camp is known as a Winter Camp. Your stay is temporary. When summer comes, each of you will be assigned to work based upon your individual skill."

Pett whispers, "Tell him I only have reservations for three days."

"He makes it sound like a vacation resort," I say, again too loud. "Heck, I may take up skiing." The corporal hears me and jerks his head in my direction. I look briefly at him, then move to the fourth row when a guard raises his machine pistol and waves it side-to-side.

Fellman couldn't keep quiet either. "Where have I heard this crap before? Another slice of black bread and a 15-mile hike to another town or boxcar. He makes it sound like we're registering for Boy's State."

"As I said," Weiss continues in precise, deliberate, but hesitant English, "the stalag to which you have been assigned is known as a Winter Camp. It has soldiers from many nations that have wronged the Third Reich. Most of you will be housed in a compound with other American soldiers until spring. Since we are overcrowded, some of you may be with different nationalities. Now, face left and follow the guards. I will see you at the top of the mountain."

Gleason says, "I hope I get with the Italians. They really know how to cook. I love pasta!"

"He sure speaks good English. Must have gone to school in America," I comment.

"He didn't go in the South, that's for sure, or else he would say y'all, and with a mouth full of grits, eh, Higg?" Pett punches me and laughs.

7

"We wouldn't let him below the Mason-Dixon line." Some of the weight of oppression lifts from my shoulders. We are not going to be shot. Not now, anyway. At least we will be in a permanent location, good or bad. I note others, like myself, begin to glance around for the first time in days; eyes swing right and left. The taut banjo string of tense emotions has snapped. It is not a jovial atmosphere; we haven't won the championship game, but a more relaxed, conversational tone of voice ripples among us.

Civilians walk around the station platform, but only a few bother to glance at us. We are a smelly, dirty, ratty-looking mob. The reason for their lack of interest becomes clear when we arrive at the camp. They have seen many prisoners arriving by train and walking through the village.

We begin to walk through town, heads toward the ground for protection from the frigid winter wind that blows down the street. Russell Huckel whispers, "Hey, look! That lady is carrying a skinned animal under her arm!"

Pett stares. "I'll be damned, looks like a dog."

Russ says, "Or badger. No self-respecting dog would live in this freezing temperature."

Freezing air permeates our bodies. We struggle and shuffle behind the guards the length of the railroad station platform and onto the streets. No one breaks into a marching song, but we do have more spring in our legs, that is if you can have spring with frozen feet in wet boots and crappy, smelly remnants of uniforms clinging to gaunt, emaciated bodies. A weak voice behind me whines, "Oh, brother, my butt is raw from all the crapping." "Hey, you guys in front, don't go too fast!"

I can feel my watch slipping down into my boot as we walk. I slow my pace, reach into the boot and pull it back up to the top. Huckel sees my motions. "Why are you slowing up, Higg?"

Before I can answer, Clete pipes in, "He's scratching his pecker. It dropped into his boot."

"If it was that long, I'd break it off and beat you with it."

I am in the front row. As we follow the guards out of town to a narrow, hard-surfaced road, I glance back and see a frozen, motley group strung out for miles. A biting, sub-freezing wind hits us in the face. Frost forms on the edges of my nostrils. My eyes run and my cheeks ache from the rawness of the cold. I pull the scarf up on my face.

I see bright lights and a hazy sun through cloudy and dirty glasses, and decide we are walking north, or perhaps northeast. The road is steep; it twists and turns through a deep forest, thick with tall trees.

Snow covers the ground. The road is slippery, so we take small steps to keep from falling. More like a shuffle. The rubber-soled shoe pacs aren't made for walking. They are cold and heavy, and your feet slip up and down inside the boot.

When the sky becomes bright, I see the majesty and beauty of the forest. The area is a picture postcard of winter. God can do great things! I ask, "What kind of pine trees are those by the road? They have shorter needles than the southern slash pine."

Gleason, who is from New England, answers, "They're northern pines. I see red and white birch, too."

Pett looks at the foliage. "There are some oaks! Look how big they are — must be 50 feet high. I can see fir trees. We have those in Michigan. This forest reminds me of rural Michigan."

The steepness of the road and this mountain air soon make it impossible to talk and walk; our breath is short and quick. Conversation stops, and we trudge along in silence.

We round a sharp turn in the road. About 100 yards to our left is a guard tower. Ominously, it rises to the heavens. I see guards inside a room in the tower, and hear a few POWs mutter, "I guess that's it." The column stops to gaze at the tower.

Stalag IXB

Russ says, "We've been walking for an hour, so the camp must be about two miles from the village and train station." As we walk along the road by the guard tower, I see 12-foot high posts. Each one is about six inches in diameter. Strands of barbed wire are strung approximately six inches apart from ground to top. We shuffle along the road past the tower for another 100 yards.

Gleason says, "Great guns! That fence must be a mile long. We still haven't gotten to the end of it."

Huckel says, "If you look closely, you'll note there are no trees behind and above the guard tower. The camp must be on top of the mountain." The road becomes wider when the posts with the barbed wire end and we come into a cleared area. The column stops. I look to the right, below the road about 15 feet.

I say to Pett, "Wow! Look at that stone building. It must be 100 years old." It is impressive; two stories high, approximately 100 feet long. Dormers protrude from four second-floor windows. A door opens onto a porch about 20 feet long at the front of the building.

Headquarters Stalag IXB — photo sent to the author by Hugo Lang in 1945

Four German soldiers, stern and somber, stand on the top step of a porch. Pett whispers, "One of them must be the big man."

I ask, "How do you know that?"

"Just look at him!" He's wearing a huge, long overcoat with four metal stars on the shoulder epaulets. His peaked cap has a large, round oakleaf located in the center, just above the shiny black peak. The spread-eagle on his cap looks like it's gold. He must be wearing riding breeches, as I can see a wide red stripe down the side. Those black boots really shine; some poor slob must have spent all night shining them. "And look at the guy standing next to the big man. He must be an officer, because he also wears a peaked cap, and two metal stars on his epaulets. The other two guys have on those huge-ass overcoats, but only wear field caps. I guess the two buttons on the peak designates their rank. Both have one chevron on the left sleeve."

Clete hisses with a tinge of sarcasm, "You're a walking world book. How do you know all that?"

"From the movies."

"You didn't look that close."

"You're right. I remember the lecture back at Fort Leonard Wood on enemy insignia. I borrowed the book from the sergeant. I enjoyed reading about different uniforms."

"Good thing we didn't go to the Pacific; you wouldn't be so knowledge-able, then."

Our guards walk to the porch and give the Heil-Hitler salute.

I see five more stone buildings, similar to barns, with windows every 10 feet along the sides, about a 100 yards down the road from the stone building.

"Say, those aren't too bad," exclaims Robert Zion.

Strubinger says, "Look to the left, about 100 feet. That's where we'll be."

On the left, past the posts with the barbed wire, is an open gate and a guardhouse. In front of it stands five battle-ready guards. The column resumes its journey into what becomes an abyss of Hell.

As I walk through the open gate, I note a dirt road on the right, leading up to the top of the mountain. A double row of barbed wire on large posts runs to the right about 50 yards, then straight up the mountain. I see another wire is three feet inside the post and 18 inches off the ground. I learn later it is an electric wire. The main street of the camp is to the left of the gate. On the right side of the road is a stone wall approximately four feet high. Some of the barracks above the wall are of stone; the rest wood, two feet above the ground, sitting on stone pilings.

"No one can dig a tunnel from a barracks that high off the ground," Huckel says.

"I bet the wind blows underneath the barracks, too," Pett says.

Looks like six rows of barracks, in a semi-circle. They go to the top of the mountain. I add with an air of finality, "So this is what a prison camp looks like. Not at all like the movies."

A large building is 50 feet to the left of the guard house. Six ratty-looking American soldiers, each dressed in a makeshift uniform, watch us with a mixture of curiosity and disinterest from the landing at the top of the steps.

A black, four-door vehicle zooms through the gate and stops in front of us. Out steps Corporal Weiss. The prisoners on the steps of a barracks above the wall jump up, clap, hoot, laugh, and yell at the corporal. He turns toward them, removes his cap, and bows. He waves one arm in a wide sweep toward the prisoners, the turns and addresses us in a loud voice. "Gentlemen, I present your fellow American prisoners. Note how happy they are, laughing and clapping."

One of the POWs yells, "Hell, Weiss, we're just drunk from all that wonderful cognac you gave us last night." Again, his buddies hoot and clap.

Registration

"Gentlemen ...." The Corporal points to the building where the six ratty American soldiers stand, located across from the barracks where the derisive prisoners hoot and holler. "You will go into the building single file. American soldiers sit at the tables. They have been here for a month or so. They will help you register and give you German identification tags. A photographer will take your picture. You will then take a shower and be led to a barracks. Finally, you'll be given a nice warm meal."

The American POWs at the door become alert. As we enter, one of them whispers, "Your occupation is *farmer* and your religion is *Protestant*. Get it? Give only your name, rank, and serial number. Do not lie. Tell the truth. Do not give your organization. Hell, they probably know it anyway; they knew all about us. The guys at the table are legit, by the way, not Krauts."

A POW asks, "Suppose you're Jewish? Our dog tags have an H."

The American prisoner answers, "Don't worry, they won't ask. When you get a chance, throw them in a cesspool. Trust me soldier, do not give any religion except Protestant!"

Pett turns to Fellman. "Do as he says. Throw your tags away when you get a chance." I nod my head in agreement, "Don't be a hero ... not now. They'll never know." Gleason asks, "How about a Jewish sounding name? Won't that give them away?"

The American POW at the door shrugs his shoulders. "I can't help you, buddy. If someone asks, tell 'em you converted. That may help; I don't know. But I've been told to tell you not to reveal your Jewish religion. No skin off my butt whatever you say."

A sharp, loud voice roars, "Raust! Raust! Raust!"

I look toward the voice and see a tall German soldier dressed in battle gear, including the dreaded SS on his lapels. His chest is covered with medals. One sleeve of his tunic is empty. In his hand, he holds a riding crop, which he pops against the wall. Another soldier is similarly dressed, but he has both arms; a patch over one eye, and a square-cut panzer cap instead of a helmet. Their eyes remind me of pit vipers, narrow slits with pea-sized black pupils in each corner. I expect pointed tongues to dart out. I sense they would welcome a chance to kill one or all of us — at least to flail away with that damned riding crop.

Heck, fellows, I think, I didn't do that to you. I just got captured. Not my fault you guys got your butts kicked.

I decide it is safer to stay away from them. I follow Pett to the table at the end of the room. Behind me at the other tables stand several members of the first squad.

Pett gives the proper answers. So do I, except in response to religion. I say, "Baptist." The fellow behind the table smiles, "They're Protestant, too."

I receive a metal tag strung on a piece of wire, with a crease in the middle. Each end has the same number.

I say to Pett, "I got number 27209. What's yours?"

He glances down, "27206."

I ask, "Wonder why the same number is on the top and the bottom?"

The soldier behind the desk says, "One part is left with the body, the other is taken by the Germans. We have already had quite a few die, and they are all buried down the road on a hill outside of camp." He points toward the gate, "If you get a chance, volunteer for the burial detail. Only way to get out of this place for awhile."

The fellow who fills out my registration form adds, "There are about 3,000 Americans in this camp in addition to 10,000 prisoners from Russia, France, Italy, most of the British colonies, Yugoslavia, and some small Chinese guys who speak French."

The prisoner who had filled out Pett's form laughs. "If the Jerries read these sheets, they will think they've captured every Protestant farmer west of the Mississippi. I bet they think the Americans are really hard up, taking all us farmers away from the plow to fight."

Huckel, behind me, snorts, "Hope they don't ask me about farming. I'm a city boy. I don't know a potato tree from a palm tree."

I snicker, "Potatoes don't grow on trees. You dig them out of the ground."

"Come on, don't give me that crap."

Pett snaps, "Shut up, you two. Just keep quiet. You'll have plenty of time to discuss potatoes, and lots of other crops, too, before we get out of this hell hole."

After registering, we are taken behind a makeshift curtain for mug shots. I hold my German dog tag in front of me, and scowl. My mind drifts back to Olin Mills and the picture taking ordeal at the department store in Mobile. But here, there is no wisecracking, with comments like 'say cheese' or 'smile for the birdie.'

We leave the building and line up, again, in rows five deep, and head up the road on the right, to the top of the hill. My heart is heavy; my breath is short; my eyes smart.

I am a POW. For me, for now, the war is over.

I can imagine how a caged animal feels as I struggle up the hill.

My existence now depends on someone else. I am helpless. We walk in silence. The hopelessness of the situation is overwhelming. It's as if a wet blanket has been dropped on top of 1,100 American soldiers.

Stalag IXB — photo sent to author by Hugo Lang in 1945

Three buildings, isolated at the top of the mountain, are enclosed in another fence of barbed wire. A gate leads into this compound. As we walk through the gate, I feel the soft cover of the New Testament in my left shirt pocket, the size of a three by five inch card. I silently make a promise to write every day, if possible, in this Bible. Perhaps a few succinct words of my limited vocabulary will help describe prison camp life. Wherever my soul goes at death will be better than the life I have thus far experienced, and I suspect it will get worse. It is demeaning to be treated like an animal.

A group of solemn-looking men stare nonchalantly at us. They wear the remnants of uniforms of an unidentifiable nation. A few have long beards. I hear them talk in a language I can't identify. One of the guards who led 250 American POWs into the compound nods toward the group. "Serbs."

We go to one of the wooden barracks in this other nation's compound.

There is a bunk with dry straw close to the door. Pett, Cole and I spot it at the same time. We all run to get into it. The guard announces each bunk will have to sleep three prisoners. Good! There are three of us in the bunk.

Later, I explore the barracks.

There are two large rooms, each of which holds approximately 250 men. Between the two rooms is a washroom with one cold-water faucet. The wash basin has no drain pipe; the water falls from the sink and runs down the slanted cement floor to a hole in the middle of the room. Behind the wash room is the toilet room. Inside is one hole in the floor, the size of a silver dollar. Under the

14

hole is a cesspool. A near-sighted person like me would never be able to hit that hole standing up, much less squatting, especially without wearing glasses.

Rows of double wooden bunks fill each room. A few bunks have a sack mattress of grass or straw; many are nothing but the boards. The straw and grass make good toilet paper, which explains why so many beds did not have mattresses. The building is damp and has a putrid smell of urine and wet straw, but it is better than the wind, and snow outside the building.

The Serbs occupy the other end of the building. I heard they had the entire barracks for five years, so are not happy about sharing their meager facilities now. One faucet for washing and one small hole in the floor as the crapper for 500 men do not contribute to a happy environment. It is obvious why they didn't exactly greet us with open arms.

Later that day, I discover there is an outside crapper up the hill, near the barbed wire fence, and close to the guard tower at the back of the camp. It consists of two long poles, each one mounted about a quarter of the way up the side of an inverted A-frame. Under each pole is a long trough. The trick is to drop your pants, sit on the pole and pray you can hit the trough. If your bowel movements are loose, crap splatters on the pole, pants, and body. The poles are usually shitty-slick from prisoners who are afraid to sit back on the pole. Later, there is a discussion and demonstration on how to hold onto the slippery pole with one hand, your pants with the other, and not fall backward into the ditch. Bowel movements are one of the most hazardous and frequently discussed aspects of prison life. Nothing can strain friendships quicker than a crappy body.

There is one positive aspect of the pole latrine: you don't dilly-dally long. No one has their knees go numb from prolonged sitting. You don't read in the crapper, either. The freezing wind blows across the top of the mountain, carrying snow or rain, with the ferocity of a freight train. Fleetness of foot and adroitness in hand movements are the keys to a quick crap and a happy existence.

After we settle in, a few American prisoners come into the barracks and yell, "Ah-ten-hut!" One climbs on a table at the front of the room, close to the door.

"My name is Kasten. I am the Man of Confidence, appointed by the Germans as the sole representative of the American POWs with the German authorities. This is my assistant, Joseph F. Littell." He adds he was among the first group of Americans to arrive at Stalag IXB, on Christmas Day, 1944.

A voice behind me yells, "Hey, how did you get that job? Looks pretty soft to me."

The MC, as we call him, answers, "I know German, and so does Joe." He points to Littell. "Both of us spent time in Germany. We were chosen by the other American prisoners to represent them. Most of the American POWs here are from the 106th Division and the 28th Division."

The Man of Confidence continues, "The camp is on the top of a mountain, three or four miles from the village of Bad Orb, in the Hesse-Nassau region of Prussia. Bad Orb is about 30 kilometers from Frankfurt am Main, half-way to the town of Wuerzburg. You will notice a few of the wooden buildings have the remains of large murals painted on the sides. These depict the purpose of the building — beer hall, dining hall, and so on. Don't worry, there isn't any beer left in that building, nor do we have a dining hall. I understand the camp is located on the estate of the descendants of Bismarck. It once housed the workers who took care of the forest and estate."

Someone mutters, "Somebody must have had a helluva lot of workers to fill these barracks."

The MC waits until the laughter subsides, then continues in a more solemn voice. "Let me explain the food situation." The mention of food gets our attention. "You will get either ersatz coffee or weak tea in the morning, made of the bark of some type of tree. I can tell you from experience, it is better to wash in than to drink." My bubble vision of a buffet at Morrison's in Mobile or the Pickwick Cafeteria in Montgomery bursts as he explains the procedure for food.

"Each barracks will walk to the kitchen, located near the large guard tower on the main street. On a slate board in front of the kitchen, the German mess sergeant lists the lunch menu for the day; 'dinner' to you Southern boys. If dinner to you is the big meal of the day, you're correct, 'cause that's what it is. Don't get too excited over the menu. It will always be some type of soup. And don't believe what the mess sergeant writes, which explains in great detail the amount of fat for each person in the daily ration — 20 grams. As you can see, none of us have gained any weight.

"For supper, just before we are locked up, each barracks will be delivered loaves of black bread by the guards. The loaves will be divided among the men. We have found that it is wise to know how many men are in the barracks. The Germans will tell us the number of loaves for each barracks. By dividing the loaves into the number of men in here, you will know how many men to a loaf. So, before supper I suggest you divide into groups. At present, there are about 300 men in each barracks, which means six men to a loaf. After the bread is issued, the barracks will be locked. Anyone caught outside after that time will be shot; no exceptions, no excuses. The barracks are generally opened at 6:30 and closed at 5:30 or when dark."

As an afterthought, he adds, "Oh, yeah, two more points. You should elect a barracks leader. He will communicate with me on everything, then talk to you fellows. The efficient Germans decided on that approach, and you can understand the reason — 3,000 people bitching all day is more than they can handle. Second, you won't get any bread tonight as the Germans weren't expecting you.

"Hold your questions. I will be in touch. Just remember, fellows, we are all prisoners of war, subject to any whim of the guards. This place is over-crowded, so these guys are looking for any excuse to shoot us. Most of the guards are here because they were wounded in battle — by Americans — so they aren't too happy. Many of them are SS troopers and are as mean as snakes. Stay out of their way. Do what they say, without any lip, or the rest of us will take your body to the graveyard down the road."

Kasten and his entourage quickly leave the barracks. The door slams. Bang! The sound of finality to freedom.

There is no conversation. Heads turn right and left, bewildered, in search of an explanation for this prospective existence of nothingness. The fatless skin over my empty stomach tightens; my bowels growl. I feel sick and fight back tears. God, how dare you let me get in this condition?

But He did.

We are sitting or lying on our bunks. I squirm and turn as if settling down for a long winter's nap. Some of those on their feet shuffle, shrug their shoulders, as eyes plead for a suggestion of how to end the hopelessness of the situation. My envelope of self-pity is ripped open by the low voice of a prisoner at the end of the barracks. I glance up at the thin soldier.

"Well, we might as well get organized. I'm Alonzo Poindexter, First Sergeant of the 375th Infantry, 28th Division. A bunch of us in this corner were captured on Christmas Day last year, 1944. I guess you might say we are old-timers, the veterans of Stalag IXB.

"We need to elect a barracks chief. I'd like to suggest Private Hugh Benner. He's a former Boy Scout leader, so he should be able to moderate our complaints and represent us to the Jerries. We are told they separate the officers and the non-coms from the Privates and Privates First Class. Our officers and non-coms have already been moved to another camp. We might as well elect someone who will probably be in this barracks. The non-coms will be moved in the near future, I'm sure." Several men cheer and clap close to where Benner and 15 or 20 others sit.

Pett turns to me, shakes his head and smiles, "Might have known it, a Boy Scout. And I never even got a Tenderfoot badge."

Gleason says, "Well, you can work on it, Pett, since you'll have plenty of time. You can learn to salute with three fingers, like the scouts, instead of with your middle finger pointed up."

Those who have been in Stalag IXB long enough to accept their fate crowd together, as do the remaining members of the first squad, B Company, 275th Infantry.

The thin sergeant yells, "I nominate Benner as barracks chief." This is immediately seconded by someone in Benner's group.

"Anyone else?"

"I move nominations be closed," says somebody in the same group.

"Second."

"Right. Nominations closed. All in favor of Benner, yell." A resounding "Yes" comes from the soldiers in the far corner of the barracks.

"All opposed? None? Benner is the barracks chief."

Pett looks at me. "So much for democracy."

Huckel says, "Let him have it. I just want to eat."

I add, "He will be pretty good. That is, if he follows the scout rules and treats everyone the same."

Benner climbs on the table and begins, "Fellows, thanks . . ."

Someone interrupts, "No acceptance speeches, just get us more food."

". . . for the vote of confidence, though I know these guys," and he points to some men in the corner, "seem to have railroaded this election through. Realistically, we have been here long enough to know that only some kind of organization will allow us to survive. So, first things first. I understand that the bread can be split evenly into six parts. That way, everyone will get a fair-sized slice. Pick your buddies and divide into groups of six. Each group should select one person to be spokesperson. If you desire, change leaders every day. No one cares — it's up to you guys."

Fellman, Huckel and Gleason in the first squad quickly gather in front of the bunk where Cole, Pett and I sit. Fellman looks around, points and announces, "Since we are standing in front of Pett's bunk, I think he should be the leader of this group."

Huckel adds, "And he was raised in the wilds of Michigan, so he knows how to survive in this weather. I say 'Yea' and close nominations."

All five of us raise our hands, yell, "Yeah, Pett's the one."

Pett says, "As I said earlier, so much for democracy."

Six others in the squad form a group near us. Oscar Penton, the only regular in the Army in the platoon, turns to Clete, who's been standing on the fringe of the 11 men, and beckons to him, "Come on Clete, join us. I want to keep an eye on you anyway. At least we know you — better than getting some yo-yo we can't trust."

Strubinger joins the group of five, which consists of Homer Smith, Robert Zion, Neal Mayfield, and Oscar Penton. The six choose Oscar as leader, without the fanfare and jovial jostling my group demonstrated.

Pett announces, "My first official act is to decide the order in which we will get the tea each morning. I'll put six numbers in my cap and we'll each draw one."

I say, "I think Pett should automatically be number one, since he is the leader. If the stuff is as bad as rumored, he should throw up first." The others smile and agree.

Since time is endless in prison camp, we learn, by instinct I guess, to fill it with trivial details; long drawn-out conversations, slow, deliberate movements. We aren't going anywhere, and when we get there it's just more of the same, spelled M-I-S-E-R-Y.

The drawing is illustrative of the endlessness of time. It takes over an hour to make the numbers, decide upon a hat with some semblance of cleanliness, then, after 15 minutes of heated debate, the order by which to draw. Fellman watches Pett with the intensity of a surgeon removing his arm. "Be sure to divide that paper evenly."

Huckel adds, "Yeah, and fold all the papers the same size."

Pett looks up with disgust, "You guys want to do this? Or let me do it my way."

Cole says, "You do it. We just want to tell you how."

Pett tears the paper into six pieces, writes a number on each one, and folds them. The rest of us monitor his every action like a starving man watching a butcher slice a side of beef. We no sooner finish than the guards arrive and scream for us to line up outside. I wonder out loud, "Why do they have to yell and scream? Can't they just ask us to do something?"

No one knows why we are to line up, so we drag our feet. It is cold inside, but not as raw and windy as it is outside. After more yelling and arm waving by the guards, we line up in ranks five deep. We trudge through the gate to a large building.

As we approach, I see steam coming from pipes on the roof. We go through a door into a large room. Fifty men are counted and led inside another room. We are told to remove our clothes and take a shower.

Fellman whispers, "Some of us better guard our clothes while others take a shower, then switch." Huckel says, "Why? No one would want to steal

19

these crappy, smelly, clothes." Cole reminds us that another POW might take them for warmth or to sell or trade, so we take turns bathing and guarding each other's crappy garments.

I have to peel my clothes off, as do others, because of the crap, dirt, and dampness that had cemented them to my skin.

The water is soothing, warm, and relaxing. I look at the other naked bodies and recall pictures in *National Geographic* of people suffering from rickets, malnutrition, or starvation. Like them, we are skin and bones. Hair that covers the face and chest of a few men make them look like mangy, hairy dogs. Eyes bulge from sockets; faces are taut against cheek bones. I notice the skeleton-like arms on many men. And we have just been captured! How will these fellows make it? I note the nipples of others taking a bath. Some are as large as a 50-cent piece; others the size of a pea. I see ribs with ridges, like rows of snow drifts — some straight, others are at various angles. I decide some day I will write a story about ears-sizes, shapes, the angle of attachment to the head.

Modesty is forgotten as we remove our bony hands from our privates to scrub off the crust and dirt. Can we lose any more weight? A few of us don't look too bad until I realize they had been huge — at least 250 pounds — when we left Fort Leonard Wood, and now are about 150 pounds. A 100-pound weight loss is as difficult on a large man as a 50-pound loss is on someone like me who weighed 160 pounds when captured.

A few POWs have razors. I borrow one and shave for the first time in two weeks. Since I am probably the tenth person to get the razor, it is like removing scales from a carp with a dull knife.

Scrunch. Scrunch. Scrunch. The blade digs into my skin. "Ouch! Ouch! Ouch!" It must be pure hell for the prisoners with thick, coarse beards. I feel specks of blood on my face and finally quit, but leave a mustache and hair on my chin. I decide to grow a goatee.

The shower of disinfectant mixed with water makes us smell like creosote. I shiver as I put on the wet, sticky, stiff underwear with dried shit. The outer garments are no better.

Pett says, "I thought maybe the Jerries would send my clothes out to be cleaned."

Russ laughs, "Dreamer. Wishful thinking, buddy."

We line up after the shower and march to the kitchen for a ladle of grass soup. We use whatever utensil available, since none are issued. I use my helmet liner, which fortunately had not been used as a toilet on the boxcar. Others frantically wipe out their helmets with snow, dirt, rags — anything to remove the frozen crap, urine, or vomit. We return to the barracks to eat the soup. It has green slime floating on top.

"Is this grass" someone gasps, as he smells, then cautiously tastes it.

I sip a wee bit of the lukewarm mess, then mumble, "Looks like grass to me."

"At least it's warm," Cole says.

"It won't burn your tongue," Gleason replies.

After dinner, a few of us walk around the compound. The tempo of bitching has increased as other POWs find places to sleep, select buddies to share their misery, and perform other chores to set up housekeeping. It is a relief to get away from the complaints. At least the wind blowing across the mountain does not bitch, moan or groan. At the top of the hill, we stare out the barbed wire at the forest, about 50 yards from the compound. The guard in the tower shifts his machine gun in our direction.

Pett turns to me, "I hope you record all this in your Bible."

"I really don't feel like it. If the guards find the Bible, they'll take it."

"So what? We'll shield you when you write. If they decide to search, we'll hide it. Just record what you can in the margins. Be careful what you say in case the Jerries do search you. Mention only a few names."

Fellman adds, "Yeah, write it down, and if you get shot, we'll come to the funeral." He smiles and hits me gently on the arm.

"If I get caught, I'll leave the Bible to you. Might make you a Christian."

I climb into my bunk when we return to the barracks, and begin to keep the promise I made myself when we first walked into the compound. On the first few pages, I write the dates and places of the company movements since landing in France, to the best of my recollection. I concentrate on the commitments to battle, capture, interrogation, and march to the boxcars. I note especially the five depressing boxcar days.

I yell, "Hey Gleason, remember the time in Landstuhl when the guard said Roosevelt was a Jew?"

"Yeah, you pulled out your Bible and showed him President Roosevelt's letter. You asked why a Jew would write in a Christian Bible. It shut him up! Good thing he was a nice guy, or he'd have shot you."

Pett says, "Just write, Higg. Quit talking. It's getting dark."

"Okay, okay, I'm writing." Skipping a few pages, I start my diary on Monday, 15 January, 1945. Good gosh, it was just 15 days since the company was committed to battle! I have been through enough experiences for a lifetime, and this is just the beginning. I look upward, and mumble, "Dear God, what do you have in store for me now?"

As darkness sets in, the grumbling, belly-aching, and bickering is replaced by heavy breathing, punctuated with sharp, quick snorts and long snores. I glance back at what I have recorded about the time spent in the boxcars. I read, "... never knew one could pray so hard and depend on God the way we have. He seems to be our only salvation."

I bow my head and silently thank God for getting us safely this far, and ask Him to keep our bodies strong and spirits high. My mind searches for a kind word for the captors, finally settling on, "We want to love our enemies. I don't know why, but how about a push in that direction? A little bit, anyway."

I cannot ask for forgiveness for the inhumane treatment that has been wrought on us. I'll leave that decision to God. It has been a long, stressful first day in Stalag IXB.

⊶ ⚏ ⊷

When the barracks doors are unlocked on Tuesday, the two POW chaplains arrive with the guards and the tub containing our morning tea. After the tea is divided for each group, my group drinks it. Benner, the barracks chief, climbs on a table and introduces the chaplains. "This is Lieutenant Sam Neal, Baptist Chaplain of the 106th Division."

Chaplain Neal waves. "Hi, men, can't say I'm glad to see you, not under these conditions, anyway." I hear a few comments like "You can say that again," and "Not glad to see you, either."

Benner points to the other officer. "This is Father Hurley, Catholic Chaplain of the 106th."

Fellman exclaims, "What? No Jewish rabbi?"

Gleason says, "Guess he didn't get captured. Why say *Father*, then *Catholic*? What do they think he would be?" Pett explains, "He could be Episcopal. Other denominations have Fathers, you know."

Chaplain Neal gets on the table and looks over the dejected, dirty group of prisoners. Some stand, but most, like me, sit on the floor. "As I said before, Father Hurley and I aren't happy to see you under these circumstances, but we're here, so let's try to make the best of it. Let me add that Dr. Eden, a dentist, and Dr. Josh Sutherland, physician, are also prisoners of war; they are available for consultation. Please, no sick calls unless your complaint is serious — like pneumonia or extreme diarrhea. When I say 'extreme,' I mean you are running to the latrine every few minutes, or are too weak to walk. Dr. Eden doesn't clean teeth, either. An emergency would be a swollen jaw, for instance. Right, Dr. Eden?" Dr. Eden nods.

Chaplain Neal continues. "These doctors will be around later to talk about their services. Now, here is the situation: each nationality is housed in a separate compound, all within a larger compound. You are in the Serb compound because the American area is full."

A voice interrupts, "Couldn't be any fuller than this barracks."

Chaplain Neal says, "That's true. All the barracks are full. You will be allowed in the American area through the one gate in the Serb compound, but only to get soup. There are about 12,000 prisoners in the camp. This camp even has a factory where shoes and clothes are repaired. It's run by a Slavic group."

I look at my shoe pacs, and think, Maybe I can get a new pair of boots.

Chaplain Neal introduces Father Hurley. He climbs on the table, and continues providing information about the camp. "There are Russian, Indo-Chinese, Italian, and Englishmen from Britain, India, and South Africa in this camp."

Pett turns to me and exclaims, "I'll be damned. Those little guys we saw are Indo-Chinese. They are the ones who speak French-Chinese. Well, kiss my foot."

I shake my head. "Not that dirty foot!"

Father Hurley continues, "The Germans have allowed one barracks to be used as a chapel. Services will be held on Wednesday and Sunday for the Protestants. Mass will be each Friday and Sunday morning. Try to attend, regardless of your religious preference. Not only will it be good for you, it will help kill time. I suspect we're confined in Stalag IXB until spring at the earliest."

There is complete silence while the chaplains speak. For once, there are no wisecracks. No one complains or gripes.

The chaplains depart after answering a few questions about the time of church services and their availability for consultations. Everyone in the barracks stands up and stretches. The sound of buckles and the cracking of bones can be heard, along with comments like, "Seem like nice guys. Glad to know the Lord is represented in this hell-hole. I need air, even if it is cold."

We wander around the remainder of the day like a bunch of dogs checking out the telephone poles and fire hydrants. Might as well get an idea of the layout, as it looks like a long winter. A blanket of resignation settles over us.

Cole tries to talk to the Serbs with grunts, grins, and sign language. After a futile attempt at conversation, he remarks, "Can't they speak English? Why are they so unfriendly?"

Pett says, "When you've been a prisoner as long as they have, you won't be so happy either. Why do you think they would speak English? Not everyone in the world speaks English."

By Wednesday, whatever relaxation I enjoyed on Tuesday is gone, blown away like the freezing wind from the mountain. A black cloud of despondency stops over me. I cannot climb out of the abyss of despair, made more so by the continual wailing, squawking, bickering, and fighting of everyone in the barracks.

That afternoon, my nerves were stretched to the limit as I try to compose an entry for my Bible. I yell, "For God's sake, for my sake, shut up, you snot-nosed twerps! Grow up. Now!" It works. My hands shake, my breath comes in rapid spurts. I swallow the saliva dripping from my mouth. It is impossible to concentrate on the events that happened that day. After an hour or so, I recall and record the key events of the day.

The ersatz coffee we get every morning is made from tree bark, tan and sticky. It is brought by a couple of guards as soon as the barracks doors are unlocked. We divide into groups of six. Pett is the leader of our six-man group, which consists of Pett, Fellman, Cole, Gleason, Huckel and me. Whoever is number six doesn't have a chance to wash or drink the tea. Dirt from the previous washers, plus pieces of bark float in the sticky, cold, brown liquid. It's better to stay dirty!

In mid-morning, some civilian who claims to be a Red Cross representative comes in our barracks. The barracks leader yells for attention, and introduces him as the Red Cross man from Berlin. I didn't catch his name, but note he is a tall, cadaverous man with a solemn expression on his face. He wears a black suit and felt hat that covers his eyes and most of his face.

Fellman exclaims, "Looks like an undertaker. He should smile at the thought of all these prospective clients."

As the fellow climbs on the table, he hands a pile of cards to Benner. He says, in English with a thick German accent, "Pass these out while I talk. Prisoners, you must fill these out to be officially recognized as prisoners of war. Until that time, you cannot receive packages of food. Your capture must be official."

Someone yells, "What the hell do you think we're doing here — visiting?"

He narrows his eyes, ignores the comment, and continues. "Your capture has to clear Berlin, then the papers will be sent to a neutral country. Until then, no action can be taken relative to living conditions, food, or medical attention."

The card doesn't leave much room to write. Gleason cracks, "I doubt these will be delivered, so might as well write something cute."

I follow his lead and write comments like, "Having a good time in the mountains, chopping wood, strolling in the forests. Wish you were here."

Benner collects the cards and gives them to the Red Cross representative. He takes a cursory glance through a few, smiles, shakes his head, and departs.

Later in the morning, the guards arrive, and give Benner a stack of paper to hand out. It is the official German form letter. I look at my form letter. The phrase "Kriegsgefangenenpost" is printed at the top of the 12-inch long, 6-inch wide paper. In smaller French type is the sentence, "Correspondance de prisonnier de guerre." There are numerous other phrases, written in German and French.

Why both German and French? Pett explains that French is historically known as the "international" language. The Germans printed the forms, so both languages are used. The other side is lined. The words at the top of the page read, "This page is reserved for the Prisoner of War."

What the hell do you write? None of us have ever written under oppressive conditions, except in school, when the teacher made you write a letter to someone in the class who was sick, or a holiday letter to your mother. The teacher told you what to write and how to do it. Thinking back, those days weren't too bad. Questions ran through my mind. "Do you reveal your location? Organization? Name of companions? Dates?"

Russell Huckel advises us to be circumspect. "Reveal only as much as you think will get by the censor."

Gleason's mouth drops open, his eyebrows wrinkling, as he says, "What does 'circumspect' mean?"

Cole grunts, "Nothing. Write whatever you want. Let the Jerries figure it out. The fancy word Russ used means just write in a circle, I think."

Somberness and quiet meditation replaces the heretofore verbal complaints and gripes. I see others, like me, stare into space, searching for a brief glimpse of pre-prison life. When a prisoner finishes, he loans his pencil to someone else. Reminiscing creates a degree of companionship and compassion rarely seen in a survival-of-the-fittest atmosphere.

I notice a prisoner who just lays in his bunk and looks at the ceiling. "Why don't you write your folks? You can have my pen. Just give it back when you finish."

He looks at the paper, then me, with a forlorn, sad expression. "I don't have no folks, nobody who gives a shit about me. Anyway, I don't write too good. You want my paper? I never wrote a letter to no one in my whole life."

I want to bite my tongue off. Big mouth, sticking my nose in somebody's business. It didn't dawn on me that some people couldn't write, and probably couldn't read. How do they communicate? Know what is going on in the world? Read the funny papers? Or the Bible? The lack of the basic skills of reading and writing are beyond my comprehension. These thoughts run through my mind as I look sheepishly at my paper.

"No, give the paper to Pett, or Cole. I can't think of much to say, anyway," I lie, as information crowds the thought processes in my head, waiting to explode upon the paper.

I write, "*Dear A. Louise & Uncle Leon: . . . .*" Damn! My pen runs out of ink. While searching for a pencil in my jacket and shirt, my mind travels back to a childhood where aunts and uncles, dozens of them, fought over custody of my brother and me. I almost tell the lonesome soldier he can have a couple of my relatives, especially the mean, hateful, money-grabbing ones. I smile, shake my head, and decide not to wish some insensitive people on anyone. I don't want to think about them, not even in prison. I shake my head to clear the cobwebs of childhood from my sight.

Ha! I find a pencil in my pants pocket; small, but with a point. I continue to write:

> *Hope you haven't worried too much about me. Hope the Red Cross notice got there soon after the missing notice. I'm alright, and out of danger, so just wait until the day I get home, which I pray will be soon. My method of capture was like something you see in the movies. I was in the mountains five days without food before giving up. I sure have seen a lot of snow & cold weather, too much for me. I've heard from you once since I came across. Yes, I heard about Jack Clolinger. Sure sorry. I've seen some good pals fall, & it is rough. Sure hope you folks had a nice Xmas. Maybe all my packages were sent back. I'll eat them when I get home. Did Frankie get to see you folks? Sure would be nice if he did. Go to the Red Cross to see how to write. Tell everyone to write me although I won't be able to write much. Try to send me some tobacco & pipe, also a razor & blades. I could use candy & food. I'm afraid you will be jealous if I told you my waist size, so I won't! I sure will be glad to see some warm weather again. Relay my letter to Charles & all the family, & above all don't worry about me. I hope to enter U. of A. next year. Give everyone my love. How is Boo? Tell her hello for me, also Bazoo. Write soon. Remember, I did my best & that's all. Sam*

I ask Pett what he wrote. He sighs. "Not much. I tried to reveal where we are without writing anything specific. How 'bout you?"

"I wrote something about the snow and cold weather 'would be glad to see warm weather, spent five days in mountains, and I am thinner.' That should let them know I haven't had much to eat, and about where we were captured. My smart-mouth older brother will read this and say I needed to lose weight anyway."

Auf diese Seite schreibt nur der Kriegsgefangene!
Cette page est réservée au prisonnier de guerre!

Deutlich auf die Zeilen schreiben!
N'écrire que sur les lignes et lisiblement!

Dear A. Louise & Uncle Leon: Hope you haven't worried too much about me. Hope the Red Cross notice got there soon after the missing notice. I'm alright, and out of danger. So just wait until the day I get home, which I pray will be soon. My method of capture was like something you see in the movies. I was in the mountains 5 days without food before giving up. I sure have seen a lot of snow & cold weather, too much for me. I've heard from you once since I came across. Yes, I ____ ____ ____ ____ ____ ____ I've seen some good pals fall, & it is rough. Sure hope you folks had a nice Xmas. Maybe all my packages were sent back. I'll eat them when I get home. Did Frankie get to see you folks? Sure would be nice if he did. Go to the Red Cross to see how to write. Tell everyone to write me although I won't be able to write much. Try to send me some tobacco & pipe, also a razor & blades. I could use candy & food. I'm afraid you will be jealous if I told you my waist size, so I won't! I sure will be glad to see some warm weather again. Relay my letter to Charles & all the family, & above all don't worry about me. I hope to enter U. of A. next year. Give everyone my love. How is Boo? Tell her hello for me - also Bozo. Write soon. Remember, I did my best & that's all - Sam

January 17. First letter home from Stalag IXB

Kriegsgefangenenpost

Correspondance des prisonnier de guerre

An Mr. & Mrs. J. L. Perry
A

Empfangsort: MOBILE, ALABAMA
Lieu de destination

Straße: 208 Kenan Avenue
Rue

Kreis:
Arrondissement

Landesteil: U. S. A.
Dépt.

Gebührenfrei Franc de port!

Deutschland (Allemagne)

Lager-Bezeichnung BAD ORB
Destination du camp

M.-Stammlager IX B   Arbeits-Kommando-Nr.:

Gefangenennummer: 37309
No. du prisonnier

Vor- und Zuname: Samuel G. Higgins
Nom et prénom

Absender:
Expéditeur

Address side of January 17 letter from Stalag IXB

"Sounds good. I did mention I wish I had brought my skis. That will let them know we are in the mountains."

"Yeah, good thinking. I didn't hint where we are, but it's too late now. This paper is too thin to correct. Anyway, I don't have an eraser."

We are told to fold the paper in the middle, address it on the outside. One of the guards and Benner, the barracks chief, explain how to complete the front in case we can't read the German and French directions. On the return half of the envelope, I write my name, prisoner number, and in the space with the words "Lager-Bezeichnung," followed by the words "M. Stammlager IXB," I checked the IXB, and wrote "Bad Orb." I decide to take a chance and designate the location of the prison camp.

I don't think the letter will get home; still, it kills time, and provides a chance to reflect on families and life before the Army.

It is a good morning. We forget our misery and discuss humorous events of the past. I find it interesting no one speaks about sadness in their lives. Perhaps we only remember joy at this youthful age and sadness comes later.

The time to eat arrives before we have time to feel sorry for ourselves. The barracks lines up and marches to the mess kitchen. We drop our letters in a box held by two guards as we leave the barracks. There is more spring in our walk down the hill to the mess hall. Maybe the opportunity to think about the past provides a few hours for thoughts other than personal misery.

After we return to the barracks and eat the soup (some kind of crushed peas) I decide to walk around the compound. Pett says, "Hey, wait up. I'll go with you. After such a heavy meal, I need the exercise."

I note some Americans on the other side of the fence, yell, and strike up a conversation with a couple of them. When I mention that most of my company was captured, one of them replies, "Hell, don't feel bad. My whole division was captured! Or, at least two-thirds of us. I think the only ones to escape were in the Division Headquarters Company. We had just moved into position; had not even removed the grease from our guns. Our artillery was overrun before a howitzer could be loaded. The damn Jerries went through us like hot grease through a dog with runny bowels.

"Let me give you guys a tip. I was in the Aleutians before the war. We had two problems up there; one was how to take a piss in the middle of the night in freezing weather outside the hut and not reveal yellow snow. That made the sergeant mad. He knew somebody was too lazy to go to the latrine. The other problem was worse, boredom, plain-ass boredom. Nothing to do with your free time. Morale got bad, soldiers became moody. Some just wandered off into the night. Others tried to drink themselves to death. My advice is to do something to keep your mind and body active. Look around you. You'll see guys talking to themselves, staring through the fence, lying around with covers over their heads, crying, all sorts of weird behavior. Participate in any and all camp activities, even if you have to force yourself."

"Even play bridge?" I ask. I hate bridge.

He nods. "Yeah, anything. Even learn to sew, or knit. Some of the stuff will be silly, but do it anyway. It is easy to let your morale drop so low you can't bring it back up. Watch out or you'll go bongos. And keep your valuables to yourself. Don't tell anybody anything.

"This place is full of thieves, crooks, scam artists. Look at the other nationalities. They've learned to make another life. Hell, I suspect the Serbs have a radio that gets all the news of the war. I know the British have one. Some of those guys were captured in Africa by Rommel in '40 or '41, so they know how to survive. Over the years, the old-timers in this prison camp have organized independent, self-sufficient communities — excellent communication facilities, laundries, PXs with all the necessities, organized games, educational courses; you name it, they have it."

He starts to turn and leave, then adds, "You guys want to buy some smokes? Five bucks apiece. What else you want? Name it and I can get it for you at a price, of course."

None of us standing at the fence buy anything, not then, anyway. We are too new at prison life to know what we want. I had hidden five dollars in my waist band, but I am determined to keep it for a real emergency, not to buy a cigarette. But my stomach aches for a smoke.

Just before dark, the guards arrive with the bread. There are enough loaves for groups of six. Benner calls the group leaders to the front of the barracks and hands out the bread. Once the bread is distributed, the arguments begin. Some loud and boisterous, others a low, steady hum of discontent.

Benner calls for attention. "Hear ye, hear ye. The Serbs have agreed to come over before lockup and entertain us with music and dancing. So, let's eat, clean up, and settle down."

The Serbs, about 25 of them, come into the barracks after we divide up the bread. The entertainment begins. They play spirited music. They sing, dance, yell, laugh. Clap, clap, clap. It is loud and noisy. I've never seen such prancing and dancing by a bunch of men. Cole laughs, claps, yells in my ear, "How do they squat like that, then throw out their legs? Looks like it would knock their knees out of joint."

I clap and laugh. "Probably been dancing like that all their lives. It's just second nature, I guess."

The group has two accordions and some type of drum, all of which they play and bang out some unknown tune. Most of the barracks claps to the spirited music. A few get on the floor and dance with the Serbs. The war, the prison camp, even the meager rations are forgotten. Scowls turn to smiles. The old saying about music soothing the soul proves true.

Just as it turned dark, the guards arrive to lock the doors, but linger to listen to the music. The Serbs dance out of the barracks with the loud cheers and clapping ringing in their ears.

The guards suddenly realize their role and yell at the Serbs, "Raust, Raust, Schnell."

As our barracks are locked, I hear one of the guards mutter in broken English, "Sweet dreams." For the first time since capture, I do just that. As I hunker down in the straw, my eyes close to the rhythmic breaking of waves over sand bars at Pensacola Beach, running to the beach, each wave with decreasing resonance, slow, quiet.

Early Friday, I am jerked out of a sound sleep as a guttural voice sears my brain. "Raust, Raust."

My hips are stiff and raw from trying to turn from one side to the other all night. As I sit up and stretch, I gaze out the window. A solid wall of dark gray clouds sit in solemn judgment on Stalag IXB. Oh, hell, I thought, another day of freezing cold, probably snow. Why can't the sun shine?

Frankly, I am glad it is morning. At least I can get up and work the kinks out of my body. I am even glad to hear the guards open the barracks.

The morning begins with the usual ritual of the division among the groups of six the so-called tea, a sticky, brown liquid. Today, it is very thick with bark from some type of tree. When my turn arrives to get the tea, I decide to neither drink nor wash with the gooey mess. I take a few pieces of bark from the liquid. I will dry them and roll a cigarette later on, or smoke them in my pipe.

The barracks chief, not his usual gung-ho, Boy Scout, let's-go self, announces with a serious expression on his face that roll call is immediate. "Now! Quick! Everyone outside."

"Hey, boss-man," a POW yells, "I'm not through my delightful breakfast. I haven't even gotten to my ham and eggs."

"Let's go, men. Hurry, hurry. Big news at roll call."

Two guards stand at the door, with helmets and rifles. Their grim expressions show the seriousness of whatever is going to happen. At the urging of both the guards and the barracks chief, we gather ourselves and walk into the cold morning.

The roll call is different. The Germans did not conduct their usual counting, recounting, and rearranging us into different rows. After we get in a somewhat helter-skelter formation, Benner yells for silence. In a hesitant, emotional voice, he says, in essence, the following:

"The Fuhrer insists the Jewish soldiers be separated from other soldiers. At 1400 today, that's two o'clock for you guys who don't know military time, we will have another line-up. All soldiers who are Jewish will step forward. They will move to the barracks at the end of the first row of barracks, down the road from the kitchen. This move is voluntary. You know if you are Jewish. It doesn't make any difference whether or not you are active in your religion. If your name sounds Jewish, and I mean first, middle, or last, you should step forward. I am told that once this move is made, the Gestapo and the German Army will take over any further identification of Jewish soldiers."

No telling what that means, but we can all guess.

Fear and hostility grip me as we return to the barracks. No one speaks. I had never known segregation of any type.

The barracks is silent for a few moments. Then, as if an orchestra conductor brought down both hands to signal crescendo, 240 men erupt in yells and screams.

"Who the hell do they think we are?"

"Strike."

"Screw 'em."

"Don't you guys go."

"No way to treat Americans."

Comments bounce off the wall. Cole screams, "Who gives a damn, anyway? What difference does it make who is what? Next thing you know it will be the Baptists."

"Not a bad idea," Gleason chimes in.

I reply, "Shut up. I'm a Baptist." Then, "Frankly, I think anyone who makes scrapple should be segregated."

"And grits, too," replies Gleason.

Someone yells, "Let's protest, write a letter of complaint."

Benner gets on the table, bangs for attention, and yells, "A good suggestion has been made. Each group get together and write a formal complaint. I will turn them in to Kasten, the Man of Confidence. Other barracks can do the same. Maybe the Jerries will listen to three or four thousand complaints."

A prisoner adds, "We can object to Geneva, and the Red Cross, too."

I ask, "Just who the hell you gonna see in Geneva? You know the address? Or you plan to get it from the Krauts?"

"First one to escape will tell them."

Cole turns to me and whispers, "These guys are just exercising their vocal chords. Best thing to do is nothing. Don't tell 'em anything."

I add, "Yeah, why even step forward? If these guys throw away their dog tags, who will know their religion? If threatened, deny it."

Sergeant Holcombe comes to Fellman. He says it is his decision whether to identify himself as Jewish. The same will be true for the Jewish soldiers in the other platoons. He pats Norm on the shoulder and says, "Whatever you guys do, we will stand behind you."

All of us in the first squad agree with Tom Holcombe. Pett and I again urge Fellman, as we had at interrogation, to throw away his dog tags if he has not done so. With no dog tags, who will know his religion? Pett vehemently tells Fellman to deny any religious affiliation.

Norm shakes his head. "No, I didn't throw them away. Thanks, fellows, but I'm not going to deny anything. When its' time to go, I'll go. Hell, I'm not ashamed of my heritage. At least I'm not a Catholic."

He looks at Gleason, laughs, and continues, "and a change of scenery might be good for me. Couldn't be any worse than living with you yo-yos." He forces a weak smile.

Cole replies, "I wonder why the bastards don't move them now? Why wait?"

Pett says, "To torture us. The Jerries are great at mental torture. What a bunch of sadists."

I don't know who is Jewish in our platoon. We don't make an issue of it. I recall, on Jewish holidays at Fort Leonard Wood, Fellman and other Jewish soldiers got passes. We kidded Fellman, saying he just said he was Jewish to get a few days out of camp. I further recall we gave him a hard time, said he should march on Christmas while the Christians took off. One time, Gleason claimed he was a Jehovah's Witness and should have Saturday off. That excuse blew up when reminded he went to Mass on Sunday.

The Man of Confidence bluntly said that when we arrived at the prison camp, we were subject to the will of the Germans. The caged feeling of being an animal stifles and chokes me more and more. I begin to appreciate why my uncle would never pen our police dog.

We spend the morning writing and collecting complaints. Word has spread fast in the American compound about complaining to the Red Cross authorities. I can hear POWs in the other barracks screaming and yelling their indignation. The barracks empty and prisoners engage in animated discussions all around the American compound.

Cold fear grips me as I see POWs gather on the road and around the barracks when we go to the kitchen for our dinner of mushy rice soup. I fear all the screaming and yelling will give the Jerry guards an excuse to start shooting. Cole alerts me to the guards dressed in battle helmets, bayonets fixed on rifles, and in strategic positions along the road and at the gates. I can see guards in the tower sweep their guns up and down the road. It is a cautious, nervous walk to dinner.

After eating the watery rice soup, the barracks becomes quiet. The lively discussions exhausted everyone. Our emaciated bodies and minds are unaccustomed to spirited discussions. I am mentally exhausted. Deep inside my soul, I feel the situation is hopeless. We are captives, subject to the whim Germans. I am despondent about the Jewish soldiers, especially Fellman. His quick wit and pointed barbs keep my mind alert. Many of the American POWs had been moved in and out of Stalag IXB, but never has a specific group been segregated.

I walk outside to shake my despondency and have a smoke. A guard has set up shop just inside the gate to our compound. His table is full of personal items, toothpaste, brushes, razors. I see a razor with a blade, flick my empty Zippo lighter, point at the razor. The guard says, "Ja," and we trade. I get a good deal, as I can't get lighter fluid, anyway.

The Germans are prompt. Just before 1400, the barracks guards arrive. I am surprised at the number of American soldiers who gather their meager personal belongings. There is no boisterous back-slapping, joking, or yelling that usually occurs when troops ship out from a group. No one knows what will happen, nor how to express regrets. This type of situation has never confronted us. Heads drop, eyes look at the floor.

Pett repeats the advice given at our interrogation when we entered Stalag IXB. "Don't go, Norm. I need another scout to help me when we get out of this hell-hole. You're so eager, you'll be shot before me."

Fellman smiles. "Thanks, but no thanks." He stands erect, pushes out his chest as if proud to be selected. He turns to those of us in the first squad with whom he has soldiered since Fort Leonard Wood. My eyes smart, heartbeat quickening, and my breathing is labored. Norm is a good buddy, a friend. We have fought side by side, survived the frigid mountain top after trudging through part of Germany, endured the wretched conditions of the boxcar ride, wise-cracking at each other and everyone else, every step of the way. His antics helped me keep a clear head and a degree of emotional stability. It is painful to see the thin, six foot and three inch frame, with arms that reach his knees and a head of dirty black hair, leave the group.

"Here is my home address, just in case you guys ever get to Virginia. Give my old man a call when you get back to the states. Hell, I'll probably beat you guys home." He hands both Pett and me papers with his home address and phone number, then looks affectionately at me. "As for you, little man, you are hereby appointed my official 'wise-ass, smart-mouth' replacement. I don't know what you'll do for a straight man, but you and Pett keep it up. With that attitude, you'll survive. The Jerries won't waste bullets on you two."

He addresses the others as he puts his arm around my shoulders. "As my good southern friend is always saying, 'Y' all come, y' hear?' The word is that we will be in the barracks just beyond the kitchen, where we'll get the sickening aroma of lousy food being prepared. No one said you couldn't visit. Just don't get too close to me."

We fall out and line up. Since our barracks is in the Serb compound, we have to march through the gates and line up with everyone from all the American barracks at the top of the hill. Four thousand American prisoners of war stand facing German soldiers. In front of them stands the Commandant of Stalag IXB. In front of the POWs from each barracks is the barracks chief. It reminds me of a division parade at Fort Leonard Wood, when 15,000 troops lined up in front of a reviewing stand, with flags to identify each division, battalion, and company.

There is no roll call. The commandant speaks to Corporal Weiss, the Stalag interpreter, who in turn shouts, "All Jews, one step forward. Now!"

Fellman, along with the other Jewish soldiers, steps forward. No one looks at them. No words are spoken. There isn't any action we can take. I am enveloped by a feeling of resignation and stifling defeat, and the horrible conclusion that my every move, my life, depend on someone else's whim.

The American Jewish POWs from our barracks move forward and join the other Jewish POWs. As they form another line, I look at the sky of varying shades of gray and plead, "God, where are you?" Clouds drift across the sky, some thick with rain or snow. "God, I know you're there. Come out from behind a cloud." The sun casts its rays from behind one cloud, then another. "Come on, God, do your thing. Blast forth on the scene and smite the heathen. Free us. Please!" God does not respond. The Jews march down the hill. We remain silent, transfixed by the incomprehensibility of the scene.

Robert Zion does not step forward.

We return to the barracks and spend the remainder of the afternoon in individual, and, thankfully, quiet reflections, apprehensive and distressed over the removal of American soldiers. My stomach quivers, my mouth has a sour taste. The evening discussion and debate is on the Nazi party. It is so heated and loud the guards beat on the doors and windows. No one can understand, nor explain, why the Jewish soldiers are segregated from the other American prisoners. Also, there is no rationale for the horrors mentioned that have been inflicted on civilians before the war, such as gypsies, political dissidents, other nationalities, and Jews.

I remember refugees from Europe when I was in high school, but never thought about which ones, if any, were Jewish. Reality is beginning to dawn on me. I am confused as I reflect, "Why would God allow this if the Jews are his chosen people?" I don't have an answer, but will ask Chaplain Neal.

I slip into the latrine to recap the traumatic day. I'm not sure the Bible won't be confiscated by the guards, so I don't write the names of the ones who left the barracks, just capsule the events around pages 72 and 73 of the New Testament.

I think about the past two weeks. One day, I am fighting for my very existence. The next day, my existence depends on the ability to act like a beast. Hunger causes me to block out any semblance of kindness to others. It is a shock to realize what I, along with others, have become for the sole purpose of self-preservation. I can sense, almost feel, men wrestling with themselves to decide whether to be an animal or be a human. Some act like animals; eyes shifting, darting, continually looking for something to steal. They complain, roam the camp from barracks to barracks seeking to trade for anything. Cigarettes replace money as the primary source of exchange. My lips break into a smile as I remember Cole is from Virginia, home of some of the cigarette companies. Ha, I think, Reynolds Tobacco and Philip Morris would be happy if they knew we place such importance on their product.

My only saving grace is to be alive. I can sporadically see the sun. Even the snow has a calming beauty which can affect one's soul. Life is what counts, and I count mine as important. I think the next day will probably be more of the same, or worse, but if I think of the future, I will lose my marbles. The future is foggy. The present is clear.

When I return from the latrine, the discussions are still in progress. Finally, exhausted, everyone in the barracks begins to settle down. Sleep is more fretful than usual. Bodies turn and toss, and cause the loose boot buckles to clash and clang. Faint snores can be heard.

As I doze off, the thought crosses my mind of the irony of the Jewish soldiers being moved on Friday, a few hours before sundown. Will they be able to celebrate their Sabbat? Well, at least they won't have to worry about cooking on the Holy Day. How about soup? Can a Jew eat it if prepared by someone else on Saturday? I decide someday I'll ask Fellman.

··· ⊷⊱⊰⊶ ···

By Saturday, life in Stalag IXB begins a pattern of sameness. So do the discussions, rumors, food, living conditions, weather. These are the breadth of our interest. There is no other world.

One of the principal topics of conversation is rumors about the end of the war. Prisoners spread, with embellishment, any tidbit of news.

"I hear Patton has reached the Rhine."

"The Russians are in . . ." and so on.

The Serbs have a radio, but it is impossible to determine the validity of their reports. They only say it is a European station. It would be helpful to know the facts.

> 16 January 1945
>
> "Eastern Front: Zhukov's forces take Radom while to the north some of his other units have encircled Warsaw and are fighting their way through the city .... Konev's troops to the south are making even better progress than Zhukov's and have reached Czestochova."
>
> [Source: page 318, *World Almanac Book of World War II*, rev. ed., Bison Books Corp., 1986.]

A rumor spreads through the barracks that we will move today. It could mean another camp, another barracks, another compound. The Serbs are anxious to get rid of us so they can have the barracks again. The rumor may be from them.

The rumor is correct. After dinner, we move from the Serb compound to a barracks in the American compound. I like the Serb compound because they can't speak English. Also, there is less bitching, stealing, yelling, and arguing. The Serbs have been prisoners of war long enough to become accustomed to this existence, or maybe they are not as volatile as the Americans.

Two-hundred-forty of us move to Barracks 42A on the top of the mountain, close to the guard tower. Actually, it is two barracks with an entrance at each end. Each barracks has a large room with a small stove in the middle, and a washroom at the opposite end from the door. At the back of the washroom is a closet-sized enclosure with the proverbial toilet — a hole in the floor over a cesspool. The room is empty.

As we enter, the question is, "Where are the beds?"

"You're standing on 'em. You sleep on the floor," is the standard answer.

I ask, "No straw? What'll I use for toilet paper?"

"Your middle finger, then wipe it in the snow," replies a POW.

"Or just wipe your butt in the snow. That will freeze the runny shit and stop the diarrhea, too."

The cleanliness of an empty barracks quickly disappears when 240 POWs get settled.

Eight of us from the first squad run to the middle of the room, to get space against the wall, under a window. For security, we get in two rows close together, remembering the maxim, "Only trust your closest friends."

Before we left the Serb compound, the non-coms had been called by name at a roll call and sent to another barracks in the American compound. We don't have time to bid farewell to Holcombe, Thibodeaux, nor Albert, only a wave and a wink. Since they are not leaving Stalag IXB, we feel we will continue to see them.

The German Army has prison camps for each rank, privates, non-coms, officers, and separate camps for Air Force personnel. We joked after being captured about going to an Air Corp camp, called "Luft" by the Germans, because of rumors about better treatment.

Kasten, the Man of Confidence, comes to the barracks and tells us to elect a barracks chief, our liaison with him and the German authorities. Benner is nominated and elected without fanfare. He has been a level-headed and competent leader in the other barracks.

A leader of each group is elected. My group of six chooses Pett to continue as leader. His initial act of leadership is to gather us around him and announce, "With the crowded conditions, we can sleep only on our sides, hopefully in a fetal position. If you slept on your back before, well, forget it. I doubt that you can sleep on your stomach, either. The floor is too hard. So, we will all sleep on the left side, then switch sometime during the night — whenever you get a cramp or become numb on your left side. We all have some habits that may be disagreeable to everyone else, but if we are going to survive, we'll have to get used to them. Except flatulence!"

Three of us yell, in unison, "Flatu what?"

Pett explains, "Farting, you uncouth bastards! Anyone that farts in another's face gets his bread last, will miss his turn to be first with the ersatz tea twice, and be the last one of our group in the soup line for a week." Thank goodness the flatus champ of B Company was transferred before we left Fort

Leonard Wood. That guy had a physical problem. He could fart taps while marching around the camp, and frequently did!

We spent the remainder of the day setting up housekeeping in the area the six of us had staked out on the floor. I pull two large nails from the floor in the latrine, nail them next to a window, turn to Pett and announce, "One of these is for you, the other for me. Keep your clothes off my nail, or I'll bust you one."

"Yes, sir," Pett salutes, laughing, and adds, "Higgins, the ever-efficient, organized, bastard. Always fretting over details."

American prisoners of war from other barracks visited just before lockup. Some ask about our capture. Others want to trade. A few just snoop around to determine if we have anything valuable to steal. I put my hand over my pocket with my Bible and think there might just be a religious man among the thieves. At least it will make good trading material.

Five prisoners identify themselves as former 28th Division, 883d Artillery. Benner says the group will entertain us. The "snoopers" leave and the group proceeds to sing a medley of songs.

"Say, these guys are good," Pett says. "Reminds me of a barbershop quartet back home."

One of the singers says, "Now, for the theme song of Stalag IXB. We'll sing it first, then you fellows can follow. It is to the tune of 'The Battle Hymn of the Republic.'"

I turn to Cole, "Not me. I'm not gonna sing a Yankee song."

"Me either." We didn't.

The leader says, "I'll say the words first.

> *"We're a bunch of prisoners living deep in Germany.*
>
> *Eating soup and black bread and a beverage they call tea.*
>
> *And we'll keep on singing 'til Patton sets us free*
>
> *And we go rambling home."*

He adds, "And the chorus is:

> *"Come and get us, Georgie Patton,*
>
> *Come and get us, Georgie Patton,*
>
> *Come and get us, Georgie Patton,*
>
> *So we can ramble home."*

"Okay, everybody sing."

The barracks erupts in song. Cole and I remain silent. Pett and Gleason, in unison, say, "Come on, forget the damn Civil War, you guys, sing!"

Cole answers, "I'm not singing, and it wasn't a Civil War. It was an Invasion of the South."

"Whatever it was called, sing. It will make you feel better."

The singing did have a certain rhythm. I begin to tap my left foot, as Cole begins to swing his arms. Soon, both of us are caught up in the momentum of the singing. But neither one of us says the words nor hums the tune. I'm not *that* bad off.

The guards arrive just at dark and run the singers out, to a rousing clapping of hands. We quickly secure our places on the floor. The first night in the new barracks is "accommodation" night. That is, we spend the night moving, shuffling, kicking, and pushing in an attempt to adapt to the floor.

"If I didn't have any arms, I might be able to sleep," Cole moans as he twists and turns from one side to the other.

"What would you use for a pillow?" I ask, as I fold a jacket to put under my head.

The moans, groans, wheezes, hacking coughs, plus all sorts of unidentified weird sounds, mingle with the dank and pungent smelly clothing of over 200 men crowded together, creating a strangling frustration.

Intermingled with these sounds is the "pooh, pooh, pooh, oomph, oomph, f-a-r-oot," of gas. I didn't know farts could have so many different pitches, lengths, decibels — some as high as a pig's squeal, some as low as a fog horn, others like the "ump-fa-fa" of a base horn. The smell makes me want to vomit; I try to hold my breath for a few minutes, without success. The air is stagnant and foul. I smile as I think that if someone lights a match, the place will explode!

And snores! They run the musical scale from double E flat to a pitch no soprano could ever reach. "H-a-a-ump," and, after at least five minutes, another "H-a-a-ump." Some snores sounded like a machine gun. Others are slow and methodical. It reminds me of a harmonica band in grade school, everyone playing a different note with different rhythm.

Buckles of the unsnapped boots bang against leather as feet shuffle.

"Get off me. Watch where you're going, half-ass. Come on, man, take it easy. That's my head you're kicking."

The floor is cold. My clothes are damp and crackle from the ice that has formed on them. My whole body aches. I wiggle my toes to stop the searing pain. I turn from one side to the other. I can feel pebbles roll from the top of my knee to the bottom. More pain. To put one knee on the other causes both to ache. My back has a constant dull pain. I stretch one leg, pull the other up against my body.

Cole yells, "Get your boot outta my face." No matter which way I turn, or stretch, I hit somebody. Come on, daylight, get here quick! I squeeze my eyelids shut and force my mind to retreat to the past.

I miss my two brothers. I haven't seen them for two years. Where are they right now? Do they live in New York? Is big brother Charles making millions in the advertising business? How many new eating places has he found in the past two years to fill his book of weird places? Wow! What I'd give now for some chow mein, or enchiladas.

My breath comes in short spurts as I attempt to hide my whimpering. I sniffle.

Cole kicks me. "Shut up."

I am both afraid and lonesome in the dark. I am abandoned.

It is worse when the situation appears hopeless and endless. If I think about tomorrow, maybe the sorrow of today will go away. But what could tomorrow bring that would be better than today? Maybe I should throw in the towel. I wonder, "Who would catch it?" Probably nobody.

My spirits perk up when I see through the window the sky turning a light gray. Black fades into lighter and lighter gray, then daylight. I listen as feet stomp up the hill to the barracks. The guard unlocks the door. Thank goodness, the night is gone.

⋯⋯≕✦≕⋯⋯

Benner announces after the morning tea that church services will be held at 10 A.M. for the Catholics, and 11 A.M. for Protestants in a building at the bottom of the hill, near the kitchen.

When a group of us get to the building, it is bursting at the seams with POWs. No doubt, many POWs who never went to church now feel their only hope is some word of encouragement from Chaplain Neal.

Since we can't get in the building, Cole, Pett, Smithy, Pray, Huckel and I walk down the main road to a quiet spot near the guard tower. We sit in a circle behind the barracks, sheltered from the wind. I read, then begin to pencil in recollections of events since capture.

Pett asks, "You read that Bible, too?"

"Yes, but I'm not sure I understand some of the verses. Like Shakespeare, which I can't understand, either."

Huckel adds, "Well, not everybody talks like you southerners. Heck, I don't understand you half the time."

"I don't speak in parables, though. I went to Sunday School for years and listened to stories about people in the Bible. I had a rough time learning the verses. It seems that only the grown folks went to Bible classes, usually on Wednesday nights. That's where you learned the Bible. I had to stay home and study."

Pett says, "You'd think studying the Bible would be more important than doing homework."

The consensus of opinion was that none of us had really studied nor understood the Bible. Parents felt it wasn't necessary. My aunts used to say the Bible was too vulgar for young minds.

We didn't get into a detailed discussion of the Bible. It's hard to be philosophical when you're hungry. Hunger leaves a large void in the brain.

Cole turns to me. "Higg, read a verse or two. You be the preacher."

Pett feigned astonishment as he protested, "Oh, no! Don't say he can be the official preacher. He preaches enough as it is without any suggestions. Every time I say something, he pulls out that Bible and says, 'You swear that's true? Put your hand on the Bible.'"

"I'm just kidding you, Pett. You're so full of bull I never know when you're telling the truth."

"Okay, I'm looking," I answer. I look at the page on which I will record my notes for this Sunday, the book of St. Mark, part of chapter 3 and chapter 4. I read the part about Jesus teaching the multitudes by the seaside, and finally getting in a ship because the people crowded around him.

Pett interrupts, "How could they hear Jesus if He was in a boat? He didn't have a loudspeaker."

Cole answers, "Maybe the wind blew toward the shore and carried his voice, or he has a strong voice. Remember, this is a parable, so you can take liberties with the words. It's the thought that counts. Go on, Higg, read."

"Yes, sir." I read the rest of the chapter about the sower of seed planting seed on bad ground, then good ground, and how the seed of the bad ground didn't grow.

"Naturally," Pett says.

". . . but the seed on the good ground did grow . . . ."

"Naturally," Pett says.

"Quiet, let me finish." I read how the disciples didn't understand the parable either. "See, I told you. They didn't understand it either, so how the hell am I . . . ."

I admonish Pett, "Don't curse, it's Sunday. Now shut up and let me give the punch line." I read verse 11: "'And he said unto them, unto you it is given to know the mystery of the kingdom of God; but unto them that are without, all these things are done in parables.' Which means, I think, that if you are religious you will understand what Jesus says, and if not, well, then get with it."

No one speaks. Reflectively, Cole says, "Can't you find something more meaningful for today?"

I flip back a few pages to page 60. "Here's a good one. I wrote on this page about depending on God and that He is our only hope. Let me read verse 35 of the twenty-fifth chapter of Matthew. Listen. 'For I was hungered, and ye gave me meat; I was thirsty, and ye gave me drink; I was a stranger, and ye took me in.' That means you gotta keep the faith, friends."

Huckel says, "Cole, how about a prayer?" We bow our heads while Cole prays.

I didn't learn much from reading the Bible as a youth, but deep inside I feel God will somehow keep me alive. I know that. He has done that once already, back on the hill, when my platoon fought to protect the captain. But, why did God take the good men, like Harry "Li'l Joe" Bergman, leader of the weapons platoon? Corporal Dupuy? Sergeant Richards? It doesn't seem fair.

Reading the Bible beats thinking about the cold, the hunger, the smell of urine and excrement. Dirt, foul odors, crappy clothes and shoes have become part of our survival. Uncontrollable diarrhea, dysentery. It is difficult to think of anything positive.

Smithy looks up and comments, with a feeling of finality, "This place is a damned mess, and I hope God damns it!"

"Amen, brother," the three of us mutter.

I sit by the fence under the guard tower as the others return to the barracks. I write the entries for yesterday and this morning. I get back to the barracks in time to line up and go to the kitchen for dinner. It is not too bad — some kind of mush soup. After dinner, Pett, Cole and I walk around the compound. We stop near the guard tower behind our barracks and examine the small wire 18 inches above the ground, about three feet in front of the face.

Cole says, "I wonder if that wire is really charged?"

Pett responds with, "I don't know, and I'm not going to test it. But I do know this: I'll be damned if I'm going to give in. Next week, starting tomorrow, we get organized and figure out how we are going to survive."

He bends over, coughs violently, and spits up bloody phlegm.

I look at Cole. He looks away. I feel a cold chill go down my back.

That night, each group gets a one-inch square piece of meat with the bread ration. Strubinger turns his small bite-sized portion over and over, then sniffs it. "Smells rotten. What is it?"

"Probably horse meat," Pett grunts. "It's red. We got some when first captured."

"Or dog," I add.

"Yeah, dog. Remember those little dogs we saw when we got off the train in Bad Orb? They were dressed out, ready to eat. I bet the Jerries took them from the civilians to cook for the big Sunday meal."

"I don't believe I want any meat. Here, Higg, you can have mine."

"Thanks. Hell, dog, hog, horse, whatever, I'm hungry!"

I take his meat and chew it slowly. Man, it's tough! I curl my lips and look at Clete. I bare my teeth and snarl, "Grrrr, grrr," then bark like the guard dogs, "Woof! Woof!"

He has a sickly grin on his face. He gags, almost throws up.

In the washroom, I write the final entry for the week. The discussion about international law, and how it applies to us, drones on and on in the barracks. The 10-watt bulb doesn't give much light, so I sit under the window to get light from the clear sky. Stars twinkle bright in the light of a hazy moon. I stare at the clear sky and pretend I can see the brisk winds of the Gulf of Mexico pushing waves, that heave like an undulating stomach with sparkling white caps, slowly toward the shore. Each wave rushes to catch the one ahead before it can hit the shore and run back into the surf.

I return to the present to see a trickle of water from the bottom of the drainless wash basin run to the hole in the center of the floor. My gaze returns to the window, and shifts from one star to another.

"Twinkle, twinkle, little star, how I wonder where you are . . . ."

"Star light, star bright, give me my wish tonight. God, help me get through this mess." My head drops. The sounds of the barracks become faint as I think, What a helluva first week. How many more can I survive?

Chapter 2

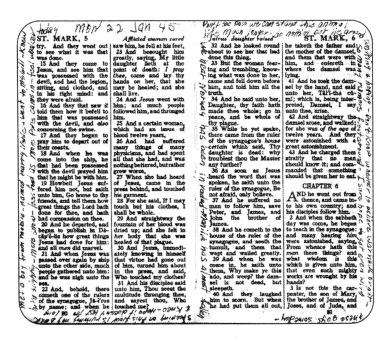

Week Two

22 January–28 January 1945

<hr>

Monday, 22 January

Met a boy from Mobile named Harry Noble. Went to McGill; knew him slightly. More snow; less footroom as more POWs come in. Feel weaker; sleep on this floor is ruining my back and knee. Hope it doesn't last for long.

Don't see how we can stand this animal life much longer. We do nothing but lie around and wait — wait and hope. Don't know whether to believe war news or not — so many rumors float around. I sure hope to get even with these guys someday. We hear Norway has been invaded; Manila has almost fallen.

Tuesday, 23 January

Had carrot soup and boiled potatoes for dinner — was a little more filling. Men are hot about food situation; we are very weak — some are in bed. We've been discussing what we hope to do after the war — I'm not sure as yet.

Some more of our company came in yesterday — almost 3,000 here now. Wrote a card to Charles today; wonder if he got it. War news sounds good on Russian front. It is a nice day. Our planes just passed over, going to Frankfurt, I guess. Everyone is looking forward to the Red Cross committee on the 25th.

Wednesday, 24 January

Outline has been made to present to Red Cross today. POWs are still weak; nothing to do. War news sounds good. My feet hurt every time I sit down — must be thawing out. Everyone else is the same.

Soup was thicker for dinner (for the Red Cross to see). He is to come to the barracks, but Jerry will probably have him see just so much. Chaplain Neal had Bible class today — very interesting. He's a professor from Lambert College in Tennessee — took five books of New Testament.

Thursday, 25 January

All non-coms left today. Sure did hate to see Holcombe & Tibby go — they were swell men — also Smithy. Hope they got a better break than we have; couldn't be any worse. This place is really disorganized now. Guess it will be this way for a long time. Feel depressed today — guess the thought of so much disorganization just when things were looking up gets me. I hate anything so messed up as this place is.

Chopped wood for three hours; was so weak could hardly walk. All of us were — couldn't lift a log two inches in diameter and two feet long — didn't know I was so weak. We have to move to another barracks soon. The war news sounds good, almost too good to be true.

Friday, 26 January

Big snow storm today. Had carrot soup for dinner; went to kitchen for it. Couldn't eat all of mine, not that it was so much!

The Red Cross men turned out to be two Jerries from Berlin. The main cause for us living like this is that our bombers have wrecked the railroads — same reason for not getting Red Cross packages. The French are the only ones getting Red Cross stuff. Had discussion on whether to join American Legion or not — was good discussion. Had good bit of jam for supper — first meal in long time.

Saturday, 27 January

Everyone is really disgusted with the Red Cross. Have to organize the barracks into companies; things are still messed up. Potato soup for dinner — it was the dirtiest stuff I've ever seen — looked like mud. I couldn't eat all of mine.

Sunday, 28 January

Last night, two men killed a guard in the American kitchen — now we don't eat or get wood until they are apprehended. Don't know if it was GIs, but we are starving anyway. We can't figure out what we've done to deserve this torture and mental strain as well as physical breakdown. 1945 has been memorable so far, nothing but starvation. I think these old guards are afraid we will try to break out, because the place is heavily guarded. Our guard is 57 years old and has six kids. One, ol' Jerry, has 16 kids. Have already gone five days without food — wonder how long it will be this time. They found the two who killed the guard, so we eat again — the Lord is with us.

By the second week, everything about Stalag IXB begins to affect the bodies and minds of American POWs. It is physically painful to leave the barracks. The 300 men in my barracks slowly stumble and hobble into the icy wind and blowing snow only when absolutely necessary. Some prisoners in my barracks crawl on their knees so their feet won't touch the floor. They have frozen feet, swollen and reddish-blue, with an oyster-white goo oozing from each crack beneath the dirty wrappings. It is too painful to wear any type of shoe, and walking or the mere touch to the wrapped feet causes a cry of anguish.

"Don't touch my ... owwwww ... stoooopppp it," accompanies sobs, whales, crying day and night.

Tears stream down a dirty, bearded face when the name of a pained and crippled prisoner is called for camp duty. Buddies answer for friends. Benner skips the name if he knows a POW cannot walk.

Time begins to take its toll. Vigor wanes, reflexes slow. Faces change from sharp expressions to saggy jaws. Eyes are cloudy and stare at nothing. Lips turn down. Noses have so much hair protruding into bushy mustaches it is difficult to see a nose. A POW walks past me with watery snot trickling through his mustache into an open mouth. I nudge Pett, "Look at the poor SOB. Why doesn't he wipe his nose?"

Pett says, "Why? Probably tastes better than the slop we get for dinner. Look at his sleeves." I stare; both sleeves are stiff and covered with frozen snot.

"Man, he's out of it. Look at that blank stare."

The man under discussion stops in front of us, stares at me, then grins. He has no teeth; his gums are a dark red, lips are cracked. Droplets of blood run into a mottled, stringy beard that is full of knots and dirt. He is about 30 years old, but the wrinkles make him look like pictures I've seen of Methuselah, who was about 900 years old when he died.

It tears my heart out to see prisoners shuffle, shoulders stooped as if carrying a ton of hay. Eyes are cast downward, which makes it easier to walk against the cold, zero-degree wind. And we've only been here a week! What the hell will we look like in two weeks? If we last that long.

Oh, my God, I think as I see the disintegration of the human body, where can I find any happiness? Maybe a day without cold? An extra piece of bread at night when a member of my group dies and we don't report his death? Or when I find a small piece of horse meat in my watery soup? An aching toe that begins to thaw? Or maybe happiness is the day I can put both cheeks of my butt on the floor at the same time and don't whimper and cry. God, how much more misery can I endure? My mind comes into focus to clear it of sad thoughts. No, God, I will *not* be despondent!

I make every attempt to adjust to the squalid conditions of Stalag IXB. True, my heart aches. It is mentally tortuous to see my fellow prisoners of war turn into animals — groveling, snarling, grabbing, pushing, and shoving. Their behavior increases my awareness of the cold, grime, and hunger. Hell, I am probably not any better behaved. We seem to be covered with a black blanket of doom. It is pervasive, like the tentacles of an unseen octopus that grabs us and forces us to gasp for breath as we flail our arms, desperate to escape. But there is no escape.

As American soldiers, we are fine-tuned instruments of battle, programmed to fight every hour of the day and night. Captured, we are caged animals, snatched from the jungle.

Company B of the 275th Infantry Regiment, along with the 274th and 276th Regiments of the 70th Division, entered the vast arena of war in late

December 1944. Most of us were untested in battle. Someone said we were, "full of piss and vinegar." In this short period, the 15,000 soldiers of the Division have been exposed to both unknown and unsuspected experiences. The rug of organized, felicitous comradeship has been jerked out from under us. We founder in an abyss of the unknown. It's like the childhood Saturday matinees movie reel with Tom Mix that broke. We impatiently sit in the darkness awaiting the next reel. We just don't have any popcorn to eat, nor gum to stick under our seats.

Prison life settles into a steady repetitiveness and adjustment to the constant whining and complaining. To me, it is useless bitching — we are at the mercy of our captors.

The major topics of discussion are the extreme cold, deteriorating health, home, war news, and food, food, food. Oh, boy! Do we talk about food! That is my salvation. I make every attempt to retain an attitude of sarcasm and sense of flippancy.

A number of events temporarily block out the extreme pain in my back and knees from sleeping on the cold floor, plus the gnawing hunger pains in my stomach. One is the psychological battle between Robert Zion and the German authorities, which began last Friday when the American soldiers who identified themselves as Jewish were segregated and moved to another barracks.

The Germans are convinced Zion is Jewish. His last name is the clincher. Each morning after roll call, the guards take him for interrogation by the prison camp officials. Robert (Bob) doesn't say much when he returns after two or three hours. His hands shake; his face has a deep scowl. After his first interrogation, he takes some cigarette butts from his jacket. "Here, you guys split the butts among yourselves." He tosses five or six butts to Pett, then walks off.

Pett turns to me, "I wonder if Zion is Jewish? Why would he hide it?"

"I don't know. It's his business. If he wants to keep it secret, so what? I wouldn't tell the bastards anything, either. We don't have to provide any information other than name, rank, and serial number." I smile and add, "Not only that, but he brings back smokes. Hope he strings them along forever."

We talk about what to reveal and what not to reveal to the Germans. Like me, some men in the barracks say don't tell the Jerries anything about anything. In the case of Zion, I suspect the Gestapo will get Zion to slip up and mention something about his past to identify him as a Jew. It is like a cat playing with a mouse. When they tire of the game, they will cast him aside.

I wonder why the Germans are so obsessed with uncovering the background on one person. Seems like they would have more important matters. Pett comments, "These people are paranoid when it comes to Jews." In the mean time, a few of us get free smokes.

Bob claims he is 'nothing.' "Hell, I never remember going to any church. I was adopted, along with a younger sister." After a few days of interrogations, Bob becomes more relaxed and talks about the sessions. "For a few days, the Jerries did all the questioning. But I guess they aren't too swift, because in came some civilians to ask the questions. I understand they are Gestapo. Relentless, they ask penetrating questions, one after the other, off the wall, changing the subject after every question."

My curiosity gets the best of me. "What are some of the questions?"

"All over the place, but usually about my childhood and church. One will question me, then another one. Like, 'When did you start going to synagogue?' When I answer 'What?' then the other one will say, 'What is the difference between a synagogue and a temple?'"

I get a quizzical look on my face, then the third interrogator comes up with something like, "When did you study the Torah?" Before I can open my mouth, another Jerry asks, "Where did your sister sit when you went to shul?"

Huckel interrupts, "Don't they notice you butt the cigarettes and put them in your pocket?"

"Sure. All three smile, then one of them gives me another smoke. I guess they think if I'm humored I'll fall into their trap. One of them smokes cigars, which I would love. They smell so good."

I reply, "Ask for one. It will be great for my pipe."

"Naw. The guy slobbers all over it."

"I can dry it out. See if you can get one."

"Okay, I'll try."

After one session, Clete Strubinger advises Zion to tell them about your first brit milah.

"My what?"

"You're no Jew, or you would know. A brit milah is when . . . ."

Zion puts his hands on his ears, shakes his head, and yells, "Stop! I don't want to know anything about Jews, or Jewish words. If I don't know, they can't trick me."

Pett points his finger at Clete, "Yeah, shut up. Just because you lived in South Philly and know all those Jewish words."

Gleason adds, "That's right. But string 'em along. I enjoy the smokes. Next time, smoke faster and get more butts."

Bob Zion mentions that in one interrogation, the Gestapo carry on a conversation among themselves about Jewish holidays and rituals. One will mention what he calls a 'Sukkot,' another something like 'shit shiv.'

Chuck interrupts, "You mean sit shiva. When a Jew dies, the family doesn't do anything for a week. They . . . ."

"Stop!" Zion yells. "I told you, I don't want to know anything about Jews or their rituals. All I remember as a kid is the Jewish kids in school take off on Yom Kippur, Hanukkah, and something called Rosh Hashanah, but I don't know why."

Huckel says the Jerries are probably fattening him up for the kill. Pett adds that Zion won't get too fat on a bowl of watery soup every day.

Gleason adds, "Maybe they are going to make soup out of your bones. Or just suck on 'em."

Zion didn't think it was funny. "You guys shut up, or I won't bring back any more butts."

Discretion is better than humor, especially sick humor. It's good while it lasts, but ends a few weeks later when Robert Zion is sent to another prison camp with all the American Jewish POWs and about 350 other POWs from Stalag IXB.

Monday morning, I see an American prisoner with "Mobile" inked on the back of his field jacket. (Many POWs write their home town or other message, such as division or regiment, on the back of a garment.) "Hey, Mobile!" I yell. We greet each other and discuss high school days back in Mobile. Harry Noble attended the Catholic high school. He is in the 106th Division, and relates how two-thirds of his division was captured.

"Wow, you did worse than me! Only my company got captured. I don't feel so bad, now."

We say good-bye after a few minutes of nostalgic discussion about home. It is useless to discuss our current miserable condition, since there is nothing either of us can do about it.

"See you around, Higg."

"Yeah, see ya."

He turns and walks down the hill.

Rumors about the war spread like wildfire through the prison camp. Many originate when the Man of Confidence meets with the German Commandant each day and gets whatever war news the German official decides to reveal. The Man of Confidence relays the news to the barracks leaders, who in turn inform the prisoners in their barracks. The news is embellished, interpreted, expanded and twisted as it passes from one mouth to another.

One American prisoner constantly darts from one group to another. His small feet move like bicycle pedals, his head moving from side to side as if he expects someone to attack him. He stands about five foot and three inches, with arms that reach his knees; he is always hunched over, and whispers into someone's ear like it's a big secret.

Once, he came up to six or seven of us and whispered in a conspiratorial tone, "I got it straight from the Serbs. They heard it on the radio — said things look good — U.S. troops made a beachhead on Luzon in the Orient someplace, and are headed toward Manila. The Serbs thought Norway was invaded and the Germans have moved out of Warsaw."

Pett snaps, "Bullshit! I didn't hear any radio last night."

"It's true, I tell you." Away he scurries to another group.

Huckel turns to Pett, "You think it's true?"

Pett shrugs his shoulders. "Who knows? At least it's something to talk about."

I add, "And give a little hope." I want to be optimistic, even in the face of what appears to be timeless adversity.

---

17 January 1945
"Eastern Front: The totally devastated city of Warsaw is cleared of German resistance by Zhukov's forces. A Polish unit fighting with the Red Army is involved in the final attack."

19 January 1945
"On Luzon, the U.S. attacks are now being concentrated to the south of the beachhead with the aim of striking to Manila. Carmen is taken."

[Source: page 318, *World Almanac Book of World War II*, rev. ed., Bison Books Corp., 1986.]

I spend the remainder of Monday feeling sorry for myself. I am miserable, cannot get myself organized, or keep my mind on one subject.

——— ▰ ———

Tuesday morning is no better. I continue to lie around, mind in neutral, drifting like a piece of wood on a smooth lake.

Dinner is announced. I drag my body from the barracks for the ration of dirty water. A few unpeeled, blackish carrots float aimlessly on top. As I sit on the ground and contemplate whether or not to eat this mess I hear a steady hum. I look up at the source of the noise. "Great guns! The sky is black as far as I can see. Look at those planes. What are they?" I drop my container of soup and point skyward. Gleason says, "They are B-17's. Must be thousands of them."

Pett jumps up, waves his arms as if the planes can see him from about 5,000 feet. "Hope they are going to Frankfurt. That's only 30 miles from here."

I cover my eyes from the sun. "We should hear explosions then."

Huckel says, "I suspect they are going to Frankfurt up north, not to Frankfurt am Main, which is closer to us."

Gleason drops his head, "Maybe someday it will be the one on that river near here." The planes move across the sky for 15 or 20 minutes. I can guess what havoc they will bring. Poor civilians, trapped victims of war.

I'll say one thing for Benner and his Boy Scout training, he sure comes up with ideas to divert our attention from our misery. He suggests Tuesday after dinner we get in groups and discuss our plans after the war.

"Where the hell does he come up with all these crazy ideas?" I ask as a number of us discuss our plans after liberation. I had a taste of college in the Army Specialized Training Program. So, I might try it. Sure beats welding in a shipyard, which I did after high school.

After the bread is delivered and divided Benner announces the Red Cross will visit us on the 25th of the month, so everyone should compile a list of grievances. He said to be sure to emphasize the lack of food, the cold, and the crowded barracks with no beds.

There is not much interest, and I say, "It's a waste of time. The Germans will do what they want to do. Has Hitler listened to anybody since he came into power? I doubt he will listen to the Red Cross."

Pett says, "Don't be negative, Higg. Loan me your pencil. I left mine at college when I was drafted. I will be secretary."

"You never had a pencil. Just remember where you got this one, buster."

"If I don't remember you will, at least when you get ready to write in that Bible. Loan me some paper, too."

"Lousy secretary, no paper, no pencil, and probably can't spell." I give him both pencil and paper. At least the discussion takes our minds off the help-lessness of the situation. Otherwise, it's a waste of time.

Gleason suggests we have some fun making up the list. "I want a private room."

"... with an ice box in it," adds Pett jovially.

"... full of beer," Strub bellows, then laughs.

Huckel says, "I'll take a large bed, with a mattress so thick you need an oxygen mask to breathe."

"That's stupid. I never heard of a mattress ..." Strubinger starts.

"You never had a mattress in South Philly." I say.

Pettingill interrupts. "Shut up, you guys. Be serious."

He adds, "It's too crowded, lying on the floor, sleeping on your side, no covers, no heat, cold."

We ignore his seriousness. I join the game. "I'd like a room with a southern exposure."

Strubinger grabs his stomach to simulate laughter, as he says, "To see what? A field of grits?"

"You wouldn't know a southern exposure from a sewer, since you're from Philly."

And so it goes late into the night. As the wind whistles across the mountain and the night gets blacker, everyone settles in his own cocoon — a dirty, damp blanket to cover our smelly clothing. Finally, Pett says, "Bull. I'll make up a list. We all have the same complaints."

— ◂╼▶╾ ▸

Religious involvement helps me keep my sanity. On Wednesday, a group of us decide to attend Bible study. Pett, Huckel, Cole, Homer Smith and I are the Protestants in the group. Strubinger and Gleason won't go to a Protestant service, since both are Catholic.

Before we leave the barracks, I ask Huckel whether the Protestant Chaplain's name is spelled Neil or Neal. "I want to write it down."

He says, "What difference does it make? The Krauts will take your Bible before we get out of here, anyway."

"Well, I might just go to Tennessee, attend his Lambert College and become a preacher."

Pett howls. "Hell, you might as well be a preacher, the way you always make me swear on the Bible every time I say something."

I express mock astonishment. "Well, first, I never know if you're telling the truth."

"Yeah," he interrupts, "I'll buy that. But why do you have to organize everything all the time? I'm glad you're not the squad leader. Let me enjoy my misery, knucklehead. That's what happens when you're an only child."

"I just don't like mess. My aunt is a stickler for cleanliness, and everything has to be in its proper place."

Russ Huckel smiles. "Brother, she should be here — would she have fun! Maybe she could get these jerks organized into some semblance of order."

I lift my head, throw out my chest, hold up both hands, and in a quiet voice, say "Please don't curse. We are on the way to Bible class."

Robert Smith, my assistant Browning Automatic Rifleman (BARman), adds, "Yeah, and while she is here she can get these guys to hit that damn hole in the latrine at night, and not crap all over the floor."

Pett says, "And push their guts back up their ass and pull up their pants so as to not drip shit all over everybody when they return to the barracks."

About half-way to the chapel I run to the front of the group, turn, hold up my hand, and yell, "Stop! All I said was that I might attend Lambert College, and all I get is a bunch of crap from you guys. Let's walk to Bible class in a more congenial frame of mind."

Smith asks, "What's congenial mean?"

Huckel replies, "Higg is using a big word to say friendly."

Pett bows, waves one arm like he is Sir Walter Raleigh laying down his cloak for a damsel, and says, "Yes, master, I will be on my best behavior, even though the snow and wind blow directly into my face, and my body aches from trying to sleep on a cold, splintery floor full of cracks. I will tune out the wails, farts, and snores in 15 different decibels; hold my breath from the smells of diarrhea and the bad breath from you guys."

He stares at us and continues, "I will ignore the twisted bodies, the knees in my back. I shall stay alert to prevent some bastard — oops, sorry, Higgs — some sweet thing from snatching my bread while I sleep."

I drop my arms and reply, "My, my, Pett, where did you get all the energy to carry on like that? Pett is in a good frame of mind today. Should be a wonderful Bible lesson."

Smith says to me, "Just don't let him sing."

"After that truthful tirade, he won't have the energy to sing."

The friendly banter helps relieve the stress of prison life.

The weather is miserable. It is cold and wet, and the snow blows in our faces as we walk to a barracks near the main gate. In spite of the misery, our spirits are uplifted, and I note a wee bit of spring in our steps.

The Germans have designated a specific barracks as both the Catholic and Protestant chapel. Wooden benches face a rail in the front of the barracks. A large wood-burning stove sits between the rail and the rows of benches. I don't know if POWs come to Bible study on Wednesday and church on Sunday to hear the message, or just to get warm in a clean building, but a little religion might filter through the hardened exterior of the soul.

Since our arrival at Stalag IXB, Protestant Chaplain Neal and the Catholic Chaplain, Father Hurley, have shown extreme compassion and willingness to listen to any and all complaints. Their activities provide mental stimulation and peace of mind to my spiritless brain.

The two disciples of Christ appear wherever a group of men gather. They are always happy and optimistic and set a good example of devout faith in God.

I recall once when Chaplain Neal left our barracks a POW remarked, "How can he be so content on an empty stomach, and in such a filthy place?"

Russ Huckel replies, "I guess both chaplains know God will take care of them. They have arrived at the highest level of spiritual contentment."

I remember the fellow who slept across from our group, thin and short, with dark, beady eyes that constantly twitched behind a jet-black beard. During a discussion the first week on religion, he whispered in a raspy voice, "I'd just like for God to give me some bread. Forget the brainy stuff."

He was dead the next morning.

It seemed to me then, and still does, that God could have given him a tiny piece of bread. No one even knew his name; he had no dog tags. I wonder if he has arrived at the highest level of spiritual contentment?

We push and shove to get on the second row of the chapel, close to the heater. Chaplain Neal opens with the comment that it is gratifying to see so many prisoners attend the Bible lessons and church services, even if it is just to get warm. He adds, "At least you made an effort to get off your duffs, and do something other than lie around and feel sorry for yourselves."

The Chaplains do not urge POWs to attend services. Their presence among the prisoners, and a quiet, cheerful, but not overbearing, politician-type glad-handling, Cheshire-grinning-attitude encourages many of the 3,000-plus prisoners to attend.

Bible class stimulates my mind. I enjoy reading my New Testament, even if I don't understand many of the words and phrases. Reading the King James version is like reading Shakespeare in high school — confusing.

When we finally settle down, Chaplain Neal reads I Corinthians, chapter 4, verse 11: "Even unto this present hour we both hunger, and thirst, and are naked, and are buffeted, and have no certain dwelling place." He summarizes the reading by urging us to have faith, "Be faithful in these difficult times."

In chorus with others, I mumble, "Amen."

Cole says, "You can say that again, Preacher."

Huckel whispers, "Might as well be naked. I couldn't shiver any more than I do now with these wet, sticky garments."

Chaplain Neal says it is easier to throw in the towel than fight to survive. He adds, "Think about tomorrow. Just hang on until tomorrow, then the next day. Take it one day at a time." Someone in the back speaks up. "I guess it can't get any worse, might get better."

A chorus of voices mutter, "Amen, brother."

Pett says, "Most of these guys must be Baptist. I never heard Methodists say Brother all the time."

"Amen, brother," I say, and wink at him.

I'm not impressed with Chaplain Neal's reading of Romans 14:17, about meat and drink not being the Kingdom of God, but righteousness and peace and Joy to the Holy Ghost are of the Kingdom of God. I say, "With more meat in my belly, I will have more righteousness and peace."

A voice behind us replies, "Amen, brother."

Pett says, "Another Baptist."

The concluding quote by Chaplain Neal is more in tune with my thoughts. He reads John 17:33: "These things I have spoken unto you, that in me ye might have peace . . . . Be of good cheer; I have overcome the world."

As Chaplain Neal prays, I ask God to help me continue my nonchalant, cheery attitude, to give me strength to survive. Humor is one of my soul's weapons used to fight for self-preservation, since I don't have a gun. Perhaps my sense of humor will give me the ability to rise above the calamitous situation. There *must* be joy in a small thing that occurs each day. If nothing else, I will pick on Strubinger. "God, let me keep a jovial frame of mind, if only for a few minutes each day."

Chaplain Neal reads Psalm 46, from which the song "A Mighty Fortress is Our God" was adapted. He leads the POWs in the concluding song. Voices drop a few decibels and quiver when we sing the words, "We will not fear, for God hath willed His truth to triumph through us."

I look at the floor and silently pray, "Come on, God, help me out. How much longer can I take this screaming, the chaotic condition of this camp, the complete breakdown of human decency?" Oh, well, I think, to hell with it. I shrug my shoulders.

I smile and stare at Huckel. "Would you mind *not* singing? A croaking frog can emit a more melodious tune. I wish Gleason was Methodist — at least he can sing!"

"Shut up, wise-ass. You don't sound so good yourself."

Pett looks pious as he leans down the row and whispers, "Please! No profanity in the Lord's house."

Huckel and I snicker, then bellow out the end of the song.

Wednesday afternoon, I stop by a group of men and listen to a POW from the 106th Division that has been at Stalag IXB since last Christmas. He explains how the Germans separate their prisoners. "The Germans have separate prison camps for airmen — 'Luft I,' for example; and for officers. Naval personnel are placed in prison camps called 'Marlag' with a number to designate the particular camp.

"The Stalag is a camp for privates, non-coms and PFCs. Non-coms are usually placed in separate prison camps." He adds that airmen are treated much better than the ground forces because Hermann Goering, chief of the Luftwaffe, thinks all airmen are the elite of any armed service.

"Balls … crap … nuts" accompany guffaws from the ones in the group.

The knowledgeable POW joins in the laughter. "I agree. Let me add that the first American POWs at Stalag IXB bitched and yelled until the officers were transferred to Oflags. Everyone pulled rank, from the colonel down to the lieutenant. Division Headquarters officers thought they were better than Battalion officers. Supply officers said they shouldn't even be here. On and on it went — it was a friggin' mess. To top it off, the privates told everybody to bug off; we're all prisoners and there's no rank, and only the guys with the guns have rank. Fights broke out all over the camp. It was chaotic. It was a blessing when this camp finally got rid of the officers. Now, if only the non-coms would leave, we'll have some peace and quiet."

—·— ≡·≡ —·—

He gets his wish. At roll call Thursday it is announced that the non-coms will move within the hour. Only three non-coms from the 1st Platoon were alive when our company was captured. Those in Stalag IXB are Tom Holcombe, platoon sergeant; Walter Thibodeaux (Tibby), sergeant of the 1st Squad, in which I am the BARman, and Corporal Joseph Albert, platoon sniper.

Second Lieutenant Francis Buttrick, my platoon leader, was shipped to another prison camp immediately after our capture, as was Lieutenant Ray Broughton, 2d platoon leader, and Lieutenant Walter Smith of the 3d Platoon. No one knows what happened to Lieutenant Groffie, Executive Officer of B Company, 275th Infantry.

Captain William Schmied, Company Commander, seriously wounded, was taken from the battlefield by the Germans. I recall First Sergeant Carlos Ramos sitting in the jeep holding the captain's head, tears streaming down his face. We never knew what happened to the other soldiers from B Company.

Among the 1,200-plus non-coms whose names were called was Homer Smith, my assistant BARman.

"How the hell did you get on that list?" Huckel asked when the barracks leader called out the names. "You're not a non-com."

Smith says, "They probably got me confused with another Smith. It's a common name."

I hug Smithy after he has gathered his meager belongings. No doubt, he saved my life many times. My throat tightens as I remark, "Well, maybe you'll get a break. It can't be any worse than this place."

Smithy recalls my frantically whispering that I had to take a crap when we were surrounded by the enemy on the hill at Falkenberg Heights. "And when Higg lowered his pants, out fell a fig bar."

"It did, too. And we ate the fig bar — you, Pray, and me. Well, if we could tolerate the cold on that hill for four days, you can take any punishment in store for you."

Huckel shakes Smithy's hand, then hugs him. "See what kind of camp they put you in. If it's a good one, claim you're a non-com. If it's worse than this — and I don't see how it could be — then yell to be sent to another camp."

"Fat chance of that," Smith answers. "I haven't had any luck so far in this doggone Army."

The group was marched out of camp before we could line up on the road to bid farewell.

We had more room in the barracks when the non-coms, and Smithy, moved out. Only about 300 men in the barracks now. No private rooms, but at least we can stretch our legs at night.

After dinner on Thursday afternoon, I get more bad news. Twelve names, including mine, are called to chop wood.

Huckel says I may be able to escape.

"I'm too weak to run. Besides, I don't know where we are."

Cole smiles and says, "Take Pett, he knows German."

"Never mind. He'd just get us shot with that college German of his. Anyway, I'd just as soon cut wood as listen to the cries of anguish and pain in this barracks. At least I can walk. Maybe it will be quieter in the woods. To get out of this barracks is a blessing, away from that sour smell of body rot and filth."

The smell of human decay causes my eyes to smart and my nose to tingle. It's sad to see men delicately removing their rotted socks from swollen feet that have the hue of a blue-black ocean. Some feet have blisters the size of pennies and a quarter-inch high, and ooze a thick, creamy liquid. I am the only one from my platoon on the detail.

As I walk to the front of the barracks I hear Pett chortle, "Luck of the Irish. Get lots of wood. I'm cold."

"Kiss my butt, all of you."

When we line up outside the barracks, I glance at the others on the wood chopping detail. One has an empty sleeve pinned to his shoulder. Another POW, about five feet and seven inches, wears the GI-issue tin glasses, thick as a magnifying glass. He has a jerky left-to-right motion to push hair out of his eyes. He doesn't wear any head gear. I can see why — he has a half-ton of straight, stiff hair that goes in all directions. I ask him how he got in the Army with two-inch thick glasses.

"I volunteered. I got tired of dirty looks. I was told my only duty would be as a clerk in some rear-action group. How the hell did I know the Krauts would capture most of the division?"

Some of the group look to be in fair shape. I note one with long blond hair, blue eyes, and thin as a two-by-four. Another has black, curly hair over his head, face, and hands. His body is probably hairy, too. Reminds me of an ape without the stoop and arms that dangle to the ground. His uniform is a mismatch of ill-fitting dress jacket, pants from a tank jumpsuit, and two different boots — one a rubber shoe-pac, the other a heel-less leather boot missing a buckle. I decide we won't get much wood with this motley group.

We stumble, in slow motion, behind two sad-looking guards, disgruntled, no doubt, because they had to leave a warm barracks. When we get to the wood yard outside the gate, behind the clock tower, one guard stops and informs us in broken English, "You can't cut all the trees. This forest is protected by order of the Fuhrer. You will only cut the marked trees."

Another guard takes an ax and puts a nick in selected trees. Then he scrapes snow from around the marked tree, points to the ground two feet below the top of the snow, and smiles and jabbers in German. The other guard turns to us and says, "No use wasting all that wood."

A POW mutters to me, "Yeah, but it would be easier to chop at the height of the snow. That way, you don't have to bend down."

The 12 of us take turns chopping wood. When it is my turn to wield the ax, my legs wobble as I stomp around in the snow up to my knees, even though it is warmer swinging the ax than just standing around. I am so weak I can't lift a piece of wood two inches in diameter and about two feet long. My knees buckle. Someone helps me get to my feet. Like the other 11, I am as week as a newborn kitten.

After a few hours, we get smart and clear a spot in the trees and pile leaves on the cold ground. When not chopping, we sit close to each other for body warmth. The guards aren't eager to work, either. They spend their time huddled together, smoking, and from the tone of their voices and gestures, complaining about the camp, the officers, the food. Typical army men, regardless of nationality — bitch, bitch, bitch.

We spend most of the afternoon picking up the fallen limbs. There wasn't much chopping. The English-speaking guard notices our inaction and grunts in guttural English, "Less wood, more cold."

As the dampness settles on the ground and the sky begins to darken, the guards put six pieces of wood on each of our outstretched arms, and we trudge back to the wood yard by the gate to the camp. We then stumble back to our barracks. I am exhausted. I fall on the floor and wrap the smelly, thin blanket around me, ignore conversation, and try to sleep, but am too sore to relax. Someone kicks me to get the bread for supper.

After I get the groups rations I toss it to somebody to cut up and curl up in my blanket. I am too sore and tired to eat. I toss and turn to ease the ache in my bones. I can't sleep. My mind jumps over thoughts like a horse in a steeplechase as I try to forget my pain. A smile crosses my chapped lips. I recall a remark by a prisoner from Chicago, who said the stench from the crap and mud, the wailing and whining, remind him of the stockyards. I could add we aren't fattened up for the kill, just starving to death. If I live until summer, maybe I'll get on a farm. Fresh milk, eggs, and vegetables! It'd be my luck to go to a shipyard.

Even the guards cannot understand the shuffling of prisoners of war around Germany. "The Fuhrer doesn't know what to do with all the soldiers we have captured." We are ignorant of events of the war. It never occurs to us that one reason for all the movement of POWs in and out of Stalag IXB is the advance of allied troops into Germany from all directions.

13 January 1945
Eastern Front. "The German defense lines all along the front in Poland are shattered by the soviet advance."

20 January 1945
Eastern Front. "The Soviet offensive against the German forces in East Prussia achieves an important breakthrough in the attacks from the northeast .... In Hungary the fighting continues, but the Soviets now control the West half of the town."

20 January 1945
Western Front. "General de Lattre's French First Army begins an offensive in the Vosges area near Colmar .... In the Ardennes, the advance of Patton's Third Army goes on. Brandenburg is taken."

[Source: pages 318–19, *World Almanac Book of World War II*, rev. ed. Bison Books Corp., 1986.]

I can feel the frustration of confinement permeate the prison camp; the cold, the putrid and tiny quantities of food, the bodies stacked like cords of wood in smelly barracks. Then, add the constant roar of Allied aircraft day and night. Everyone, guards and POWs, are edgy.

I caution those close to me to not make the guards mad. "They are so jumpy they will shoot at the slightest provocation." Then I add, "I don't believe the zookeepers know what to do with so many of us crowded together. They run around like headless chickens. Note how they look at us with their eyes moving back and forth, afraid to stop and talk, hands poised on the clubs that hang by their sides. I doubt it helps their morale to see our Air Corps flying over all day, hear the drone of our planes at night. POWs keep coming into the camp, then some move out. I suspect some higher-up is making life miserable for the ones who run this camp."

Strubinger snarls, "Piss on 'em. Turn us loose. Look at the Italians; those guys run in and out of camp all the time."

Pett says, "Ever notice how no one pays any attention to them? Are they prisoners, or what? They wander in and out of the camp just like the French."

Huckel adds, "I thought the Italians were on the Germans' side."

Cole shrugs his shoulders. "This war is so screwed up I don't think anybody knows who is on whose side." He adds, "It makes me nervous. I'm never sure what the guards will do. They act like we'll riot, and they could get trigger happy. Although there aren't too many guards in this camp, from what I can see."

Clete says, "Yeah, but they have the guns."

The food ranges from just tolerable to putrid, which would be a good cause for a riot. As a POW in the chow line once said, "From nose-holding to gag, from heave to vomit." I never experienced such unpredictable weather. One day it is freezing cold; another day it snows; then it warms up, the snow melts, and the camp is a sea of gooey mud.

＊＊＊

I survive Saturday, but don't remember much about it.

＊＊＊

Sunday morning, just as the sky begins to turn from black to light gray, the door to our barracks flies open to shouts of, "Raust! Raust! Raust!" The ear-shattering barks are followed by screams, in German and English, "Now! Outside. Line up."

Guards stomp into the barracks in complete battle gear. Some of the bayonet-capped rifles wave around the room. Others poke men closest to the door. Boots kick us.

The reflection of searchlights from the guard tower bounce from wall to wall around the barracks. The shadows of the guards flash on and off the walls.

I sit straight up. My heart pounds as I think, oh, hell, this is it. I begin to gather my meager belongings. I feel we will either be shot or marched out of the camp. I feel my shirt pocket for my Bible. There is no time to think where I can hide it. The barracks erupts with shouts of "What the hell is going on? What now, for cripes sake? Are we going to move, get shot, or what?" Again, I make sure my Bible is in my shirt pocket. Thank gosh it's only the size of an index card and easy to conceal.

Corporal Weiss, the interpreter, is in battle gear. He waves his pistol from side to side, up and down. I've never seen him scowl like this. He yells in his British accent, over the roar of the other voices, "Take nothing. Leave everything in place." Then he adds, "Outside! Quick, double time! Line up in columns of five."

We stumble and bump into each other. Guards push the point of their bayonets into our backs, forcing everybody into the raw, cold, morning. The wet snow, with flakes the size of pancakes, hit each of us in the face. The sky is a mottled gray-black. Daylight peeks over the mountain as we stumble, but faster, to the top of the hill behind the barracks. The guard tower is 50 feet from where we line up, five deep.

Cole glances at the tower. "Uh, oh. The guards in the tower are in battle gear, and those machine guns are aimed along that beam of the searchlight to us." I get in the middle rank, pushing Cole in front of me. "This may be it. If that Kraut in the tower sweeps his machine gun down the line, the guys in the front row might fall on us, so get in the middle row."

Pett adds in a panic-stricken tone, "Be sure to get on the bottom of the pile if you aren't hit with the first blast." Eight or nine of us push and shove to get in the middle of the five ranks.

Our barracks guard is normally a quiet man. He is about 50 years old, with an angelic smile that reveals only a few teeth. This morning, however, he is in full battle gear. His eyes are hard, almost hidden under a huge helmet that covers his face. The helmet is tilted back on his shoulders, so it won't fall off. A prisoner in the front row must have noticed how absurd he looked in a coat and helmet about two sizes too big. "You look silly in that steel helmet and overcoat. Both are too . . . ."

Wham! Our normally quiet guard hits the prisoner in the stomach with the butt of his rifle. "Shut up! Just do as I say. Line up like this." He trots to the end of the first row and extends his arms up and parallel to the ground. "Each row will have this much distance between them," he snaps.

Another prisoner ventures a question. "What's going . . . ."

A German officer interrupts, "Quiet! No talking. Line up."

The sky loses its gloom of darkness. The eastern sky shows a tint of pink, but the searchlight continues to sweep the rows of prisoners. Everyone falls silent. Stark fear grips me. I pound my feet on the ground and beat my arms against my body, along with the others, in an attempt to get warm. We act like geese flapping their wings when rising off a pond in the winter.

The guards stare intensely at us as they walk around the perimeter of the five rows of prisoners. The sky becomes brighter. When there is sufficient light, a tall German in that dreaded SS uniform and a sleeveless tunic slaps his riding crop against his boot. Behind him is another SS trooper, patch over one eye. Both have those hard, mean stares. They didn't seem any nicer than that first day in the interrogation room. They still remind me of pit vipers.

"Oh, hell, that's the son-of-a-bitch who yelled at us when we were interrogated," whispers Hugh Cole, "and there's his buddy, next to him."

The SS guard spoke in a voice as cold as the wind that roared through the barbed wire. Corporal Weiss interpreted in a softer, but stern, voice. "We will walk down each row. As we approach, hold out your arms and slowly turn them."

A prisoner near him smiles and asks, "You checking fingernails, Corporal? Mine are clean. I scrubbed them before I took a shower last night."

"Quiet!" The hard voice of the SS officer cracks like a rifle shot. "Bring that smart-mouth to me. Now!" he screams in German.

I'll be damned! The bastard understands English. I hope he can't read minds, too.

Two guards run to the source of the comment. As the prisoner is snatched out of the ranks, Cole says to me through clenched·teeth, "Glad you kept your smart mouth shut."

"I'm learning."

The guards inspect the POW who mouthed off. Slowly walking around him, peering into his clothes. He takes off his wool cap, looks at the head of twisted, long, black-and-gray hair with a flashlight. He is frisked from head to foot. As he is motioned back into the ranks, the SS officer can't resist the temptation. He hits the prisoner on the back with his riding crop. The fellow stumbles forward into the arms of his friends.

We stand in a broken line, five deep, as the guards slowly walk between the ranks. An officer and two guards inspect each prisoner, motioning to hold out and turn arms, remove headgear, and be frisked. Another guard looks at the back of the prisoner in the row under inspection.

No one speaks. The hard stare of the SS officer as he looks into the eyes of each person would melt a steel bar. When he gets to me, I stare back, eyes open, careful not to even blink. I think, damned if you're gonna stare me down, you bastard. I shiver as the cold wind penetrates my clothing and runs up and down my bones. I want to put my hand over my shirt pocket to protect my New Testament, then decide I'd better remain immobile.

The lips of the SS trooper part just enough to reveal yellow teeth. His snarl reminds me of a Doberman. Another thought runs across my mind. He thinks I'm scared of him, that's why I'm shivering. Actually, I'm freezing. My lips tighten. I think, I hope I get another crack at you, you SOB. Damn, I hate your lousy, sadistic guts. I don't finish for fear my lips will move.

I hold out my shaking arms, turn my hands over, open my jacket. Thank goodness the guards didn't frisk us, just stared at our garments. My watch and Bible are safe. I hear voices as the guards walk through the barracks, no doubt poking and turning over anything moveable. A German soldier is even sent below the barracks to look into the cesspool and stick a rod in it. Someone near me mutters, "I'd hate to be that poor SOB. Wonder what he did wrong to get that detail?"

Time drags on. We can hear yelling, screaming, the guttural snap and bark of the guards, the banging of wood as doors open and close. The Germans, in full battle gear, kick, stoop and peer into every crack and cranny in all the American barracks.

Cole asks, "What time is it?"

"Eleven-thirty. We've been standing in the cold and snow since about six this morning. I wonder how much longer we can stand here, freezing, with no food?"

He sighs, "We spent four days on that hill without food. You remember, Higg? And since then we've only had bits and pieces of food. I guess we can take it a little longer."

I mumble, "Yeah, I guess so. My stomach has shrunk so much I couldn't eat all the soup we got the other day. What we have gotten this week is full of rotten potatoes that smell so bad I can't eat the slop, anyway."

About 2:30 P.M., the two chaplains come around the barracks below us and stop in front of the group. The Man of Confidence, his assistant, the camp commandant, and approximately 15 soldiers in battle gear follow them.

Everyone becomes quiet as one chaplain speaks. "Last night, two American soldiers broke into the kitchen. The German mess sergeant awoke and found the men. He was severely beaten with an ax, at least 20 times. He was found dead this morning. We have been told that no one gets food, water, or can return to their barracks until the assailants are found.

"Men, if you know who did this atrocious act, you should turn them in. Or, if you know of or see any blood on clothing, report it. If you see anyone washing blood off their body, report it. Why should 4,000 men suffer for the cowardly act of two, maybe three, men?"

Someone asks, "Hey, Chaplain, how do you know it was Americans?"

"Because it happened in the American compound, close to the kitchen. No other nationality could get through the locked gates that separate the various compounds."

A number of comments follow.

"So that's why we're standing here."

"Hell, turn 'em in."

"Turn in a buddy? No way."

"Kill for this lousy food? Must have been hungry!"

"The potatoes are rotten, anyway. That mess sergeant ought to be killed for serving such slop."

"My old man would have hit my mom with a hammer, too, if she fixed the kind of food that we get here."

The German officer bellows, "Shut up! Stand Straight!"

Minutes become hours. Time drags on and on. Bodies begin to sag. A number of POWs sit on the ground, a sea of mud after stomping around in the snow. The guards don't seem to care.

Huckel, his voice hoarse and cracking, asks, "How would anyone get out of a barracks this far from the kitchen, sneak down the hill, break into the kitchen, kill somebody, and then sneak back up here? It must have been prisoners near the kitchen, like maybe a person who knows how to break into the kitchen without detection."

Just as the gray sky turns dark, and the wind of approaching night becomes noticeably colder, cheers come from the bottom of the hill, one barracks, then another, up to our barracks at the top.

A prisoner runs up to our group, accompanied by two guards. "They got 'em. Found the clothes in the cesspool under the barracks across from the kitchen. Bloody clothes were also found under a mattress in the barracks. There are two of 'em."

We break ranks. Voices rise in cheer. Hands clap. There are yells of, "Finally ... thank God ... kill the jerks ... I'm freezing, let's get inside ...." It is an effort to gingerly walk into the barracks. Everyone is stiff from standing

10 hours in the snow. Upon entering the barracks, I see our belongings scattered all over the place. It takes an hour to sort out and rearrange ourselves into groups. We are exhausted.

There are only a few moans when Benner announces that we will not get food that night. No one cares. Rest and warmth is what everyone wants. A prisoner yells at Benner, "What happened to the guys who killed the mess sergeant?"

"I understand the Germans marched them off. Said they belonged to them. The Americans won't get to decide their fate."

As quiet settles on the barracks, Pett, half asleep, says, "It has been quite a week. Cold, no food, a killing. It can't get much worse."

But it does.

Chapter 3

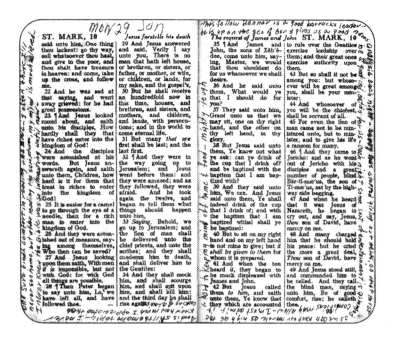

Week Three

29 January–2 February 1945

Monday, 29 January

One sure finds comfort in reading the Bible. I often think I'll never see home, but after reading the Scriptures, my mind is much relieved. I never knew the Bible was so interesting until now. Food is still the main topic. I never knew how much I appreciate the cooking of A. Louise.

This fellow Benner is a good barracks leader. He is up on the geography of Germany, and gives us a good news analysis each night. Jerry has stopped giving out news, so that must be a good indication for us. Each night some sort of entertainment is arranged so we can keep our morale as high as the conditions allow. I admit it is hard to keep my mind off home and food — mighty tough.

Tuesday, 30 January

We wrote letters home again today — this is the second letter and second post card — I doubt if they'll ever reach their destination anyway. I have a bad cough that I can't seem to get rid of; must be the sawdust from the bread lodged in my throat. I've made up a menu I hope A. Louise will prepare for me. I'm sure tired of this animal life: yelling, bickering, arguing over nothing. Trying to exist on the minimum of bread and soup; always hungry and dreaming of food. It is really hell — I never lived like this before, and I sincerely pray that I shall never have to repeat it.

Wednesday, 31 January

Went to woods today to cut wood. Two men fell out, but we had to carry them anyway. We are so weak that we can hardly move; the guard was rough and worked the hell out of us. Guard hit two men and drew his gun on one; we were ready to kill him. It was too rough for me.

The Czechs donated their Red Cross packages to us — we are supposed to get them tomorrow. I hear Von Ribbentrop is in London; also, Roosevelt and Churchill in Moscow — the news is so good I'm almost forgetting how tired I am. Faith in God seems to have been rewarded. I've had almost all I can stand of this stealing, arguing, and so on — I hope and pray the end is near.

Thursday, 1 February

The weather has broken; snow has almost melted overnight. I hope it doesn't hinder the Russian drive. During the day, it has turned cold and windy. We don't get our Red Cross packages until tomorrow. I sure pray the war is drawing to an end; I'm sick of this life, if you want to call it living. Two men had a fight, but were so weak neither could hurt the other. Men are more on edge; I feel nervous and sarcastic myself.

Friday, 2 February

Much warmer today; snow has gone and very wet. Feels like more men are getting colds and dysentery; I have a cold. This is good flu weather — an epidemic would wipe the camp out. There is nothing in the hospital; they can do nothing for a sick person — sure is pitiful! Too bad we can't be as happy always as we are today; the Red Cross packages brought our morale way up. It is a pretty day, and our planes have been coming over all day — wish I had room to describe this day.

Saturday, 3 February

I have dysentery. I'm miserable. Traded my corned beef for cheese, and cig-arettes for chocolate. Everyone is sick from eating the Red Cross packages. Even though we didn't get much, no one can hold the rich food. I also have a horrible taste in my mouth; feels like flu coming on. I hope not, as this wet, rainy weather will play havoc. I pray an epidemic doesn't break out.

Sunday, 4 February

I feel little better; awful weak, terrible headache. I had chills and fever yes-terday; I had nightmares. I think the fever is gone. This is the only time I've been sick in the army, and it has to be in a POW camp. Didn't eat at all yesterday, but tried some soup today; got to have something to help this diarrhea.

The misty, dirty gray daylight seeps ominously through the barracks window early Monday. I don't know whether or not I'm happy to be alive. Maybe I'd be better off dead. I can't sleep. My mind relives the events of the previous day — the killing of the Jerry mess sergeant, all day in the cold and snow, the menac-ing sweep of the machine guns from the guard tower, the guttural screams of the prison guards as they run from barracks to barracks, and finally, my elation over the discovery of the killers.

Hope, then despair. Up, down, up, down. Accompanying these emotional ups and downs is the fighting, bitching, screaming, snarling, and stealing. I have to retain my sanity. None of us have training in how to survive as a pris-oner of war; how to cope with the demeaning physical and psychological con-ditions. Sure, I'd seen films on how to kill, but nothing on survival. Yes, I was told if captured I only had to give name, rank and serial number, but the Ger-mans already knew that. In fact, when interrogated, my interrogators had the company roster!

Maybe we weren't supposed to survive. The people who wrote the Army manuals had never been captured, so how would they know? Then, too, it was embarrassing to be captured. I joined the Army to fight, not languish in some God-forsaken prison camp. My childhood wasn't all peaches and cream, but I had clean clothes, good food, and the freedom of movement.

My search for survival is indescribable. I wrap the blanket around my crappy, smelly garments and try to get comfortable on the cold floor. I pull my knees to chest level. Pett utters a sharp, "Ugh, that hurts, Higg." Down come the knees. I search for any snippet of past happiness. "Oh, God," I meekly pray, "Please block out the cold, filth, and continual carping of others. Hide the constant reminder of prison life."

It is difficult. The reality of prison life begins to envelop me. The first week was one of highs and lows, good times, bad times. If I am to survive, an emotional adjustment is necessary. Physical survival is in the hands of the Germans. There is nothing I can do about the quantity or quality of food, the living conditions. However, I can try to adjust emotionally to prison life. But how? I can dream and talk of better days. I can retain a sense of humor.

Every night is both miserable and frightening. We are locked up like caged animals. The claustrophobia begins when the doors and windows are locked, made even more unbearable when I have to contend with the pungent odor of cigarettes, the smells of filthy garments, vomit, runny bowels, and endless farts. I didn't know there were so many types of snores — short, long, loud, jerky. The boot buckles jingle like spurs and bring screams of anguish from the bodies stepped on when men stumble to the latrine.

My eyes close tightly to hold back the tears. I think of homemade pimiento cheese, and suck saliva from my dirty chin into my mouth. The dirt tastes like mayonnaise. I love those sandwiches. I shake my head to clear the cobwebs. I sit up. "Fellows, if we're gonna survive, we have to get with it. Let's explore this camp. We may find a way to escape. Let's see how many different divisions are in Stalag IXB."

Pett gathers his knees up to his chest and mutters, "Oh, shut up and go to sleep."

"Yeah, who gives a damn," mumbles Hugh Cole.

Daylight arrives. The old man, who is our barracks guard, delivers the ersatz tea, looks at the floor, then comments to Benner he is sorry about the events of the previous day. No one responds.

As we sit around waiting for the group to get its ration of tea, Huckel asks me, "Are there any rules to your stupid game of division identification?"

"Yes. List only the divisions designated by a patch on someone's shoulder." He wants to know about other nationalities, as they don't have patches.

"Let's just walk around camp, talk to people, observe, then gather before soup and name the various divisions and nationalities. I will write them in my Bible." It is refreshing to walk around in the cold, fresh air and talk to other prisoners. I decide if anyone starts to complain, I will walk away. This will be a happy event.

The group gathers before dinner and names the divisions they have seen: "70, 42, 36, 100, 106 (lots of them!), 28, 45, Red Devil British paratroopers, 79, Serbs, Russians, Czechs, French, Italian, French Moroccan, 84, 14 AI, 9 AI, 90, 87, 96, 94, 8, 35." I sketch each patch in my Bible to help identify the division.

After the barracks is locked, the leader, Benner, gives a summary of the news he received that morning in a meeting with the Man of Confidence. I am amazed at the knowledge of the men in the barracks about the geography of Europe, until Huckel says that many of the POWs are first and second generation Europeans, so they know about various European countries.

"When I was a boy in Mobile, I only knew a few Syrians, a couple of Greeks, and a Japanese family."

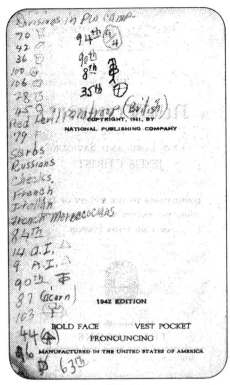

List of Divisions

Strubinger needles me. "Who would want to settle in the south, anyway? In Philly, there are people from all over Europe. Each nation lives in its own ghetto, and many still talk in their native tongues. And buddy, let me tell you, those ethnic delis and eating places are great."

Benner continues with attempts to keep morale high and prevent fights among the animals. He's creative with all sorts of topics for discussion, on subjects as diverse as the role America can play in the post war to the growth of baseball. He ends each evening with the theme song of Stalag IXB. The guards often beat on the sides of the barracks for us to quiet down. I guess we aren't supposed to be happy.

"Outta my face. That's my blanket, you bastard. Gimme more room" I sit up, listen to the screaming, yelling, and bitching, then cover my head as I lie down in my cocoon. What a miserable way to start the day. I went to sleep last night with a song on my lips and a heart vibrating with happiness. Today, I sink into the dark cave of snarling, faceless animals. God, where are you? This is no life for humans. Are these humans? Have you removed our ability for compassion and replaced it with an animal's innate sense of survival?

My restlessness causes Pett to turn over, then kick me in the knees. "For God's sake, stop hacking in my face and turning back and forth like a pig on a spit."

"Pett, what's going to happen to us? I wasn't brought up in a world of gimme, gimme, gimme . . . ."

He interrupts me with another kick. "Take the silver spoon out of your mouth, Mr. Innocence. Welcome to the world, friend . . . . Shed your skin of lovely people and wiggle along with the other snakes of life."

The mumbling awakens Gleason, who says in his New England accent, "Shut up, you guys. Pett, I didn't know you were such a philosophical talker before daylight. Damn, I'm glad I'm not married to you and have to listen to all that crap so early in the day . . . gimme a piece of the blanket . . . ."

"Here, take the whole damn thing. I'm outta here." I throw off the blanket and get up.

"Just where the hell you going, downtown? Or across the road to the commandant's warm, cozy quarters in that stone building?" Gleason yells as I gingerly step over bodies to get to the front of the barracks.

As I stand by the door, my thoughts return to those lonely days as a boy in Warrenton, Florida, where the most hazardous part of my early morning paper route was avoiding the ruts in the sandy streets. I guess that's about what I'm doing now, trying to avoid the ruts of depraved humanity and stay on the smooth path of life. I wonder how long I can do this before my nerves snap? The rubber band of calmness and reason is about stretched to the breaking point.

Bang! The door rattles as it is unlocked. "Hot stuff. Outta the way, soldier. Let me get the tub; breakfast has arrived."

The sounds of life snap me back from a dreamy yesterday. I move out of the way as the barracks chief and a couple of eager-beavers prepare to get the tub of hot liquid when the door opens.

Another cold and bleak day begins.

--- ※+※ ---

After washing in the tea, the Jerries bring cards and paper to write home. I decide to use some of it for toilet paper, as I am skeptical about letters getting home. However, it's a boost to my morale. I take a long time to write the letters and cards. I'm not going anyplace, so why hurry? Sentence structure is important to convey information but not reveal our location. I wonder if this letter will ever reach home.

I dream of various dishes my Aunt Louise used to make in an attempt to detract from the aching body and hunger pains. Perhaps, I think, I'll feel better if I list what I'd like to eat my first day home, so I spend most of the afternoon crouched under a window recalling menus. My enthusiasm was so high, I decide to write out a menu for the second day.

I return to the group and show it to Pett. He looks, then reminds me that it is not the twenty-eighth of January, but the thirtieth. "You lost a day when we stood in the snow." He adds, "Great gods, Higgins, how did you think of all that? Hey, fellows, listen to what Higgins plans to eat the first two days home."

Everyone "oohed and ahhed" when I read my list. Huckel says, "Say, let's dream up menus and foods. Higg, you write them down."

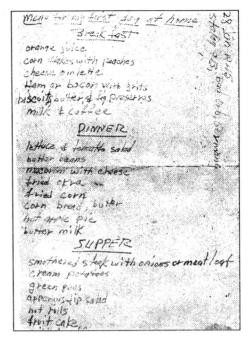

First day home menus

When I have filled a page, I exclaim, "That's all I can get on this page. Let's stop."

Pett says, "Yeah, I'm full." He burps long and loud.

"And look at the saliva on me," Cole says as he slurps.

I inquire of Gleason, "Tell me again, the recipe for that malted milk drink. I want to be sure I get it right."

"Okay," he says, "You can use malt or butterscotch. Put in marshmallows; mix in a pint of pure whipping cream with lots of malt or butterscotch; add scoops of chocolate ice cream; then pour in chocolate syrup and a raw egg."

"Raw egg?" Clete exclaims, "Why the hell add an egg?"

"I don't know. My old man always added one. For health, I guess."

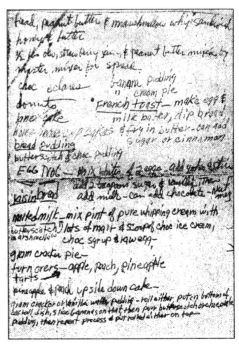

Recipes

Clete concludes, "Think I'll just leave out the egg and add more malt."

It is a great afternoon. Even the six-inch thick slice of black bread my group of six gets for supper doesn't create any argument. The one by two inch piece stopped the gnawing in my stomach.

Pett burped again and asks to see the supper menu for the second day. He reads out loud, "Cold ham, potato chips, pineapple salad with cheese ... what kind of cheese, Higgins?"

"Cream."

"Cream? How 'bout Swiss?"

"Who ever heard of pineapple salad with Swiss cheese?" I am indignant.

"Nobody. But whoever heard of eating so darn much food in one day?" He continues, "But I will take the candied yams, loaded with marshmallows. No bread. It might be made with sawdust. But pie? Oh, yeah, apple!"

Cole interjects, "You had that for dinner the first day. It's all gone. Pick another one."

Pett laughs as he replies, "Oh, yeah. I ate it all! How about blueberry?" And on and on it goes most of the night, until I drop off to sleep.

When my name is called after breakfast Wednesday for another work detail, I am anxious to go, even though my stomach is in knots and the diarrhea makes my butt as bloody and raw as a freshly-butchered cow. I walk outside the barracks like a roll of barbed wire is between my knees — slow, deliberate, legs as far apart as possible. However, work is preferable to idleness, and it keeps me from brooding over the hopelessness of my situation. Then, too, clean air is better than the foul smell of the barracks.

The guards are lethargic and in no hurry. Our work detail moves like sea turtles — slow, cautious — axes dragging in the snow. Two prisoners collapse as the detail leaves the camp. The rest of us keep walking. The four guards halt the detail, and, with various motions, tell us to carry the fallen men. Sixteen of us take turns half-carrying, half-dragging them down the road. Thank goodness we didn't have to go too far.

The snow is two feet deep where we stop to cut trees. We only have three axes, so I stand back in the crowd. I didn't get one; luck is with me. The three unfortunate POWs who get the axes start to chop the trees at the top of the snow, two feet above the ground.

"Nein, nein," a guard screams. He grabs the ax, pushes the snow from around the tree, and, with motions of the ax, says to cut at the ground level. A second guard inspects the trees and indicates which ones to cut. Two of the three prisoners proceed to cut after brushing away the snow; the third one chops at the level of the snow.

Wham. Pow. Bang. The rifle butt slams the face of the ax-man. He falls to the ground. Whump! Another prisoner is hit in his chest with the butt of a rifle. "Uggghh," the prisoner moans as he drops to the ground. Another guard jerks his pistol out of the holster and points it at the third prisoner with an ax. Click! The safety is off.

Screams. Yells. Rifles wave at us. The guard continues to point his pistol at the prisoner. He drops his ax and puts his arms over his head.

Someone says, "Oh, shit, this is it." Two of the prisoners are so scared they lean against the trees. We, the remaining 11, start towards the guards, mad as hell. I figure we can rush them, grab the guns, shoot 'em, and take off to the woods.

Quickly, the guards back up the hill and point their rifles toward us. Click. Click. Click. The rifle bolts snap shells into the chambers as the safeties are released. The guards stand close to each other, raise their rifles, then wave them back and forth in a motion that tells us to get back on the road.

A POW exclaims, "No way will we take all of them," as he moves toward the road. The rest of us shrug our shoulders and follow him. Whew, I think. Another close call. Someday, I'll get shot if the guards get any more nervous or trigger-happy.

We march back to the camp. The wood cutting is over. No one looks back at the four POWs still in the woods. The prisoner who was hit in the chest, the one who cut wood at snow level, and the two prisoners too weak to walk with us eventually return to the barracks. Nothing is ever said about the third prisoner, the one bashed in the face and knocked cold. I guess the Jerries shot him.

Benner says after lock-up, "I just heard from Corporal Weiss, our interpreter, that Churchill and Roosevelt are in Moscow to discuss the war, and Von Ribbentrop is in London."

"So what?" I say to no one in particular. I relax on my pallet and listen to the excited conversation among others in the barracks. Frankly, I am so tired I don't care whether it is true or not, but it gives me a few minutes to dream of freedom.

---

30 January 1945

"Allied Planning. Churchill and Roosevelt and their advisors met in Malta to make preparations for the Yalta meeting with Stalin. They leave for Yalta on the 2nd."

[Source: page 321, *World Almanac Book of World War II*, rev. ed.Bison Books Corp., 1986.]

I try to read the Bible every day. It provides peace, contentment, and the opportunity to lose myself in thought and contemplation. The concentration shifts my mind from physical discomfort to more pleasant thoughts.

Why did God let us suffer like this? I often muse. Why didn't He stop the war? Why am I denied such pleasantries as food, recreation, warmth? What have I done wrong, God, to be subjected by such treatment? How long will I suffer before death arrives? Does God even want me? I sometimes feel that God nudges me and whispers, "Survive!"

I can't memorize any particular verse or passages from my Bible. It is the rhythm of the words that provide a sense of calmness. I write in the margins, around the printed text. I don't write many of the names of my fellow prisoners. You never know when the Jerries might decide to search and seize the book. I carry it in my shirt pocket, and so far have not had it confiscated. Since I'm not sure just how long we will be prisoners, I only allocate two pages to each day. I date the pages for four months. I could date further, but decide that after four months I will be liberated or dead. The statements are terse and succinct. I list as many events of each day as I can recall. I write when it's convenient, but attempt to write late in the day or at night if the latrine has a lightbulb.

My spirits go sky-high when I hear the Czechs will give us one of their Red Cross packages. We aren't sure how the boxes will be split up, but that is a minor problem. The idea of good food makes me happy, so I don't worry about how much I'll get. I dream of food as I fall asleep with a smile on my face.

The Red Cross packages are delayed because of the overcast day. A cold wind blows all day. It is too cold to go outside. We huddle close together to retain some body heat, ignoring our smelly bodies. Cold takes precedence over smell. I put my blanket around my head, pull the wool cap over my face, and place my face and head between my knees. The sights and smell of other people is too much to tolerate. I wish I could read my Bible. It might make me feel better. I move it from one breast pocket to the other one to be sure no one can find it. My left hand is over the pocket.

The pitiful ration of bread we get for supper doesn't help any of us. We are jumpy, argumentative and quibbling. I am as restless and edgy as an animal in a zoo during a full moon. Luckily, no one says anything to me, or I will bite their head off. I watch two men fight, but their blows are as effective as slapping a cream puff. Both fall in a heap on the floor, panting, grunting, and hugging each other like two playful brown bears.

Strubinger watches in disgust. "Thank you, Max Schmelling and Max Baer." I smile as I recall the great German boxer Schmelling and the American boxer Baer.

The Red Cross boxes are delivered to our barracks early Friday. The joy of real food temporarily eliminates my feeling of remorse. Pettingill, Cole, Huckel and I form a group when it is announced there will be four men to a Red Cross box. We appoint Cole "Big Chief Divide" because of his Indian reticence and honesty.

Cole returns from the front of the barracks with a big smile on his face. "We have twelve pounds of food for the four of us. Just look at what we have!" I write in my Bible the contents of the box as Cole puts them on a blanket:

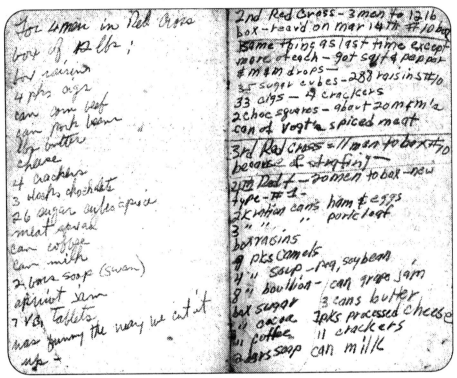

Contents of Red Cross boxes

1 box of raisins

4 packs of cigarettes

1 can of corned beef

1 can of pork and beans

1 pound of butter

1 tin of cheese

4 crackers

3 blocks of chocolate

26 small lumps of sugar

1 can meat spread

1 can coffee

1 can milk

2 bars of soap (Swan)

1 tin of apricot jam

7 vitamin tablets

Cole decides that each of us will split one item into four portions. We draw straws: Pett is first, Cole second, Huckel third, and I'm last. The 16 items are selected for division, following the order of the straws. It is agreed that no items will be eaten until everything is divided. The vitamin tablets are loose, so we decide to divide and eat them. I get one tablet.

We divide the canned items first, then the bulky butter and chocolate. Cole divides the milk and coffee into the three empty cans that contained the meat spread, corned beef, and pork and beans. The top and bottom of my mess kit serve as a container for some items.

The milk switches around in my mouth. I close my eyes and smack my lips. I had forgotten the soothing and sweet taste of milk! We observe Cole divide the butter, cheese and chocolate. We watch him like a hawk. My eyes follow every move while I mentally calculate the width of each piece. Huckel makes a ruler from a piece of paper because of the distrust.

No one wants the apricot jam, so we draw straws to determine who gets the darned stuff. Short straw takes all. I get it. Everyone laughs as Pett says, "Higg, save it. Maybe your aunt can figure a way to use it." Later, I trade it to a Frenchman for four cigarettes.

We decide to go outside and have a picnic after the food is divided. It is a beautiful day. There is no snow. Cumulus clouds drift across the robin-blue sky. Suddenly, B-17 bombers fill the sky on their way into Germany. The drone of the planes is music to my ears. Cole squints his eyes. "Those planes must be at least 20,000 feet up. I can just make out that they are B-17s. I should be flying one rather than sitting in this hell-hole."

I can't resist. "Hugh, the leaders of our great Army know you were needed to lead us through the catacombs of confusion, chaos, and crap."

"Oh, shut up and eat."

There is no bickering, arguing, or fighting all afternoon. It is a picnic in the park as we gorge ourselves and watch the planes overhead.

All night I pay the penalty for eating like a pig. My stomach aches and growls; my mouth tastes like bile; and I am wet from the runny crap that oozes out of my butt and down my legs. I stay by the hole in the latrine most of the night. Everyone who comes in slips in the crap and urine. Finally, a POW takes a knife and frantically makes another hole. Within two hours, the 10-by-10-foot latrine has holes all around the walls.

Early Saturday, I swap my corned beef to Cole for his cheese, and my cigarettes to Pett. "Grrrr ... grrr ..." my stomach growls. Up I jump and run outside, drop my pants and lean against the barracks. My bowels spew like a fountain. I notice other prisoners lined against the barracks wall. We look like a bunch of crows on a phone line.

My face is hot. My clothes are drenched with sweat. I shiver and shake, and my teeth rattle. It is useless to complain, since all 232 men in the barracks are in the same condition.

Darkness is worse. The sounds of groans, burps, spewing of bowels, and a foul smell fills the barracks. There is no circulation of air. Sleep is in spurts. During one fitful sleeping period, I see my mother rise up from her coffin and beckon to me. As I start toward her, a red, black, and yellow coral snake races from the coffin and grabs my arm. It starts to chew. I scream.

"You hit me, Higg. Calm down!" says Cole. "You're crying and sobbing, and talking about snakes and your mother. Man, you had a nightmare."

I sheepishly whisper, "Thanks for waking me. What did I say?"

"Forget it. Nothing but a lot of gibberish."

There is no church Sunday. I guess God and the preachers take a rest so we can recover.

God knows we are thankful.

Chapter 4

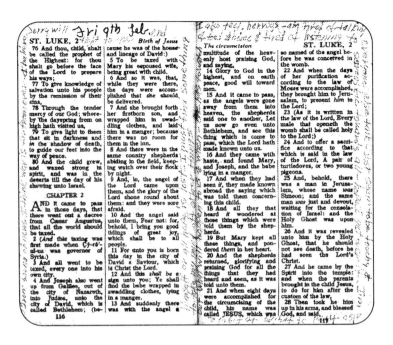

Week Four

5 February–11 February 1945

—◦—❖❖—◦—

Monday, 5 February

Still weak, but feel better. Walked around a little in the mud, but my feet froze. The ground is very muddy and cold. Haven't been able to eat all my bread or soup; I have no appetite.

Tuesday, 6 February

About 400 men are leaving today, supposedly to work in a factory near Leipzig. Of course, that comes from Jerry, so I can't believe much. I hope our group doesn't break up. We are to be deloused today. Allies are still driving, so we are informed. I hear the big three are meeting. I've been captured a month today — seems like a year. We think Jerry doesn't want Allies to catch us in the hell hole, so we all may move out.

Wednesday, 7 February

P-47 strafed the camp yesterday; killed three GIs and wounded 11; also, a number of French, Russian, Serbs. It really scared us to death. A protest has been made. Probably a couple of hot pilots.

Stealing is getting worse — two in my group had their bread stolen last night. All GIs are supposed to evacuate this camp in the next two weeks.

Thursday, 8 February

Took a shower and delousing this morning; feel much better. Some of the boys left today. Our Confidence Man went also. I heard the big three delivered an ultimatum to Jerry — I hope he accepts it, although I don't think he will. Got my hair cut for the first time in two months; I feel quite different. Weather is still unsettled.

Friday, 9 February

From the sound of the news, I think the war is far from over. I believe Jerry will fight to the end. I also feel nervous; I'm tired of talking of food and home, and tired of listening to everyone else talk. Just seem to be tough and sarcastic towards all. I hope I get over it. I'm also tired of trying to figure out what will happen to us and when. One has to watch himself, or all hope is lost. I must find something to take my mind off other things.

Saturday, 10 February

Five GIs to be buried tomorrow — two died of malnutrition, three from the strafing. Sure is tough to die in a POW camp. We hear Manila has fallen; hope so. The war news sounds better. If we stay here until the last of the month, our chances of being freed are good — if we move, we'll probably sweat the war out. My nerves are more on edge; we are beginning to bite each other in my group and have petty fights.

Sunday, 11 February

Started snowing again; hope it doesn't stop the Allies. Lots of argument about the end — most think by May. Buried the five GIs; sure was tough. One has to keep hope and faith, or all is lost. It is tough sometimes, especially with each day the same.

A Keystone Cops movie of the 1920s would be slow compared to the fast-paced events of the fourth week in Stalag IXB. Most people will not be subjected in their lifetimes to the pathos, death, trauma, helplessness, even humor, we POWs experience daily in prison camp.

Monday, I delicately struggle outside on shaky knees to wash my smelly, crappy clothes in the snow. I am weak from gorging on the Red Cross food last Saturday and Sunday, then vomiting and crapping, sometimes simultaneously. My stomach aches and my butt is so raw I try to keep the cheeks apart, but the only way is not to walk. I can't eat anything. I just lie around in pain, feeling sorry for myself. Time drags on. Finally, darkness and fretful sleep.

⊷ ⊷

The Tuesday roll call is a jolt to my sense of false happiness. It is announced that at least 400 men will go to a factory near Leipzig. We stand at least two hours while the names are called. I feel totally helpless. Remnant self-confidence in my ability to survive under the heavy hand of an all-powerful enemy falls like a hammer on a nail. I glance skyward and silently seek strength from God. Faith! Faith! I have to keep the faith.

All 80 American soldiers of actual, or suspected, Jewish ancestry are on the list. Conflicting stories circulate among us about the composition of those to be shipped. One POW says all the misfits and unhealthy will be among the prisoners of war leaving Stalag IXB. However, the Man of Confidence, Kasten, and his assistant, Joe Littell, are on the list. They certainly aren't sick, misfits or complainers.

A number of men on the list are from our barracks, including Robert Zion. He's certainly no misfit, nor are others in our barracks whose names are called. After the roll call, we go back into the barracks for our morning tea.

Later that morning, I hear a scream, "Here they come, here they come! Watch out! Duck! Run for it!" All hell breaks loose. Like a fool, I run outside as I hear the "rat-tat-tat" of machine guns and the whine of engines. I look into the blue of the sky. Great gods! There is a dogfight between an American and a German plane, both screaming and roaring from the sky, one chasing the other.

Our barracks is on top of the mountain, so I get a good view of both planes. Suddenly, the Kraut fighter blasts through the clouds and dives straight towards the camp. I watch in horror as the German plane zooms in low, engine screaming. It races down the street below us.

The American P-47 weaves right and left as it trails the German fighter. Fire and smoke follow the "pow, pow, bam" and "rat-tat-tat" of the P-47's cannon and machine guns. It is over in seconds. The Jerry plane shoots straight up, the P-47 in pursuit, close on the tail of the German plane.

Huckel screams, "Where is Cole?"

Wide-eyed and breathing rapidly, I yell, "He went down to the kitchen on the main road."

Prisoners of war yell, cry, cringe close to the barracks, lie on the ground, try to dig a foxhole in the snow. Some run around like headless chickens. Someone yells, "Get next to the building, the planes might return." Along with the others, I crouch against the barracks, hoping to be out of the line of fire.

The P-47 tries to get close to the weaving and darting German plane as the two fighters go out of sight.

As we regain our composure and go back into the barracks, some wise-ass yells, "Protest! Protest! They aren't supposed to fight over a prison camp."

"Balls! This is war, buddy, and anything's fair. I just hope the pilot knocks the Jerry out of the sky."

Cole comes running up the hill. I can see him enter the barracks. Crying and yelling, I hug him. Huffing, puffing, wide-eyed, he tells us the details of the attack. "I crouched next to the wall along the road. The shells went within five feet of me, kicking up dirt all over the place. After the planes went into the sky, I saw bodies all over the road, some with American uniforms."

It is reported after dinner that 3 Americans were killed, 11 injured. Many Serbs, French, and Russians were also killed or wounded.

⟶ ▰▰▰ ⟵

Gleason awoke Wednesday morning, rooted around his clothing like a cocker spaniel after a field rat, then yells, "How can somebody steal my bread from under my head?"

Huckel jumps up, throws his blanket aside, unrolls a coat he uses as a pillow, and moans that his bread is also missing. Both whine at the same time, "We wanted that in case we get a chance to escape!"

Pett says, "Or to stay alive."

Now we are suspicious of each other, watching every move so no one can sneak a bite. I don't trust anybody.

The rest of Wednesday is spent complaining. I am nervous and jittery from the strafing, lack of food, cold, and the fact that my friends will be leaving. I get in a corner of the barracks and try to recap the traumatic events of Tuesday and Wednesday. It is difficult to read anything in my Bible, I just write succinct comments.

It's quiet after the evening bread is delivered. No one wants to see their friends leave, even if it might result in a better life. It sure as hell can't be any worse than here. There are a few weak attempts at humor, but most of us remain deep in our individual thoughts.

Before daylight Thursday, we are awakened and ordered outside. The men whose names were called Tuesday are ordered to get their belongings and line up on the road by the kitchen, ready to leave Stalag IXB.

Pett kicks the ground as he exclaims, "Damnit, Higg, you and I told Fellman to throw away his dog tags and not leave when the Jerries asked the Jewish fellows to move to another barracks. Remember?"

"Yes. Since there are others on the list, maybe the Jerries aren't after the Jews." I turn to Bob Zion and say, "Sorry to see you go."

As we walk back into the barracks, Cole says to Zion, "Well, there go our free smokes." He smiles and adds, "Ask the Gestapo if I can take your place and be interrogated every day."

Zion is one unhappy man. He has been interrogated every day since our arrival the previous month. The Jerries are convinced he has some Jewish blood in him. As he gathers his belongings and prepares to leave along with Fellman and the others whose names were on the list, Pett says, "You gave 'em fits, friend. They never did break you if you are Jewish. Thanks for the smokes."

Zion's owlish eyes become moist. He smiles and shakes our hands. "Thanks, men. I gave you guys fun for a month, didn't I?"

Cole advises him, "Change your name when you get home. If you are Jewish, then get yourself a y ..." Zion puts his hand over Cole's mouth and whispers, "Don't say it! I don't want to know any Jewish terms."

The designated men line up along the main road, then walk out of the camp. I can hear murmuring but no loud cheering. Later, I hear that some of those watching saluted. Neither Pett, Cole, Huckel, nor I walk down the hill to watch the 400 exit Stalag IXB. We are sad to see our close friends leave for an unknown destiny. I certainly don't want to see Fellman leave, although he probably would make a smart crack to me.

Pett sighs, "I wonder if we'll ever know what happens to them? Or whether we'll ever meet again?"

I add, "May be better not to know. We have enough problems trying to stay alive in this hell-hole. If anybody survives, it will be Fellman — as long as he keeps his mouth shut."

Yeah, I think as we break ranks and wander back inside, I have got to look at today, not live in the past, except for happy thoughts. No use worrying about tomorrow. When it comes, I will decide what to do. I glance over my shoulder at the fence, and try to see beyond it into the valley, across the snow-covered mountains. I shrug, smile, and turn to Cole. "By the way, what is that word you started to say when Zion told you to stop?"

"You mean a 'yarmulke?' That is the little skull cap the Jewish men wear when they go to synagogue. Some wear it all the time."

"Even in the winter?"

"Sure. They wear it under their other hat — I think."

"I'll be damned."

We get deloused after the shipment of POWs. The Jerries probably don't want to waste the creosote-smelling water. When we are in the shower, someone remarks that the mixture is strained cesspool residue mixed with creosote. But it is warm, and cleans my filthy body. I even hum a tune. I feel good so I decide to get a haircut. A fellow in the next barracks hacks away with rusty, dull scissors for 10 cigarettes.

When the bread is divided in the evening, all eyes concentrate on the cutter. Pett says, "What a lousy way to exist. I refuse to get suspicious of you guys. My gosh, I have to hold on to some semblance of humanity, or I'll be like those guys who walk around shaking their heads, mumbling gibberish from slobbering mouths, with eyes that stare and never blink."

I add, "Yeah, it's time to start over, not be so suspicious."

Eight of us squat like Indians around a campfire and discuss the war news. One rumor is that we will move out as soon as possible, since the Jerries will not want the allies to find us in this hell hole.

Where do all these rumors start? How do we get them so fast? Are they true? The rumors go from group to group, barracks to barracks. Remind me of a forest fire in gale force winds. Huckel comments, "I think the rumors pass by osmosis."

Strubinger asks, "What the hell is 'osmosis?'"

Huckel replies, "Infiltrate, or permeate. These rumors just go through the air and land. I don't know how or where they come from."

I add, "All I hear is 'someone said' or 'I heard.' But I don't know who said what, or who heard what."

Cole says he's seen a more relaxed attitude in the Jerries. "Their tone of voice is less autocratic and bellicose." We can roam the camp and go in and out of barracks to visit. One side of me asks if any of the rumors are true, the other side says, "Yes, yes, believe them."

> 4 February 1945
>
> "At Yalta, in the Crimea, the second phase of the Argonaut Conference (in code, Magneto) begins, attended by the heads of the governments of the United States, the Soviet Union and Great Britain, i.e., Roosevelt, Stalin and Churchill. The Allies discuss common strategy, especially political questions and the 'division' of spheres of influence when the war is over."
>
> [Source: page 661, *2194 Days of War*, Mayflower Books, W. H. Smith Publishers Inc., New York, 1977.]

We are surprised when we get cards and are told to write anything we want as long as its not negative about the German soldiers. I decide to write my Aunt Nettie in Montgomery, Alabama. She is the most modern, so we kids used to say, of the seven daughters and two sons of my grandparents.

Recalling her brings joy to my heart. She is only four foot, eight inches. She puts pillows on the seat and behind her back in order to drive her huge Buick around town, cigarette dangling from her mouth. She was the only female I knew who was a traveling salesperson. She sold mayonnaise in Alabama and north Florida, and would hitch a ride with whatever salesman was available if she couldn't catch a train or bus. I sat for hours while she told stories about her travels. I recall the times when she bought me a new suit. She'd take me into the boys' department of Hamil's, or the Montgomery Fair, and tell the head clerk to "Show this young man the best suit you have. Let him pick it out. Get him a shirt and tie, too."

Wow! What an aunt!

I close my eyes and dream of happy childhood Christmas dinners at her house. My nostrils quiver as I smell a 25-pound turkey. My aunt's lively discussions of the advantages of cornbread over toasted or untoasted plain-white-bread dressing, and the arguments over the use of Lea and Perrins to make gravy. Should giblets be fried before being added to the dressing? On and on about every item on the huge menu. Christmas dinner always included rice (never potatoes), cranberry sauce, butter beans, snap beans, fried corn, pineapple and cheese salad with grated yellow cheese. I drool every time I think of those meals. My stomach aches as I taste each item as if I was still eating. God, I missed those days.

I break into a grin when I write 'Lane cake.' That was my Aunt Nettie's specialty. She didn't have the time nor patience to make white or dark fruit cake. These were left to the non-working, housewife aunts, who started the process in October, soaking the fruitcakes every week until Christmas.

Kriegsgefangenenlager M.-Stammlager IX B   Datum 6 Feb 1945

Camp des prisoniers

Dear folks; Just a card to let you know I'm out of danger. Am in a scenic part of Germany, but don't care for such cold weather. I dream of the day I can sit down to a good Griffith dinner. Please save all my fruit cake as I love it! Hope all of you are in good health. Give everyone my love & don't worry about me. Just be prepared to cook all sorts of pies, lane cake, waffles cookies, & candy when I get back.

Love, Sam

Years later, I found out why the kids did not get any Lane cake. My aunt loaded the filling with bourbon. My grandfather, a teetotalling Baptist who never let alcohol past his lips, loved that cake! He would eat three pieces, then sleep the rest of the afternoon.

Pett interrupts my nostalgic dream. "Why are you laughing?"

I tell him and conclude my story with, "No one ever told him about the bourbon."

I then tell Pett of other pleasantries of Christmas as a kid in Montgomery. "Three or four of my uncles always went in the bedroom to 'talk' until their wives told them to 'stop that right now — it's Christmas.' But they were much happier, sucking mints and smelling like that Lane cake. I was grown before I realized they were nipping at the bottle."

As we turn in our postcards to the barracks chief, I remark to Pett and Cole, "I remember the first Christmas I was in the Army. I had leave and went to Montgomery. My Aunt Nettie announced before dinner that since I was home from the war, and may not be home for the next one (she called a spade a spade, whether you liked it or not), I could sit at the big table rather than in the breakfast room with the kids. My cousin Mary Frances was next in line. She started to complain, but Aunt Nettie calmed her with the promise, "Since you are a college girl, you may have a piece of Lane cake."

Cole asked, "How do you make Lane cake? Sounds good."

"Beats me. My aunt never told anyone. All I know is you could smell the whisky in it on everyone's breath, and the family seemed happy all afternoon."

Five men died, two from the strafing earlier in the week. They will be buried Sunday. All the American POWs — at least 3,000 of us — line the main road of the camp. We silently bow our heads, then salute, as the funeral procession passes. The bodies are taken to a cemetery outside the camp, which I understand is on the side of a mountain. Since no one in our division or company died, we did not become involved in either the grave digging or the funeral procession. I heard the ground was so hard and mostly shale, that only a pick could break the ground, so the graves aren't very deep.

Most of us have a detached view of death. It is something that just happens. I do not get upset or concerned over people dying. I have the stoic view that such is a fact of prison life. The funerals are a nuisance. We have to stand in the cold and snow for an hour or so. On the other hand, they are a diversion, and provide time for reflection and medication.

As I return to the barracks at the top of the hill, someone behind us says, "I hear that Manila has fallen, and we might get out of here by the end of the month."

I turn toward the comment and ask in a sarcastic tone of voice, "Where do you hear all this crap? Tell me, will ya?"

I am edgy and tense as I continue, "Either say where you heard it or shut up."

"Brother, ain't we nervous? I heard it from a guy next to me in line when the funeral passed. I don't know where he heard it."

All the bickering, combined with the cold, put me on edge. I am so damned tired of these rumors. I just wish I knew if one rumor was true. I want to believe, but need something more than, "I heard."

---

4 February 1945

"Philippines. On Luzon, advance units of 1st Cavalry Division reach the outskirts of Manila from the north while units of 11th Airborne Division approach from the south.

"Western Front. The Allies announce that all German forces have been expelled from Belgium. First and Third Army units are attacking toward the Roer River around Duren."

[Source: page 322, *World Almanac Book of World War II*, rev. ed., Bison Books Corp., 1981.]

After the funeral, I walk to the top of the hill and gaze through the fence to the white snowcaps of the adjoining mountain. I take an old, ripped and repaired piece of paper from my wallet. I read parts of the poem, "Invictus." Memorizing it keeps my mind off the surroundings

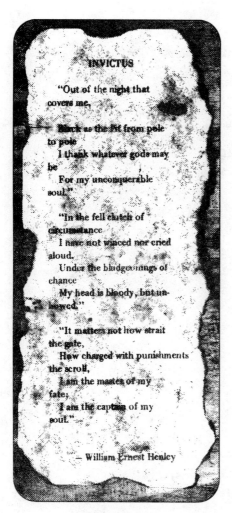

The tattered poem

Invictus

Out of the night that covers me,
Black as the pit from pole to pole,
I thank whatever gods may be
For my unconquerable soul.

In the fell clutch of circumstance
I have not winced nor cried aloud
But under the bludgeonings of chance
My head is bloody, but unbowed.

It matters not how strait the gate,
How charged with punishments the
scroll,
I am the master of my fate,
I am the captain of my soul.

William Ernest Henley

When I recited it in high school, my teacher informed me the poem was not Christian. I asked why, and she said the poem placed your destiny in yourself and not God, nor Christ.

I gaze through the fence and think about her comment. It seems like both God and I have something to do with my fate. I am not a theologian, or even a student of the Bible. All I know is the poem calms my nerves, gives me positive thoughts about survival. I look at the sky and reverently ask, "God, you don't mind, do you?"

I remember a verse from Psalms which goes something like, "The Lord is both my steady rock and a fortress, and my strength, and I will trust in Him always." I have to trust in something. Might as well be God — man hasn't been helpful.

Chapter 5

Week Five

12 February–18 February 1945

━━◆※◆━━

Monday, 12 February

Someone stole my bread last night. Sure wish I could catch him — I believe I would kill him. Our barracks has camp detail today — sure is a mess; a couple have already passed out.

Tuesday, 13 February

French got Red Cross package, so lots of trading going on. The war news is still good; according to most, the end is about March 15. Small, petty things are getting on our nerves. Serbs and Russians have so much GI clothing they don't trade much. Had an election in the barracks for the best all-around GI. It was like any election; guys vote for anybody.

Wednesday, 14 February

Cole and Gleason are leaving in a GP to go. Sure hate to see them go; we've been together so long, and have made plans for the future. We may not run into each other for some time. Bombers came over last night. Sure wish we could be recaptured. We are always sweating out something. Pettingill and I will be on the next shipment — we dread the boxcar ride. Yank planes are around too much.

Thursday, 15 February

Rumor of Red Cross packages again. This barracks is on alert to ship, so they will probably wait until we leave to give them out. I can hear planes day and night now; the weather is a lot better. I'm really skin and bones. We hear through the Serbs that Berlin has fallen and street fighting in Frankfort. Optimism is very high; some think this month will tell the tale.

Friday, 16 February

No planes today; the weather is foggy. Some guys think the war is over. I wish my morale would boost up; no news given today, so may be a good indication. My nerves are more on edge — I wish something would happen.

Saturday, 17 February

Such a pretty day; I can't understand why AC isn't out. I hear rumors of war over from the Serbs. I look forward to our two meals so our group can sit and talk. We have some good discussions on all subjects; talk all about our families. Some guy keeps pounding on a rock making something, and it is about to drive me nuts. I'm sick of dreaming of food.

Sunday, 18 February

Some more GIs came in — no one has seen them yet. I hope they have some up-to-date war news. It's a very misty day; bad for AC. We are sweating out our shipment; I hope Cole and Gleason don't leave — we have too much to look forward to. I went to church; it was good. Chaplain Neal set my mind at ease after a week of choking up. He gives a good sermon. Talked about truth and freedom today; I sure feel a lot better after hearing him speak — he is doing a fine job.

Prison life is nothing but boredom and crowded barracks. The lousy food keeps me alive, but barely. I can count my ribs through the dirty shirt and smelly jacket. My waist measures about 15 inches — on the outside of my clothing. It hurts to sit, as there is no fat on the cheeks of my butt. Both hips are black from lying on one side, then the other.

Rations are the same — a piece of black bread, dirty soup with rotten potatoes, pieces of cabbage or bits of unpeeled carrots, and "tea" made of tree bark in warm water. Occasionally, we get a gram of horsemeat or grayish, smelly cheese.

The weather changes as often as a newborn baby's diapers — snow one day, warm and wet the next, then windy the next day. And cold! It's a biting, bone-chilling cold that penetrates every bone and muscle of my body. I shiver constantly. I see my breath when I exhale. The only warmth is the closeness of our bodies when we sleep.

Accommodations are the same cold, rough floor, colder at night, every night. Diarrhea, fleas, lice, or both, as well as stomach cramps, are always with us. The grayish-white dawn of Monday appears through the dusty window-panes on 240 bodies, like a bag of pretzels dumped on a table. I turn from my left to my right side. My right arm automatically goes under my head for support; also, to feel the bag of bread I have saved. "Oh, my God, where's my bread? Somebody stole it, right from under my head!" I get on my knees, shake my blanket, and then fling it against the wall. "How? When?"

I sob and sniffle as I whisper, "I better not catch him, or he's dead, I promise you." My eyes dart around the barracks from person to person. The other five in my group jump up and rummage through their clothes.

Cole sardonically says, "Welcome aboard. It was Huckel and me a week ago; now you. Somebody has it in for us."

Gleason whispers as he looks around the barracks. "I wonder if anyone heard us planning to escape, then decided to go themselves?"

I clench my teeth to mask my disappointment. "I don't know. We've discussed it for some time. Let's keep our eyes open to see if we can discover the bastard."

Gleason laughs as he says, "Yeah, see who takes a crap and it goes 'plop.' That means he has eaten so much bread his shit don't run."

Pett stares at Gleason. "Now, that's smart! You're elected to stay in the latrine at night and watch."

The exchange breaks the tension. I guess as long as we see humor we can survive. Five men all speak at once, jostle each other and point to Fred. "Yeah, I second it. Go, Fred, go. Good thinking, you got that right."

However, I'm pissed. I don't like disappointment. I retreat into my cocoon of privacy against the wall. My Bible comes out of my breast pocket, and I write down the event but can't concentrate or write coherently. I look at the other five and recall the excitement over the idea of escape. We had made elaborate plans since capture, but something always interfered — sickness, weather, too many guards, no food.

Everyone had an assignment. Pett had a year of German at Albion College, so he can read the signs and say a few words to civilians, if necessary. Just don't ask him to engage in conversation, Huckel once advised us. Cole has a good sense of direction. As a patrol scout, he can read a compass, if we can find one.

I had learned the details of the uniforms worn by the French and Italians, both of whom went in and out of the camp without guards. Especially the Italians. I guess it was because at one time the Italians were allies of the Germans, so there was no need to worry. The Germans probably decided there would be fewer mouths to feed if they didn't come back to camp.

Gleason, Strubinger, and Huckel are from big cities, so they know how to navigate the alleys to keep us out of sight. Our health is fair, except for Pettingill. His cough sounds like a gravel truck. If we can keep him quiet, he'll be able to read those signs.

None of us have traded any part of our American uniform, so we would be treated as soldiers, not spies. Strubinger argued we would be better off in a mismatch of uniforms. He was voted down when Huckel said, "I'd rather be shot as a soldier than as a spy."

Clete asked, "Where are we? All I know is that we're somewhere near that town of Bad Orb. We never go anywhere, and the guards won't tell us."

"Ask the Italians or French. Both nationalities are in and out of the camp all the time," I replied.

"And the Brits. Those guys will know which way to go," Pett says. "Will the German civilians hide us? Shoot us? Turn us in? I have heard those so-called 'Terry' guards are worse than regular soldiers."

"It can't be any worse getting shot than dying like caged animals."

Cole looks at the group of six and says, "We have enough men involved in this escape to take over the prison camp. Hell, we'll sound like a troop of elephants going through the forest. How will all of us escape at the same time?" We spend days analyzing just how all of us would get out at the same time. Then some bastard stole my bread.

I wipe away the tears of disappointment and return to the present. Everyone in the group is curled up in his own blanket, deep in private thoughts. All that the planning had accomplished was that a bit of hope had entered our lives.

Par for the course. Nothing had gone right since our regiment landed in France — living in the cold, rain and mud, sleeping in pup tents in a pasture outside Marseilles, Christmas dinner on that cramped boxcar during a three-day bumpy ride to the front, sitting in a foxhole on the Rhine River, traveling in a night so black even the convoy got lost, one battle, sitting on the hill for five days, capture, interrogation, walking and walking, and finally the ride in that damned 10-by-33-foot cattle car for five days to Stalag IXB. Now, this crappy existence.

I ask myself, how did I get in such a mess? I glance at the ceiling, close my eyes to hide the tears, and sob, "God, you aren't looking out for me. Are you just letting me stew in my own juice?"

My mind and eyes focus on today. I shake off the remorseful thoughts like a dog shedding water. I get up from underneath the window and look at the smelly, crowded cold shack in which we try to exist. I snap at Pett, "You're hanging your clothes on my nail again. Stop it, you hear? Use your own nail. This place is worse than a pigpen. Not even pigs whine and whimper and snarl at each other like we do."

Pett yells, "Ah, shut up, Higgins. Quit your damn bitching. You're always talking about being happy. Well, be happy. What's done is done. We'll get out of here yet."

Strub gets up and turns to Cole. "I hear the guards unlocking the door. Come on, Hugh, it's our turn to get our breakfast."

He turns to me, "Give it up for lost, Higg. We'll never find the guy who stole the bread. Who's first on the breakfast list today?"

Pett says, "Me. I can hardly wait to wash my face in the sticky, gooey mess." As Cole and Strubinger go for the tea, my eyes narrow; I look quizzically at Strub's back. I recall the comment of my great uncle Nick, Confederate Army Veteran, "Never trust anyone from north of Richmond, Virginia."

Pett washes in the lukewarm tea. When he finishes, Cole, next in line, says, "Damn, you're dirty. You all mind if I throw it out? No one else can wash in it."

The conversation is of how to escape, but eventually returns to just survival and dependence on each other. I add, "And trust." I look at Strub and smile, then continue, "There has to be something in which we have trust. Might as well be each other." A bond has developed among the few remaining members of the 1st Platoon of B Company, 275th Infantry. "We depend on each other for survival, so let's have faith and trust in each other, or we will be talking animals."

"But without a south Alabama accent," Clete adds, smiling.

While everyone is drinking or washing in the tea, Benner announces the barracks is on camp detail today. Strub yells, "Oh, boy, the shit detail. Why don't you just say it, Benner? There ain't no other detail. All the cigarette butts been smoked or chewed."

Names are called to line up outside the barracks. I hold my breath. No one in my immediate group is called for the honey-bucket detail. By now this detail has become almost unbearable. The cesspools under the latrine floor overflow; the ground underneath is a sea of mud and excrement. Those who get pulled for the detail complain bitterly. Some pass out from the sight of the muddy crap. Others vomit or have dry heaves. Many put a cloth over their mouth and nose.

I am jumpy and nervous all morning, so I decide to just sit in a corner and feel sorry for myself. The dinner of slimy, dirty potato soup doesn't improve my spirits. I am cold, hungry, and my body is aching all over from sleeping on the floor. It is impossible to read or write. I refuse to enter into any discussion. I am afraid I might get into a fight, so I wrap up in my blanket, cover my head, and put my mind in neutral.

Monday ticks away into Tuesday.

Somebody screams that the French got Red Cross boxes when the morning tea was delivered. The wise-cracks flow like runny bowels.

"Why the hell do they get a Red Cross box, especially since Americans probably donated them?"

"Wonder if the French will have red wine or champagne with their food?"

"At least the trading activity will pick up."

It does, too. All day, POWs trade clothes for food. The Russians and Serbs don't need any more American clothing. Some of them already look like American POWs. I don't understand why they want American clothes; their garments are heavier and warmer. By Tuesday afternoon, the barracks is full of POWs from every nationality looking for something to trade or steal. Pett says, "Better stay close to your belongings. These guys remind me of a pack of vultures hovering overhead, just waiting for someone to leave their stuff alone for a second."

Why do Americans steal from other Americans? Our so-called buddies are the worst thieves. It is disconcerting to have to keep an eye on my belongings every minute. I was not raised to distrust people, but damn if I haven't learned in this lousy place.

Late in the afternoon a guard distributes post cards and stationary. Strubinger says the Jerries want to clear out their supply room before the Americans arrive. I decide to write a girl I had known throughout high school. She'll pass the word around about me.

Quiet reigns in the building while letters are written. It reminds me of Sayre Street grammar school in Montgomery when the fourth grade teacher made everyone put their heads on a desk and sleep for about 30 minutes while she slipped out for a smoke. I write a postcard to a girl named Boo DeVan.

Note to Boo Devan on post card provided to prisoners of war

"Boo! Where did she get a name like that?"

"I don't know. Her real name is Myrtle Lee."

"Say, why do southern girls all have double names, like 'Virginia Lane' or 'Mary Beth?'"

"To be sure both sides of the family are recognized, I guess."

When I write my aunt and uncle in Mobile my mind slips to the food. My aunt's love to cook, and Christmas was cook-time. Their specialties are desserts. Each one prepared her own specialty the same way, with the same ingredients, in the same pan. My letter home reflects my desire to return to those wonderful cookies, cakes and pies. My mouth moved as I chewed on a piece of pecan pie. Saliva dripped from my lips as I recall stealing a piece of divinity from the candy bowl, and it melting in my closed mouth. A smile forms as I recall how I would help Grandfather eat his second piece of Lane cake. Those were good days. I shake my head to erase the sad memories.

The letters and cards are collected. Everyone reminisces about their letters and homes. After the one-inch piece of bread is rationed to us for supper the barracks leader calls for attention.

"I hear from the guards that the American Army is pushing this way." Before he can explain the barracks erupts into cheers, foot stomping and clapping. "Go, man! Yea, Patton. How long?"

"Probably by March 15," Benner yells.

I'm not sure I can last that long — it's a month away. I tell myself, I *can* last a month.

Benner wants to keep the barracks in a jovial mood. He says, "Let's elect the outstanding POW in the barracks."

"Come on, spare me, Benner. I'm already the most popular fellow in here," somebody yells, followed by cat-calls and laughter. Everyone mentions his own name. I yell out my name, then remark to Cole, "At least he tries to keep our spirits high. Must be the Boy Scout in him."

"Yeah. Next thing you know, we'll be playing capture the flag."

"I'll volunteer to take the flag — about 50 miles from here!"

Somebody yells, "I nominate the Fuhrer."

Hoots, hollers, and derision follow this nomination. Finally, order is restored. A group from the 28th Division, located at the front of the barracks, nominate one of their group. He is elected without much input from others in the barracks. No one is interested in such a silly ritual. A wise-apple comments on the results, "What's he gonna get, a day in Bad Orb?"

"Let him sit on top of the honey-bucket detail all week and wave to all his subjects."

"Give him a red beret from a British paratrooper and the Commandant's great-coat."

The laughter and jostling continues for an hour or so. The poor slob who is elected has a silly grin on his face, blushes as he gives a wave, and drops his head. No doubt he feels sorta silly, but it is nice to hear laughter. It's surprising how good news about the war or a Red Cross box — even if it was to the French — and writing home lifts everyone's spirits.

Many POWs believe every rumor. As I settle down for the night, I say to Pett, "I refuse to believe all the crap about when we'll be free until the Americans actually tear down the gates."

"Don't be such a cynic, Higg. You gotta believe in something."

He's probably right. It's hard not to be happy over the good news. Deep down inside me my soul screams, "Believe! Believe!" but my practical nature tells me to wait for the facts. Is a rumor the whole truth, half truth, or no truth? Please, God, tell me one rumor is true.

> 4–11 February 1945
>
> "Diplomatic Affairs: It is now clear to all that the war in Europe has been won, but both Britain and the U.S. believe that they will have much to do to defeat Japan .... The postwar borders of the countries of eastern Europe are also largely determined at the Yalta meeting ...."
>
> [Source: page 322, *World Almanac Book of World War II*, rev. ed., Bison Books Corp., 1986.]

At roll call Wednesday Benner announces the next two shipments. Cole and Gleason will be in the next group. Pett and I will be on the following shipment. No one is sure when the shipments will take place.

Pett yells at Benner, "How do they make up those lists? Why can't we go as a group?"

"Don't ask me. All I know is this is the list."

My German tag number is 27209. Pett's is 27206, but Cole and Gleason's numbers are more distant.

Pett's eyes are damp when we return to the barracks. He shakes his head and moans in a barely audible tone, "I'll never survive strafing. I don't want to die without a chance to fight. I'm not going if my name is called. I'll try to escape, probably get shot. So what? At least I'll be buried in a grave, not thrown off a boxcar like a piece of wood, left to rot in the forest."

Pett and I avoid Cole and Gleason the rest of the day. No use crying over spilled milk. What's to be will be. I am mentally exhausted from being jerked from elation to depression. One day everything is fun and games; the next brings another disaster.

When Strub returns Thursday with our five-inch slice of bread for eight men, he says Red Cross boxes are on the way, then adds, "This entire barracks is to leave soon, probably before the Red Cross boxes are delivered."

The weather is much better, so I spend the day meandering around the camp listening to rumors of the war's end, looking up at the specks of black in the sky. The steady hum of American and British planes is like icing on the cake of happiness. I can taste freedom. All night I lie on my pallet and dream of food, freedom, and family. I guess I slept.

Friday we awake to a cold, damp, windy day. I try to stay warm by moving closer to Pett.

Fred returns from the latrine laughing. "Just like good old Boston; one day sunny, next day cold and rainy."

His attempt at humor doesn't hide the more frequent twitching of his left eye, a sign of nervousness I'd noticed since capture. No one responds. The usual stone-faced expression on Hugh's face begin to sag. He drops his eyes, refuses to look at me.

All day Friday, I isolate myself from the group. I am tired of talking and listening to optimism about the war. When the end comes we'll know it. No use dreaming. It just makes my stomach churn, my bowels growl, and my eyes water. I wrap myself in my cocoon of desolation. I am as tense as a violin string. I will explode if anyone says a word to me, so I cover my head.

"Here, Higg, eat your damn piece of bread. Cheer up, happy-boy."

"Oh, shut up, Don, and leave me alone."

"Okay, stew in your own misery-juice. I'll eat your bread. I love it!"

"Kiss my butt, but first stuff my piddlin' piece of bread up it."

The sun came out Saturday. My spirits improved. I feel better on bright, sunny days.

I jump up, bright-eyed and bushy-tailed.

"Hey, let's get outside and pick lice and talk about food and family."

After dinner, a group of us gathers in the sun to talk. Along come the Serbs with the war news. "I guess their radio is broken. You think they hear all that stuff, or make it up?" Cole asks.

"I don't know, but it cheers me up," Pett says.

I am both happy and jumpy. I wish I really knew what was going on in the war.

13–15 February 1945

"Europe, Air Operations. On the night of 13–14 February, there is a massive RAF attack on Dresden by 773 Lancaster bombers. This is followed by the daylight attacks by 8th Air Force on the 14th and 15th involving 600 planes altogether. The greatest damage is done in the RAF attack when the city, crowded with refugees from the Eastern Front, is devastated in a horrific firestorm. Various authorities give different figures for the number of casualties, ranging from 30,000 dead to 200,000 dead. The best estimates suggest a figure around 70,000 is more accurate. The raid becomes very controversial because Dresden is not an important military target and has been a city of much historical interest."

[Source: page 324, *World Almanac Book of World War II*, rev. ed., Bison Books Corp., 1986.]

Little things make me jittery and nervous — the sucking of breath, the smacking of lips, even the 'swish, swish' of the wind whistling through the toothless mouth of another POW, the hyena laugh from a prisoner. I can hear the constant beating of a rock on another rock. The 'bang, bang, bang, thud, thud, thud' goes on for an hour. "What the hell is that noise?" I scream at no one in particular, then walk outside to discover a Mexican-American POW making tortillas from some messy-looking glob. He smiles and continues. Well, at least he's happy.

Sunday, more POWs arrive. Rumor has it the Germans are moving prisoners from one camp to another to avoid capture. The Allied forces are closing in on Germany from all sides, but Stalag IXB remains under lock. I feel the world is closing in on me. Rumor, sickness, and departing friends. Maybe church will cheer me up.

I urge everyone to go with me. We attend as a group, since this might be our last time together. Even Gleason and Strubinger, two staunch Catholics, go with us. Pett says he won't tell the Pope, and Clete and Fred both shake their heads and smile.

I see a large number of American prisoners of war come into camp as we walk to church. They are a sad-looking group — dirty, hollow expressions hiding eyes in sunken sockets. They wear clothing from various nationalities on bodies that would make skeletons look fat.

Huckel asks, "I wonder what ever happened to Fellman, Zion, and that group?"

Cole replies, "No telling. And the non-coms. I miss Zion and those free cigarettes."

I add, "Wonder where the 70th Division is located? Was B Company reformed when all of us were captured? Is Gartenmann still alive?"

Cole says, "Gartenmann will make it. Knowing him, he's probably already back in Switzerland."

"Is that where he's from?"

"I think so."

---

17 February 1945

"Western Front. The XV Corps of the U.S. Seventh Army continues its limited offensive to eliminate the German salient at Gros Rederchin and Wilferding. The 70th Division is now going in on the left flank of the corps, attacking hills to the southwest of Saarbrucken . . . ."

[Source: page 668, *2194 Days of War*, Mayflower Books, W. H. Smith Publishers Inc., New York, 1977.]

"Wonder if Van Horn and Landells got through to Battalion? I know Captain Schmied sent them back before we were cut off," he adds.

"And that mess sergeant. I guess he's fixing those sticky buns for another company. He is one good cook. I enjoyed KP back in Leonard Wood." I smack my lips and suck in the saliva.

Cole laughs, "You must have — you were on KP enough. You never did learn to clean that Browning Automatic Rifle for Saturday inspection."

"It should be against Army regulations to have to clean a BAR for Saturday inspection after firing it all week."

As we enter the chapel, I sarcastically whisper to Cole, "I hope we don't sing 'The Battle Hymn of the Republic.'"

"That's not a religious song."

"You got that right. I'll look in my Bible and pick out a song for us to sing when Chaplain Neal asks for suggestions."

Chaplain Neal quotes from the book of John. There are four books of John in the New Testament — Books I, II, III, and just *John*. I often wonder if the same person wrote all of them, and why all the numbers? I make a check mark in my subconscious to ask Chaplain Neal someday. I'm not sure I understand everything the Chaplain says, but his words and voice provide some comfort to my weary soul. He says something about the truth making me free. He reads this from one of the books of John. Well, I think, I'm tired of waiting to be freed, and I'm not sure how *truth* will do it.

Chaplain Neal quotes Jesus as being the truth, and adds we have to believe in Him and His words. I turn to the first page in my Bible and read the words I wrote the first week in Stalag IXB:

> *When we've no power to fight alone,*
> *nor even strength to call our own,*
> *Thanks be to God, for it is He*
> *through his Son gives victory.*

The words that lift my spirits the highest are from a passage in the book of Psalms. The Chaplain talks about God protecting and keeping me safe. *That* I believe devoutly, deeply, and with conviction. Along with the others I bow my head in a closing prayer. My mind slips to the poem *Invictus*, and the part about "I am the master of my fate, I am the captain of my soul." I close my eyes as I think, yes, God, with your help, I will make it. I do not believe that death is the only path to freedom.

Cole punches me and whispers, "Yell out a song to sing from your Bible."

I open my New Testament to the front, and yell, "Nearer My God to Thee." As we sing, Cole and Gleason look at each of us with tears in their eyes. My voice chokes, tears cloud my eyes. I look at the floor. No words can express the love we have for each other.

After the service, we silently walk outside toward the barracks. Clete finally breaks the silence. "Damn this lousy weather." It is misty. The wind blows at what seems like 40 miles per hour as we walk to the hilltop. Clouds drape like wet sheets over the mountain. No plane activity today, I think as I look skyward.

We get a bowl of muddy-looking soup with pieces of unpeeled potatoes full of spots which stare at me like pieces of whole black pepper. The potatoes taste as bitter as gall. I throw mine on the ground when I get to the barracks. "I'd rather starve than eat that crap."

The lousy weather and the crappy food compounds my disgust of other prisoners. The uncouthness of many of the men in the shack, called a barracks, tightens like a boa constrictor around my throat, as I lay around all afternoon shivering and aching from the cold.

Why does God put me in this position. "Help me! If this place is a sample of hell, I'll take the alternative. Whatever is necessary to go up, not down, show me the way … Please, please, please, dear Heavenly Father."

This feeling of frustration combines with anxiety to sit heavy on my shoulders. My nerves are as raw as uncooked steak.

When the evening's allotment of bread is delivered to the barracks, Pett points to me. "Your time to cut the bread. Bring back the largest piece you can get." I look at the slice of bread for my group when passed out by Benner. It is a half-inch thick, and the sawdust content even has splinters. And six men have to share it. Shit!

Strubinger squints at me as I prepare to divide the tiny portion. His square face is pockmarked, with splotches of black and blonde stubble. "That's all you got, you measly little bastard?"

I'm not in any mood to listen to his crap. The blood rises in my cheeks. My face gets as red as an over-ripe tomato. My breath is short and rapid. I explode. "Shut up, you unpolished turd. I take it back. I wouldn't insult a turd by calling you one. You're worse, but I can't think of anything." I often wonder why we don't throw him out of our group. However, as Pett said once, "We know him, he can be trusted, and will fight for our protection."

I cut the bread. One of the rules in our group is the person who cuts the bread gets the last piece and all the crumbs. I carefully place each piece of bread on a cloth on the floor. Six sets of eyes watch my every move.

All of a sudden, Clete screams, "Wait! That piece is larger than the others. And look at the crumbs you're making. You trying to get most of the bread?"

"Shut up, Clete, and let me cut."

As I start to cut another slice, Clete yells, "Wait a minute. You are still cutting the bread uneven. I'm number five. I'll get a handful of crumbs."

I stop and look at the bread. The last two slices are not as large as the others. The cloth is full of crumbs. I shrug my shoulders. "I'm sorry, fellows. This bread has so much sawdust it crumbles. And the knife is dull, too."

I calmly give each of the other four a slice of bread. I stand up. The knife is pointed upward. I turn it over, grab the handle and raise it over my head, look into Clete's face, and start to thrust it downward.

Clete's eyes become wide with fear. "You don't dare." My hand quivers as it starts downward. I stop. I slowly drop my arm and stare at Clete. I want to kill him, but decide he isn't worth getting shot over. I whisper in a shaking voice, "Right. No use busting a good knife on your lousy hide!"

I kneel, scoop up the crumbs along with the remaining two pieces of bread, get on my feet and slowly crumble the bread on his uplifted face. "You want bread? Here, eat this!"

I stumble to the latrine, sit on the cold, crappy, wet floor, pull my knees under my chin and whimper, God, what's happening to me? I can't take much more squalor and hostility.

It's useless to think about health. Diarrhea, fleas, lice, cramps are part of this existence. And this is living? I shake my head to clear the cobwebs of despair, and smile. Boy, I really scared the pee out of Clete. I don't think he will carp at me for awhile. No one looks at me as I return to the group. They just turn over and adjust their bodies when I squirm onto the floor.

A good fight cleanses the soul. I am at peace with myself.

Chapter 6

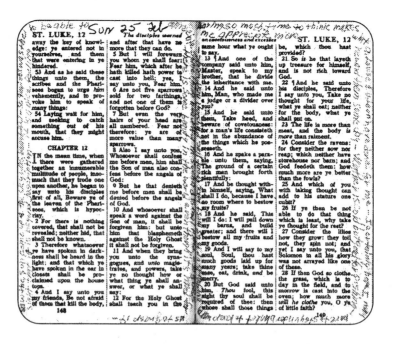

Week Six

19 February–25 February 1945

——✠——

Monday, 19 February

I blew my top last night. My nerves couldn't take any more. I'm sorry I blew up. The old chow question is up again. Some think all the trading comes from the kitchen. We aren't getting the amount of potatoes in our soup. The traders are getting bread someplace and the kitchen is the only place GIs have access to. It will all lead to nothing.

Tuesday, 20 February

Starting coughing again last night. Couldn't sleep all night. My stomach and chest are sore from so much coughing. Sure disgusts me. Still chilly and damp. No planes for two days; news not much better. Soup was thicker at noon, so everyone is satisfied. Tomorrow the same old gripes will be heard.

I'm sure sick of the bickering, and now fights break out frequently. Cole and Gleason are leaving tomorrow. Sure hate to see them go. We have so much planned for after the war in the States.

Wednesday, 21 February

Cole and Gleason haven't left yet. Sure hope they don't, but imagine any day now they'll go. Snowed last night and colder. All afternoon the skies have been filled with B-17s; I hear the Yanks are on Corregidor. Hope they bomb tonight, as it is pretty, but still pretty chilly. Still have that hacking cough. Almost gets me — my stomach and chest ache from so much coughing. My knees still hurt a lot.

Thursday, 22 February

Cole and Gleason left at noon. I cried when I shook hands and my eyes are still red. Cole and I have been eating and sleeping together since September. I admire and like him as a brother; I sure hate to see him go. Cole and I have sworn to notify each other's family when we are freed. That I'll do, in case something happens which I pray to God doesn't. My first meal will be dedicated to we four. I'll go to Richmond to see him, too. We are to leave in a few days, but I think our chances of being freed are better if we stay here. Pett and I are still together.

Friday, 23 February

Met Raymond Hoagland yesterday. Sure was glad to see someone from home, especially that I went to school with. Hope to see more of him. We had camp detail today — I was on the cesspool gang. Was smelly and filthy, but had two old men as guards. They are ready to go home, too, and say the war should be over in not more than two months. Nice day; still chilly, but sun is out. We didn't get extra chow as we might have known. We had built our hopes up so much that it was a severe blow. I felt like crying when I didn't get any more soup.

Saturday, 24 February

We hear the big push has started on First, Ninth, and Third Army fronts. Even the Jerries say it is the big fight for the war's end. Hope it is soon. Today we plan to write down the clothes we want when we get back. Only 100 men in here now, but still have fights and arguments all day and night. Sure is hell to sit here and listen to that stuff. The building is cold now that only a few men are in here. We finally got our seconds on soup — it was surely appreciated. Of course, some still complained.

Sunday, 25 February

Saw the sun come up, and the sky was beautiful. So good was the sight that it is beyond description. It is a nice feeling to be able to appreciate something beautiful in such a dismal place. I guess there is some beauty in the world, even though it's hard for us to grasp it. Having so much time to think makes me appreciate more what A. Louise and U. Leon have done for me; I certainly hope I may reward them some day. Weather is cold, but good for pushing. Have to stay under blanket to keep warm. Our guards up to 65 must have front line physical next week.

━ ━━━ ━

I wake up from the first beam of light which peeks into the barracks. Why did I act like an animal toward Clete last night? The loss of self-control humiliates me. Each week my behavior becomes less civil, less flippant, less humorous. No doubt God's reaction is 'tsk, tsk' as he shakes his head. Certainly not exemplary, nor commendable. I squeeze my eyes, look up and promise I will regain an attitude of bon vivant. My prison mates always enjoy my stories of the past, many of which I embellish to get a smile or a chuckle. I am determined to recall the good times, block out the bad ones. There is humor in anything. You have to search for it and, if necessary, fabricate a story.

I lean across three bodies.

"Psst, psst. Hey, Clete, you awake?"

He rolls over.

"I'm sorry, Clete. I didn't mean to take the stress of this damn prison camp out on you. It's getting to me. I even curse more. I just can't stand all the noise, filth and bitching. I know I have to get hold of myself. And I will, so help me."

"Yeah, you better, or some slimeball will knife you, you damn hotheaded Irishman. South Philly is full of guys like you, except you aren't fast enough, nor strong enough, to 'hit, hurt and hurry,' as we used to say. Thanks for all the crumbs you dumped on me."

I get philosophical. "It's bad enough to try to exist today without clogging the brain with the miseries of yesterday. We have to take one day at a time,

111

grab the ring of beauty and joy as the merry-go-round of misery passes us. Yesterday is gone. Tomorrow is uncertain. My aunt used to say, 'don't worry about spilt milk.' She then proceeded to preach about carelessness for an hour."

Clete grunts.

I continue, "Did I ever tell you about the dog food caper?"

"No, but I have an idea I'm going to hear it." He moans, sits up, wipes his eyes, and in a tone of exasperation speaks loudly to the other six still curled in their blankets, "Higgins has a story to get your blood running before the barracks is opened. Might as well listen to it."

"This is the truth. It was like this. One time before my aunt and uncle went out of town, she said to eat the corned beef hash in the icebox."

"We call those *refrigerators* in the north," Gleason interrupts.

"Well, whatever. They left and I fried the corned beef hash for supper, even put a poached egg on top. Upon their return the next day, my aunt looked in the ice-box-called-refrigerator-in-the-north and exclaimed, 'Why didn't you eat the corned beef hash?'"

"I did eat it."

"No, you didn't, it's still in the bowl."

"Then what did I eat?"

"You ate the dog food!"

Clete laughs, then adds, "Now I know why you growl all the time."

"Did you smell like garlic? Dog food is full of it," Cole adds.

"How do you know, Cole, you eat dog food?" Strubinger asks.

"No, but I could smell it when I fed the hounds."

Thus, the week begins on a happy note. It gets better when the barracks leader reports the Yanks landed on Corregidor. Somebody yells, "To hell with the Pacific. How about us?"

"This is authentic. An Englishman told me when his group brought the tea. Remember, those guys have a short wave radio set up for the news every night."

Huckel is skeptical. "I doubt it is true."

Clete replies, "You gotta have faith, friend." He looks at me, smiles, and adds, "Or you get dog food for lunch."

I can't resist listening to the war rumors. My heart always beats a little faster. Each one provides some measure of hope and a reason to last another day.

16 February 1945

"Philippines. Two battalions, one seaborne and one dropped by parachute, land on Corregidor Island in Manila Bay. The attacking troops land successfully enough, but a bitter struggle soon develops among the tunnels and gun emplacements of the island. The U.S. troops are quickly reinforced. Since the battle for Luzon began, 3,200 tons of bombs have been dropped on Corregidor."

[Source: page 324, *World Almanac Book of World War II*, rev. ed., Bison Books Corp., 1986.]

A feeling of apathy pricks my soul. The cough won't stop. My stomach muscles ache. Pain pierces my chest with every breath like a hot knife. Sleep is fretful. My knees ache constantly, even worse when lying on the cold floor. Before daylight I thought about getting up, but where would I go? If I tried to go to the latrine, the screaming, cursing, and bodily blows would stop me.

I get more irritated at the actions of other POWs. My stomach aches from hunger. The freezing rain, wind and snow won't go away. My body is always damp. It's a constant battle not to sink to a vegetable-like state and just give up. The next world couldn't be any worse than this one; warmer if I went down, and not as cold if I went up. I sit alone all morning, feeling sorry for myself. No one bothers me.

As I hurry from the kitchen Monday to prevent my puny ration of soup from freezing, I see the Big Dealer, whose name I never knew, walk past me. He looks like an overstuffed Buddha on a six-foot frame. I scream at him, "You in cahoots with the Jerries? Where the hell do you get all the potatoes to trade? Somebody in the kitchen is wheeling and dealing."

My hands shake, become sweaty even in the 15-degree weather. He shrugs his shoulders and swaggers down the street toward the kitchen. Cole and Gleason grab me as I start to throw my soup on his clean uniform. Cole whispers, "Stay calm. You may need him someday to trade for something."

"I can't understand how he lives like a king outwardly and with his conscience inwardly. The two approaches to life are incongruous. He wears an American officer's pink coat (a heavy overcoat) to his knees, twill woolen army pants, a green shirt, and a tie! It's bad enough to dress like an officer when he's only a private, but a tie! That's rubbing it in." The Big Dealer wears paratrooper boots, always shined. His clothes are pressed. He is clean, hair trimmed — the epitome of a West Point general at a division dress parade.

As we walk back to the barracks, I remark to Cole, "I've heard he lives across from the kitchen, sleeps in a bunk, has a footlocker full of tradable items, plus money! Three Mexican-American POWs stand guard over his bunk and footlocker 24 hours a day."

Cole remarks, "A couple of the POWs who live in the same barracks say he is a nice guy — just resourceful, creative, and with the initiative to make a buck and just capitalizing on a difficult situation."

"Bullshit! Anybody who tries to exist on top of this wind-blown mountain can't have any compassion for some asshole who takes advantage of his fellow prisoners." The debate stops as we try to eat the dinner slop. All afternoon and evening there is continual bitching about the lack of food. It's the same argument over and over. I roll up in my blanket and shiver. I try to sleep. There is nothing we can do about anything. Our captors have all the cards. Might as well take what life deals us and make the best of it.

—•—■●■—•—

At roll call Tuesday Cole and Gleason's names are on the list to leave tomorrow — the only ones from our platoon. I look at the ground as my eyes cloud over. I squeeze them, tight to keep from crying. Gleason looks at the dark sky and clouds so low the mountains are invisible, and attempts to be nonchalant. "We won't leave today. The Air Corps can't fly in this weather. Those guys will probably have to sit around all day in a warm room in England and drink, eat, and sleep. I sure feel sorry for them."

"Oh, shut up, Fred. I don't want to think about it," Cole snaps.

Each of us avoids talk about the breakup of our group. All day, Cole and Gleason gather their meager belongings and try to stay busy. It is useless to talk of the future when you don't know what will happen 10 minutes from now. Longing for the good times of the past only makes the present more unbearable. The only thing left is to complain and gripe about the current situation. Even that is a waste of time, so I just sit against the barracks wall and shiver. My mind is in neutral. The constant bickering and bitching continues throughout the day and night. With 200 or so men in a 40 by 60 foot room, there will always be somebody to complain.

I didn't go for the noon ration of soup, nor take any of the bread for supper. I feel so sorry for myself, I don't want to do anything. I just want to be alone with my own miseries.

—•—■●■—•—

Wednesday the sky is clear and filled with B-17s. Huckel looks up and yells, "There won't be any ground movement today. The Jerries don't trust the American planes, even when they are 20,000 feet in the air."

114

Gleason says, "I don't understand this weather — black and overcast one day, warm the next, then snow, then rain."

My stomach aches from the hacking and coughing. Huckel advises me to go to the infirmary, "Frankly, I'm tired of listening to you."

"I'm not going. If I die it will be here, among some friends." I glare at him and smile. My knees ache so much I put my blanket between them and try to lie on my side. I can't get comfortable, so I get up and go outside to watch the B-17s, a beautiful sight. I just hope they will fly all night, and level all the buildings in Germany.

At roll call Thursday, it is announced the names on the list a couple of days ago will leave after dinner. When the time arrives, Cole and Gleason pick up their belongings. The farewells are short. Our existence depends on so many factors it is not wise to anticipate nor contemplate our fate. Cole and I have been close since Fort Leonard Wood five months ago. The fact I am alive is due, in part, to Cole. He relieved me of my pack while climbing up Falkenberg Heights chasing Germans. I recall the incident.

"You said, 'Here, you little twerp, let me have that pack. You can't dodge in and out among the bushes and snow with that Browning Automatic Rifle, plus a pack.'"

"And I was only too willing to let you carry it."

The Browning Automatic Rifle, BAR for short, weighs 20 pounds. I also carried an ammunition belt with eight magazines, each of which weighs four pounds, two hand grenades and God-only-knows how much clothing.

He says, "Yeah, you handed me that pack so fast I didn't have time to reconsider my stupid offer."

My eyes get watery when we hug. I don't think we will ever see each other on this Earth. He has a sad look in his moist eyes. He sniffles, then asks me to look up his family in Richmond after the war. He tells me to write their names in my Bible. "Now. Not after I leave," he commands.

Gleason gives me a hug.

We all promise to dedicate our first meal to the four of us: Pett, Cole, Gleason and me. Gleason adds, "Send me that list of your meals the first day at home, Higg. I'm going to eat each meal, vomit, then eat the next one. When I finish there will be a 10-gallon bucket of vomit and one happy soldier. Hell, I might even eat the grits, and without sugar, too."

I get my Bible from my shirt pocket and write their names and home addresses. When I look up, they are gone. The guards won't allow the men in the barracks to go outside while the POWs line up. Pett and I look out the window. Both Cole and Gleason are at the far end of the line. On command, they turn right and march toward the main road of the camp.

As we turn from the window Pett says, "Well, we have more room now, since there are only about 100 men in here." He wipes his eyes on his sleeve and sniffles. We spend the morning rearranging our surroundings, spread out without too many territorial fights, and discuss just who will be in the bread group.

Survival and faith are paramount in my mind, although there is still the question of just why I have to experience this torture and anxiety. The close relationship with Cole and Gleason is over. Something has to replace the void in my prison life, or I will go crazy. Pett and I are on the next shipment, but Pett will never make it. I'm not sure if I will either. Regardless, I need to prepare for the prospective trip to wherever. Faith in the future is the only way to survive. I curl up in my blanket and read the Bible.

After dinner, I walk around camp. I see beauty in the snow capped mountains. They reach up and kiss the grayish-white clouds. My spirits go up when I see a POW with "Mobile" on the back of his jacket. I catch up with him. Lo and behold, it is Raymond Hoagland, whom I knew at Murphy High School in Mobile. He still has a resonant voice and the look of the serious student. We walk around Stalag IXB most of the afternoon, recalling old times.

It is a good afternoon. Not only is my mind diverted from Cole and Gleason, but it is fun to talk about the past. We only retain the happy memories. The sad ones we bury.

The new men who join our group are introduced. One is Lucius J. Mahoney, the other Tutwiler Ulysses Tutherow. I sullenly examine the newcomers. The one called Mahoney is taller than me, about five feet ten inches. He has stooped shoulders, bushy eyebrows, and a peaked French army cap that looks silly perched squarely in the middle of a small head loaded with curly, black hair.

"My name's Mahoney, Lucius A. People Call me Luke for short." Mahoney's flat 'A' accent makes words like "narrow" come out "nero." He is definitely from New England. Unfortunately, he reminds me of Fred Gleason.

I look up and mutter, "Where you from? Know it's not Atlanta, Georgia."

"South Boston."

"Another bean guy. Might have known." I wasn't happy to have someone remind me of Fred, but that's life. In prison camp you don't pick your associates. Hope he doesn't smell."Guess you are Catholic, too."

"Right." His stern face breaks into a quick smile. His eyes twinkle. Maybe he won't be too bad, after all.

The other POW appears to be about six feet and five inches. I think he is taller than Hugh by three or four inches. I notice his left eyebrow arches when he speaks. Both eyes are half closed, and cast a haughty, superior look downward. He tilts his head upward just enough to give the impression that he smells something foul in other people. This air of superiority is confirmed when he speaks.

"I am referred to as Tutwiler Ulysses Tutherow."

Strubinger can't resist, "And suppose we don't *refer* to you? What do we call you?"

"Tut for short." His short, English-accented voice reveals class.

Clete interrupts. "Oh, hell, another damned southerner. You probably eat grits, too. At least I can understand one of you." He nods to Mahoney.

When Tut replies, I notice his left eyebrow rises at the start of every sentence. "I was born in Tyron, North Carolina, but since my father and mater — mother to the uneducated — spend so much time traveling, I've been in boarding schools most of my life."

Pett says, "And just where did his highness 'board?'"

"A school in Westtown, Pennsylvania."

I say, "Surprised you are in the Army. Couldn't you say you were a pacifist?"

"My farther informed me I should be a patriot. I was a cadet in the Air Corp, but I got sick and got thrown out of training. My farther . . . ."

I interrupt, "You got to quit saying 'farther.' It's a short 'a,' like 'father.'" He ignores my correction. As a corner of his mouth cracks the beginning of a smile, the left eyebrow rises. I'm sorry I opened my big mouth.

"I was to join the congressional staff of a senator when I finished flight school, but it didn't work out."

Pett bows and says, "Well, I am so happy you joined us. Maybe you can write your whatever you call him and get us out of this stinking pit." I get tired of the conversation. I miss Fred and Hugh, so I get up and go into the latrine. It stinks, but it's quiet.

The bread is cut and passed out. I don't know who did the cutting. When I return to my blanket, the two newcomers have gone to their blankets.

———— ❈ ————

Friday our barracks gets the camp detail. If there is any activity that will prevent remorse or self-pity it is the cesspool detail. I volunteer since it is an alternative to a day of monotony. You have to have a clear mind and steady hand to dip the long bucket into the cesspool under each barracks, then put it carefully — and I do mean carefully — into a huge tank. Some wag named it "honey-bucket" detail. "Honey, you better not get it on you." How true that is! You lose friends fast when you smell like a latrine.

The guards are not anxious to work. We move slowly to fill the tank and pull it outside the camp. There is only one trip all morning. While in the woods, one of the Polish guards tells an American POW who speaks Polish that the war will be over in the next two months. He adds that the Allied Forces are already in Germany, but is not sure of the location.

The cesspool detail only works half a day, and is always first in the dinner line. We get an extra dipper of soup. I guess no one wants to see and smell the crappy bodies. It certainly isn't compassion.

When we line up, the guard at the kitchen says we will only get our normal dipper of soup. I yell, "What! We were promised an extra ration." The other members of the detail surround the guard, ready to kill him.

Everyone yells at once. "Dirty bastards ... you promised ... no more volunteering ... we were tricked ..." and so on.

I look at the piddling helmet of soup. I hate myself for getting upset over such a small matter. Then I think, no, it isn't small. It is a big matter. I was *promised* an extra ration. You can't trust anybody.

＋──◄◆►──＋

Saturday at roll call, the barracks leader said those who worked on the cesspool detail Friday should get in line first for dinner. We would get our extra ration of soup.

Somebody asks, "How will you know who is entitled to the extra ration?"

Some wit replies, "You can smell 'em."

While getting our ersatz tea, the war news is announced by Benner. It sounds good, but I doubt if it is true.

The barracks is colder with fewer men, but we do get to spread out. My mind searches for something to do to keep from thinking about the cold. Finally, I hit upon an idea. "Hey, men, after dinner let's write down the clothes we want after the war. Maybe a list will warm us up, or at least keep us from feeling so darn miserable."

Pett says, "Good idea. Everyone make a list this morning and then after dinner we'll sit around and compare notes. Be sure to include the prices."

I sit against the window and make a list. Once I look up and comment, "I wonder what's really happening in the war?"

Pett answers, "I don't know, but since I don't hear any guns I assume the Americans aren't close."

23 February 1945

"Western Front. A major new offensive by U.S. First and Ninth Armies begins with heavy attacks along the Roer, especially in the Julich and Duren areas .... Farther south, there are also attacks by units of U.S. Seventh and Third Armies."

[Source: page 326, *World Almanac Book of World War II*, rev. ed., Bison Books Corp., 1986.]

I enjoy my extra ration of soup for dinner. My helmet is almost full. I burp a few times, then have diarrhea. As I return from the outdoor latrine, I can see the sun sink behind the clouds, and say we should compare our lists. A stomach full of soup and hopeful war news lifts my spirits. Pett, Huckel, and I enjoy comparing lists.

Since my list is more precise, Huckel suggests I read it to the others. "You must have been a Beau Brummel. I never saw so many clothes or such high prices. In New York, we buy them at Macy's, in the basement."

"Well, yes, I do like clothes. I remember my grandfather Higgins and my Dad always had a handkerchief in their coat pockets."

Pett says, "Hell, I never had a handkerchief, muchless in a jacket pocket."

"What did you wipe your nose on if you didn't have a handkerchief?" I inquired.

"My sleeve."

"Must have been a snotty mess. Here's my list."

Huckel looks it over. "My God, look at the clothes. All I really want is a discharge. I might even have it enlarged and wear it as a gown." Then he adds, "Why do you want an ETO jacket and a field jacket? Here, you can have my field jacket. It's a little dirty, but you can have it dyed along with the ETO jackets. How are you going to line it with fur?"

"Aw, you guys don't know anything about clothes. I don't mean *this* type of field jacket. I mean one of those raincoat-like things."

"You already have a raincoat listed. You want a fur lined toilet seat also?"

Pett laughs, "You want those garters to hold your socks up to your underwear?"

"Kiss my foot, all of you."

Strubinger joins us and reads my list. "You're going to spend $263 on clothes? You must be mad. I might spend 50 bucks." The remainder of the day is spent talking about clothes. My mind gets numb. The discussions stop. We just sit around dreaming until it is time for the bread for supper.

As the sky darkens I fight despondency. I try not to think about Cole and Gleason, but their faces keep clouding my vision. The affection I have for them weighs heavily on my mind. My despondency is so deep I can't participate in deciding on a new group. It would have been Cole's turn to cut the bread.

——◄█►——

Before our barracks is opened Sunday, I drag myself from the floor, weave across the legs and arms of the sleeping POWs, and look at the sunrise through a dirty window. Puffs of clouds chase each other in a pale blue sky. My mind wanders back to the early mornings in Warrenton, Florida, when I would stop my bike after delivering papers and gaze across a calm bayou, glistening from the sun that peeked under the railroad bridge to Fort Barrancas. The sun winks at me as each small wave of the bayou gets in its path.

I wish desperately for a return to my youth in Warrenton. Only pleasant memories remain. Maybe that is what dreams are made of — memories. I shake my head and look around at today's crappy existence.

The pleasures of prison life are few — extra bread, a warm day, a delousing, and now, more room in the barracks. These are tangible, not a dream nor an illusion. Each one helps my self-preservation. What tangible evidence did I have of a pleasant childhood? Someday I'll make a list. Yeah, that's a good one for the group.

I shiver. It is so damned cold. It penetrates every garment. My bones ache. Oh, well, I decide, I'll just lie around today and dream of the Gulf of Mexico and those slow, lazy waves hitting the white beach. The water is probably 70 degrees, at least 50 degrees warmer than this place. No mountains for me if I ever get home.

I skip supper. The thought of one more meal of black bread turns my stomach. I just want to feel sorry for myself. Nights are the worst. Hours seem like days. They just drag on and on and on.

Finally, my eyelids get heavy.

I begin to fall asleep, trying to think of more pleasant days.

Chapter 7

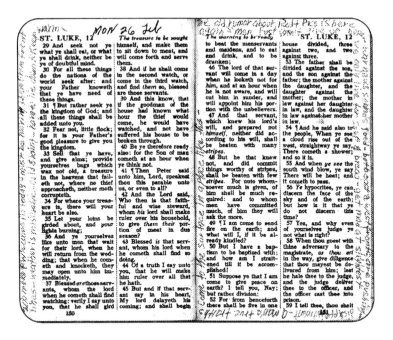

Week Seven

26 February–4 March 1945

———✦✦———

Monday, 26 February

Two hundred more POWs came in today; must be moving from the front lines. Weather is miserable — cold and rainy; have to lie down to keep warm. The old rumor about Red Cross packages is here again. Men just won't give up hope. War news sounds good — both East and West fronts are pushing. We only live for soup and bread, and get mad at slightest disappointment. A man's true traits come to the surface in a place like this.

Tuesday, 27 February

Around 200 POWs a day are coming in; 2,000 are due here; lots of British. They say the Russians were in Berlin on February 8. Yanks have been pushing since February 1. All are very optimistic. Next month should be the month. The new POWs say one to two months. I'm beginning to think of food again. I hate myself for letting my mind get so low. I see myself being stingy and selfish as far as food is concerned. I use my helmet for soup instead of mess kit because I'm afraid some may be spilled, and every drop counts now.

Wednesday, 28 February

Nice sunny day, lots warmer. The English said they got Red Cross packages at their last camp. I'm sitting in the sun. Some guy is playing the accordion to the Serbs. I washed my shirt as it stunk so badly. My Higgins legs sure have disappeared right now. Spent a very pleasant day talking about food. Sure will be glad to get back to A. Louise's good cooking; I didn't know how much I appreciated her home. Sure will appreciate it more when I get back. Still lots of arguing and fussing going on. Some of these guys are lower than snakes.

Thursday, 1 March

I hear the Ninth Army is across the Rhine. It is cooler today, with a strong wind. From reports from other POWs, this camp is pretty good. At one camp, 397 died and only 10 percent should have. Other 90 percent was from starvation, malnutrition, etc. They did get Red Cross package, but all in all we are lucky here. We have to air the barracks and get outside every day to try to get some sun. The doctors are afraid of a flu epidemic and so am I!

Friday, 2 March

Had a good discussion last night on Catholics and Protestants, also on heredity and environment. Pett and I talked until late — I enjoyed it. I hear Turkey and Egypt declared war on Jerry. Real cold today; have to stay in bed to keep warm. It is trying to snow. Guys just stand around and snap at each other. Sure is rough to have to listen to them all the time. I shall donate to the Gideons without hesitation, because this Bible has been my salvation. Without it I would be lost.

Saturday, 3 March

It is snowing hard and extremely cold; I guess March will be a miserable month. I hope it doesn't hinder the war. This is the first time I've ever been around anyone who is always sickly, as Pettingill is. Sure is rough to listen to him cough all the time, but he can't help it. He looks terrible. Sure is cold in here. To look at my teeth makes me want to cry. I hate to think what condition my body will be in after this existence.

Sunday, 4 March

Three more men being buried today. Snowing with great ferocity today. I hope we can last through this month without too many deaths. The soup was extra thick today, but had no salt, so naturally lots of guys had to complain. I went to church. Chaplain Neal talked about making vows to God in time of need and then breaking them after returning to normal living. I shall strive to keep mine. He spoke of cursing and breaking marriage vows. The chaplain sure does a swell job, as do the doctors and medics. Two more were baptized today.

The bright sunlight awakens me. Damn, I'm tired and sore. I sit up and rub my eyes. The barracks is a beehive of activity. I can hear the familiar sounds of runny bowels and urinating from the latrine, accompanied by moans, groans, and yells of phrases like, "Don't piss on me, shithead — outta my way, here it comes — oh, brother, I can't take much more of this . . . ." The "clank, clank, clank" of boot buckles fills the air as men climb over each other to get to the latrine.

"Gentlemen, your morning tea has arrived. Please arrange to have a designated member of your illustrious group come to the front."

"Aw, come on, Benner, just say the damn tea is here," Pett yells. "Cut the crap." He turns over and kicks me. "Up and at 'em, Higg. Another day has arrived, full of fun and frolic. Arise, and prepare thyself."

"Aw, shut up. What have you got to be happy about? Let me sleep, or die, whichever comes first."

"Hey, it's tea-time, and you're first, Higg. Just think of it — you can drink or wash. What a choice!"

"To hell with that sticky tea of tree bark. I don't want any. You can have mine. I'm freezing. Let me alone, please."

It's Monday, another day, and hopefully, one more week of life. The weather is miserable. The gray, overcast, misty day makes me even more despondent. I don't want to get out of my cocoon of warmth. There doesn't seem to be any solution to the deprivation of our basic human needs. I decide to get up and get the darn tea. But first, I tell Pettingill and Huckel that we have no control over whatever lay in store for us. Events happen, and there isn't anything we can do. "All we can hope for is to attempt to survive within whatever parameters some greater power has set."

Pett sits up, stares with barely discernable eyes from two deep holes on each side of his nose, shakes his head, and says, "You have lost it. I don't know what the hell you're talking about. You understand him, Huckel?"

"I think he's saying we better keep our marbles and find something to do besides feeling sorry for ourselves."

"In that case, shiver, shake and go get our ersatz tea. My clothes need washing. As last man that's all it's good for."

"Go to hell," I mutter. After moaning a few more minutes I finally get up. "Oh, bull, I'll go get it, but I don't want any of the stuff." As I get on my feet I look at Pett. He doesn't look or sound good. Under my breath I mutter, "Please, God, don't let him die on me. Enough is enough."

When I get the group's tea, one of the guards who opened the barracks says in an irritated tone of voice that over 200 POWs arrived at daybreak. When I mention this to the group Pett comments, "Oh, how wonderful. Just what we need, more bodies in a spacious windy shack. Maybe they carry a different species of lice to mate with the ones that cover our bodies."

Huckel says, "For a fellow who wheezes and coughs all the time, you sure are full of it today."

"I'm dying, so I might as well be in a good mood when I go to the great beyond."

I roll up in my blanket deep in my own misery and watch the others pass the tea from one to another and wash their faces. The rumors start as each group comes alive. I try not to listen but cannot help it. Rumors, rumors, rumors. They are driving me up the wall, starting at daylight and increasing throughout the day. The rumors career off the barbed wire, bounce from barracks to barracks, group to group, person to person. Even the guards get caught up and pass rumors as they walk around camp.

"I can't take it any more. I'm outta here. It may be cold outside, but at least there aren't any stinking and smelly bodies."

Pett throws off his blanket. "Hey, wait on me. I'm going with you. Maybe the wind will carry the smells downwind to the commandant's quarters."

The first rumor heard from a group outside the barracks is that 1,000 POWs would arrive from Stalag 12A. Each new group of prisoners, like the 200 that arrived before breakfast, causes an avalanche of questions, such as "When do we get out of here?" "Where are the Americans?" "How much longer, for Pete's sake?"

I asked Pett, "Why was it necessary to move Cole and Gleason out of Stalag IXB last week, and then move prisoners into this camp?"

Pett says, "The Germans don't know what is going on either."

Our barracks guard had said earlier that the German army was trying to keep its prisoners intact as they retreat in one direction, then another, to avoid capture by the advancing armies of America, England, and Russia.

There are British among the POWs that arrive on Tuesday, announcing that at least 2,000 POWs are on their way to Stalag IXB. They are highly organized, especially the paratroopers, who are mean and ornery as a bed of excited hornets. Even the Jerry guards are wary of the Red Devils, so named because of their red berets. These guys are confident, arrogant, and tolerate no interference.

The proud, almost arrogant, British POWs march into the Serb compound. They immediately set up a kitchen, even with stoves. A commissary is in operation within two hours to sell, exchange, or buy anything desired. One Brit has a table with razors, scissors, a toothbrush, and some type of peppermint cake about four inches in diameter. I be damned. It is toothpaste. When we finally get to walk around the Serb compound, I immediately go to that table with the toothbrush and toothpaste.

I stare at the items, then ask, "How much? I don't have much money."

"What you got?"

I put my hand in my pocket and feel zilch. Darn if I'm going to trade the five bucks hidden in the seam of my pants. So far, neither the Germans nor the scumbags had discovered it. "Nothing."

Another POW pushed me aside and said, "I have two dollars."

"Sold." The two exchange money for toothbrush and paste. He immediately spit on the cake to create some saliva, then brushed vigorously. "Hey, mate, you're bleeding all over the place. Get over there out of the way."

"Oh, boy, this feels nice."

He bleed like a gutted deer. I decided the removal of the yellow stains from my teeth wasn't worth it. But, I sure did want to clean my teeth.

The most astounding British operation is a short wave radio that is operating within an hour after they arrive. By Wednesday morning, they send out reports about the East and the West fronts moving into Germany.

These guys are amazing! I am less cynical about their reports than other rumors I've heard.

Huckel, Strubinger, Tutherow and I join a group talking to some of the newly arrived POWs, who speak of deaths at the other prison camps. One POW said about 397 died in one camp, 90 percent from starvation. Huckel turns to me and says, "I figure it's part of life to suffer. Nobody's going to suffer for me. You aren't, and I'm not going to suffer for someone else. Look at those poor bastards who starved to death. That's the toss of the dice."

"Yeah, I guess so. My survival is up to me, and to help it along, I think I'll continue to use my helmet for the soup rather than the German mess kit. My helmet's bigger, might catch the drippings from the ladle."

I don't steal, not yet, but my eyes watch closely the movement of fellow POWs to see if anyone hides something edible. I sit with my back against the barracks wall to watch POWs walk past me. Often I think, He walks stiff-legged. Wonder if that bulge in his pants means he has food on him? After dinner Wednesday I express my interest in food to Pett. He laughs.

"Higg, you're paranoid about food. You going to steal now? You don't know how to pick pockets — you'll get caught. Take it easy. You'll crack getting so worked up over food."

I know he's right, but my mind won't bury my thoughts about food. Cake, brownies, sugar cookies, chocolate pie race through my mind. Saliva drips on my chin from the thought of each one. The only way I can eliminate these thoughts is to listen to others talk about freedom. Even the complaints work to drown out my thoughts about food.

The sun is warm enough to sit outside, but we must keep our backs against the barracks to avoid the cold wind. My spirits perk up from the sun. I even wash my smelly shirt and lay it on the ground to dry. I look at my chest. "My gosh," I remark to no one in particular, "I can see my ribs. And look at these toothpick legs. They would be the envy of the big-thighed, fat-legged Higgins clan."

A group of us gather around the steps to the barracks and discuss various dishes. None of us knows the ingredients, much less the proportions, but we speak with great authority. Mahoney, who was raised near Boston, mentions Boston baked beans and brown bread. I ask if the brown bread is just burned bread.

"Of course not. It's a special bread, made that way."

"How?"

"Hell, I don't know. It just is."

I tell a story about eating boiled shrimp and crackers. "When I was in high school a group of us would go to the Gulf just below Foley, Alabama, across the bay from Mobile. When the shrimp boats came in early in the morning, I'd wade out and get a bucket of shrimp — usually for nothing — then fish all morning. The ones left I'd take to the house, boil and eat for dinner."

"Didn't you remove the intestines?" Russ asked.

"What intestines? We just peeled and ate 'em. I didn't see any intestines."

"That's the thin, black, thread-like strip down the back, under the shell."

"That's dirt. I don't mind a little dirt."

He laughs, "Boy, how'd you learn so little and be so old? Hear that intellectual comment? Higgins says shrimp don't have intestines, only dirt!"

All I get is snickers, smiles, and heads shaking.

I hear the accordion from the Serb compound. It is relaxing. Thoughts of prison camp are negated. My body tingles from the warmth of the sun. The bantering among friends is a delightful way to spend an afternoon. Sure beats the sounds of griping.

Mahoney's recipe for what he calls "Ice Cream a la' Éclair" is a mouth-watering and far-out dessert. I asked him to repeat it so I can be sure to write it correctly on a piece of paper.

"Put a pint of vanilla ice cream on a plate, place four chocolate eclairs on the sides, pour nuts on top, then hot chocolate syrup with pecans over it, then put peanuts and crushed vanilla wafers. You pour hot fudge over the whole mess. Delicious."

Pett groans, burps, and moans, "I think I'm going to vomit."

I burp, slurp up the saliva on my chin. "I'm so full I don't think I'll eat any supper." And I don't. The talk of food satisfies all of us. No one from our group of six eats the bread ration.

That night, I roll and toss in an attempt to stop the hunger cramps in my stomach. I'm not sure which is worse — hunger, or the constant hum of voices complaining. As I cover my head I ask God to freeze their tongues, but not mine. Won't the light of day ever come?

⚊ ⚌✦☰ ⚊

Thursday, while eating my soup and watching the other POWs struggle up the hill from the kitchen, I see a troop of Germans march toward the Serb compound. "Oh, hell, the Brits are in for it now. Hope they aren't shot in front of us. It'll ruin my dinner," warns Tut.

The Germans have picked up the radio signal, I guess. The Jerries, in battle gear, march into the British barracks. Tut and I watch the search through the fence. A Brit standing close snickers, "The blokes won't find one piece of a radio. We were captured in North Africa in early '39, and have moved up, down, and across this bloody country. We've received a broadcast every night and haven't been caught yet. The Jerries won't go into the paratrooper barracks. They might not come out!"

I strike up a conversation with him. He shows snapshots of his wife and a small daughter. He looks at the pictures and speaks of them as if he had found the photographs on the ground — no longing, no concern about their survival. He has forgotten how to be compassionate.

The tempo of the rumors has increased, each one more encouraging. I can feel optimism in the voices and springy walks of everyone. The rumors range from the Russians' arrival in Berlin, to Turkey declaring war, to the movement of the Ninth Army. Each bit of news is greeted with comments like, "I wonder where my outfit is now? Which divisions did you say were involved? Where are those places located?" The rumors are easier to believe. I want to believe them, but the realism of prison life makes it difficult.

---

28 February 1945

"Western Front. In the U.S. Ninth Army sector, the offensive of the 35th Division (XVI Corps), 84th Division (XIII Corps), and 29th Division (XIX Corps) goes on without pause. The 9th Armored Division also crosses the Ruhr."

[Source: page 674, *2194 Days of War*, Mayflower Books, W. H. Smith Publishers Inc., New York, 1977.]

1 March 1945

"Western Front. Munchen, Gladbach and Neuss fell to the U.S. Ninth Army, which is now advancing rapidly toward the Rhine. The attacks of First Army toward Cologne are continuing, as are the efforts of Third Army near the River Kyll and south of Trier."

2 March 1945

"Western Front. Trier is captured by units of XX Corps from Patton's Third Army."

[Source: page 328, *World Almanac Book of World War II*, rev. ed., Bison Books Corp., 1986.]

I wander around Stalag IXB all afternoon to escape the cloud of despair. I finally return to the barracks. I'm still in prison, the food is terrible and it is cold. I roll up in my blanket and try to avoid thinking about destiny I cannot affect.

Night is hell. I get a caged-animal feeling. The walls close in on me. I become panicky, reminiscent of the five days spent on a closed boxcar. I can hear the "clack, clack, clack" of those square wheels against a background of whines, sobs, and moans. I even sway back and forth.

It is impossible to escape the arguing, complaining, the general cantankerousness of confined men. My nerves are frayed. I snap and jump at the least sound. Only talk — about anything — will keep my mind active.

After eating my bread, I join a group in a corner of the barracks to engage in an intelligent conversation. No arguments, no fussing, just mind-stimulating talk. One of the subjects under discussion is heredity and its relationship to the environment. None of us has much to say, since Huckel is the only one whose knowledge on the subject is even one step above ignorance. Of course, I have to say something. I comment, "I think a person's genes determine how that person will act. The environment doesn't account for much."

Tut adds, "Maybe so, but the environment can affect how one acts. For instance, if you are around people with good manners, or who only use proper English, then you will learn those habits." He cocks that left eyebrow and rolls those bovine eyes skyward, then down at me.

The snob, I think, but say, "I never thought about that. Maybe you're right, but a person must have the will to learn those habits, and that's what I mean by genes."

Huckel sums it up. "You are both correct. Since none of us knows what we are talking about, let's move on to something else."

So we discuss the Protestants and the Catholics. Mahoney and Strubinger explain why they eat fish on Friday. The arguments pro and con get loud and belligerent. Huckel, the conciliator, says, "I think we better leave that subject alone or we'll be in a fight." He stares at the group, "We have to help each other if we want to outlive this lousy life. Religion is best left alone."

Everyone shakes their head in agreement, although I do want to argue with Mahoney about the Catholics. He gets so excited he shakes all over when he gets mad. His blue eyes spread open like a baby robin's mouth. His long, thin nose quivers and his nostrils flare like a thoroughbred race horse after running six miles.

Somehow, we get on the subject of clothes. Pett can't resist a crack in regards to my father and grandfather always wearing handkerchiefs in their pockets. "I notice how well-dressed your people are. You send your shitty uniform to the cleaners every morning, shave and bathe each day. If they dress like you look now, I'm glad I don't."

"Oh, shut up. You know what I mean. My older brother is also a sharp dresser."

Huckel asks, "What about your younger brother?"

"He's a slob when it comes to dressing. Couldn't care less. But he's color-blind, so that may be the reason."

"See," Pett exclaimed, "I told you, environment!"

We are too tired to continue the discussion. I go to the latrine, sit near the window for light, and try to ignore the smell while I write in my Bible. I note in the front it is donated by the Gideons. I will give to them if I get out of here. It's my only route to God and peace of mind.

――――✦――――

"So much for summer," Chuck announces Friday morning. "Look at the snow blow across that mountain. I'm not going out today. I believe I'll have breakfast in bed then read a good book. I got a couple of good ones from the library yesterday in Bad Orb." He shivers, pulls his thin blanket around him when he returns from the window.

"All that intellectual talk last night froze my brain."

The weather goes from bad to worse to tolerable. One day it is cold and dreary, then it snows, then the sun comes out, but it is always cold. There is nothing we can do.

After the tea is delivered and divided among the groups, I ask Huckel to name some books for a library. I find a piece of paper to list them on. I want to rekindle the pseudo-intellectual discussion of the previous evening.

I write: Books I would like to have as a start to a good library:

Robilias Collection

Joseph in Egypt

The Prophet by Gibran

Das Kapital by Karl Marx

Saki Collection

Collection of Eugene O'Neill's plays

Medici Family

Faust

The Origin of Species by Darwin

East of the Sun

Leaves of Grass by Whitman

Thomas Wolfe collection
Christ in Concrete
Emerson's essays
Set of Great Greek dramas
Life and Times of DeVici
Works of Shakespeare
Works of Shelly & Byron & Keats
Great Orations
Aesop's Fables
Good set of encyclopedia (Britannia, New World, America)
Works of S. Vincent Benet
Works of Victor Hugo
Great American Play
Collection of biographies of great artists

When I finish writing Huckel remarks, "Higg, you read all these and you'll be educated."

"I never heard of some of these. Have you read them?"

"No, I got 'em from an English Lit professor. I'd like to read them some-day. That's why I carry this list around with me."

Tut asks, "How about Boccaccios' *Decameron*? That's a winner."

"Never heard of it."

I reply, "I have. My English teacher told the class it was a dirty book, and not to read it. So we did. I found it in my uncle's library. About half the class read it — in secret, of course."

Huck asked, "Was it dirty?"

"Naw, just risqué."

"What was it about?"

"It's about a group of people who took a trip in the 15th Century. To kill time, each one told a story, generally about nuns and priests. The best one, I remember, was about the gardener who revealed himself while asleep in a monastery garden. Some younger nuns saw this, hid him, and then used him as a stud."

Pett sits up. "Wow! Must have been fun."

"It was until the Mother Superior caught them."

"What then?"

Tut concludes the story. "The old gal took him for herself! Finally, he was so worn out he escaped."

Pett moans, "I knew I should have been a Catholic. Clete, is that what the nuns and priests do?"

"Beats me. I just go to mass."

—— ✠ ——

Saturday the weather is worse. I look out the window at the blinding snow storm raging down the street, and listen to Pettingill's hacking cough. I shiver and wrap my blanket around my shoulders. I wonder, "Think the Air Corp will fly in this weather?"

Huckel replies, "I wouldn't if I was in the Air Corp. Might get shot down and have to live like this."

I borrow Pett's mirror and looked at my teeth.

"My gosh, they are yellow and all sorts of stuff between each one."

As I hand it back to Don I note he looks worse than me. I don't know how all this will affect me, but it is questionable whether Pett will even make it. His eyes have sunk so far into his head that I can't see his eyeballs. The stringy pieces of hair on his head droop onto his shoulders. His black, coarse beard is caked with mucus from slobbering and coughing.

Pett wheezes and coughs violently as he turns to Russ and me. "Don't you guys come see me when I go to the hospital. I couldn't stand to listen to such educated bastards. If you do come, bring the funnies and a comic book — nothing heavy."

Pett will die for sure if he doesn't get something solid in his stomach. The diarrhea has left him too weak to rise off his bed on the floor. Our group has covered for him on details, refusing to let him go on sick call. We know he will never return. The infirmary is just a place to die.

I get up and go into the latrine. I turn my face to the wall so no one can see me and get my five dollar bill from inside the seam of my waistband. In their searches, the Jerries had never found it. The scumbags hadn't suspected, or a couple of them would have rolled me for my pants.

Only a baked potato will stop, or at least slow down, the diarrhea.

I return to our pallets and nonchalantly say, "Think I'll take a walk."

Pett wheezes, "In this lousy weather?"

"I need the exercise, and I just love to play in the snow." To the sound of snorts, laughter and a crack from Clete, "Bullshit, you can't stand the cold," I walk to the front of the barracks.

As I start down the steps, the Big Dealer walks toward me. I know he either has potatoes or can get one. I stop as I reach the ground. His 'I got mine' expression is reinforced by the clean, creased pants, pink officer's knee-length jacket, and gloves on his hands, even though he wears the soft cap of an enlisted man. If contempt were daggers, he'd be full of holes.

I turn, walk to the fence, and whistle at a Brit paratrooper. When he arrives, my eyes moisten as I whisper, "You got a potato? Not for me, for my buddy. He needs one to stay alive."

His reply crushes me. "Ten American dollars or three packs of American smokes."

My voice cracks as I bring a crumbled five-dollar bill from my jacket, "I don't have any smokes, and this is my last five dollars."

He looks at the bill and then into my eyes full of tears. "Hold it. Stand right here, bloke. Let me see what I can do."

He turns and retreats into a barracks. In a few minutes he returns with a huge potato. It looks at least nine inches long.

"Here. Give me the money. And don't say what you paid for it — bad for business. If I hear you brag about it, your bloody butt is gone. And your buddy's too."

"Don't worry," I exclaim in a gleeful voice. "Thanks, fellow. God bless you."

"From the way you look, He better bless you."

I put the potato in my jacket, rush back to the barracks and roast it on the stove at the front. I stand guard over my gold while it cooks.

Shifting the potato from hand to hand I take it to Pett, kick him, and say, "Here, eat it, but slowly so you don't vomit."

He struggles to rise on one elbow. "Where'd you get this? How much did it cost? And where did you get the money?"

"It cost seven-hundred-million dollars. I robbed a Wells Fargo armored car last night when it brought our pay."

"Don't be funny. You don't have any money."

"I stole it."

"No you didn't. You don't have the guts to steal."

Huckel and Clete Strubinger listen to us, then say, "Just shut up, Pett, and eat the damned thing."

Clete adds, "Or I'll grab it and run."

Pett eats the potato while we stand guard.

At Sunday morning roll call, funerals are announced for three more American POWs. Everyone is urged to stand on the road while the procession passes, even though the blowing snowflakes are the size of lemons. Huckel says to Clete, Tutherow, Mahoney and me as we walk to the main road, "I never knew snow could swirl like this."

When the funeral passes I bow my head and pull my cap down around my ears. Clete glances at the canvas over the bodies. "How can they bury them in this freezing weather? You can't dig a hole."

"What do they do in the north?"

"Either put the body in a mausoleum, or in some sort of cold storage." I hadn't thought about the disposition of the bodies. None of our group has died, so I look upon death in a detached fashion — just another event over which I have no control.

Huckel, Tut and I attend church. I want to be sure I say a word for Pett at prayer time. The comments by Chaplain Neal really strike home, that people seek God only when they need him. I recall asking God for help to win a football game. We needed all the help we could get. Now, I wanted some help for Pettingill. The preacher's words on cursing cause many men to shuffle their feet and look down to avoid the preacher's stare. I, too, had forgotten the admonition, "Don't take the Lord's name in vain."

I can't recall any Bible passages about cursing. I wonder if he just made that up. Reverend Neal read Mark 10:2–12, then asked us to follow it if we had a Bible. The key verse was, "What God has joined together, let no man put asunder." Since I wasn't married, this part of the sermon didn't get my attention. It's true, my older brother has been married three times, but he seems happy. The cursing thing did make sense. Like my aunt preached, "Bad words are an excuse for poor English."

Two more POWs join the church. We clap and yell, "Amen," after which we sing "Abide with Me." I read the words from my Bible as others look over my shoulder. The service finishes on a resounding rendition of "Onward Christian Soldiers."

We bend double to keep the snow out of our faces as we struggle back to the barracks.

I shiver and write in my Bible. I spend all afternoon against a wall feeling sorry for myself. It is so cold not many go outside or even get out of their blankets to get the bread at supper.

I don't want mine.

I just want to feel sorry for myself.

Chapter 8

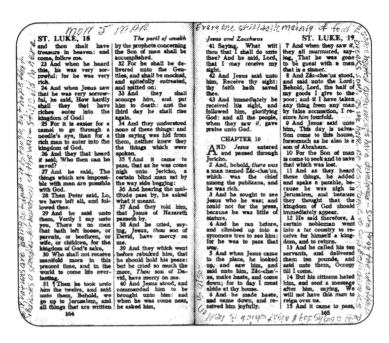

Week Eight

5 March–11 March 1945

⇥⟞⟝⇤

Monday, 5 March

Rations are being cut down. It is tough, but I hope that it indicates a speedier termination of the war. Still cold in here. Everyone still talks mainly of food, and some heated arguments have developed. I sure pray the weather breaks soon, as we have no resistance to cold and epidemics. Pett coughs day and night, which is hell on us also.

Tuesday, 6 March

Been captured 60 days; seems like 60 months to me. We hear that British Second Army has been committed. We also hear that the radio has been telling people that Yanks aren't such bad guys after all. I hope that means the end is near. I wonder how much things have changed at home. I pray all the time that everyone is well. I often wonder if we'll do all the things we plan in here. Three months in a row, something has happened on the 6th. We are holding our breath today. I went to a forum on jobs in postwar America; it was very interesting.

Wednesday, 7 March

One more buried today. I paid my respects by saluting as the funeral procession passed. Went to Bible class and enjoyed it. Snow has melted and now ground is muddy. It's a little warmer. I bet A. Louise never thought I knew so much about her cooking as I've expressed here. I sure brag about her cooking, which is the best by taste test. The Yanks are in Cologne on Rhine, so we hear. We can hear the bombing in West by Northwest again. My legs hurt a good bit at night, probably from the floor.

Thursday, 8 March

I thought we were going to move today to let the Russians come in, but we didn't — I sure am glad. We can hear the bombing and artillery from Patton's drive to Koblenz. I hope it ends before long. Everyone is optimistic again. The Limeys think it will be two more months; I hope it's sooner. I still fear an epidemic; I pray each night that such a thing won't occur. Two men died of spinal meningitis — I'm scared to death of an epidemic. I pray to God that it won't spread. We moved to another barracks. Sure makes this meningitis scare more applicable to us. What a mess this place is — 215 men in a much smaller place. Only a small latrine and faucet for over 500 men.

Friday, 9 March

Last night was rough. Men were crawling over each other yelling and fighting. Our nerves will be completely gone in a few more weeks. I have that nervous feeling in my stomach again; I guess all the changing around did it. Some men are supposed to move out of here; I pray they do to make it easier. The news sounds good. I pray it won't be long. The sun is out. I pray it stays out and the weather breaks.

Saturday, 10 March

Everyone has to walk around for one hour each morning and afternoon, which is a good idea. The weather is dubious, being different each day. We can hear the rumbling continually day and night. The guards say it is

*artillery, and we hope so. These guards sure are a bunch of old men — they
can hardly walk. The main topic of discussion is still food, and many new
and fancy recipes have been contrived. I wonder if we'll ever try any of them.*

Sunday, 11 March

*I went to church — good sermon on founding of the church and taking
part in church activities. Corporal Weiss, the German guard, was there. He
is a fairly nice fellow, sociable. There are all sorts of rumors about news.
We got more Limeys in, and from what they say, we are lucky at this camp.
They walked 31 days to get here. They received Red Cross packages at the
other camp. Some think the artillery is closer, even at Frankfurt, 132 miles
away. Weather is still misty and rainy — pretty cold.*

Monday, there is the announcement of a cut in rations. I think, Cut to what? If
you divide zero by zero you still get zero, and that's about what we get now. A
four-inch thick loaf of bread cut eight ways only gives a half-inch of bread for
each person, no matter how you cut it!

The camp is a sea of mud. The warm weather melted the snow during the
night. At tea time (breakfast), Benner announces that the funeral for two who
died last night will be after dinner. He urges everyone to line up on the main
road out of the camp.

It is impossible to sleep. The floor is cold. The barracks is cold. I am
cold. Factor in the snores, the clanging of boot straps as men climb over others
to get to the latrine, accompanied by cries of anguish, and you have one big,
miserable way to start the week.

I decide the POWs in this stinking hell-hole are at the bottom of the
trough of the living dead. A feeling of despair envelops me like the thin, grayish
blanket around my skinny body. I am reminded of a line from the poem *Invictus*:

"In the fell clutch of circumstance . . ." which is exactly my situation, the
line, ". . . master of my fate" is a bunch of crap.

I see a light at the top of the trough in which I lie. I can claw my way to
the top with hope and determination. The war news provides hope. It is more
frequent and optimistic. Hourly, prisoners, wide-eyed and breathless, announce
in the tone of a town crier to any who will listen, the location of American
troops. We laugh at the smallest effort at humor like a bunch of hyenas. A sense
of cautious anticipation moves through the prison camp like leaves fluttering in
a quiet, soft breeze.

I find myself more bitchy about the lack of food. The weather doesn't help. The frigid wind races across the mountain top and deposits icy flakes of snow in every crevice of the shanty-type barracks. In these conditions only a brave man, or one in fractured intestinal pain, uses the outdoor latrine.

There is a stupid rule that the latrine in the barracks should not be used during the day. How the hell do you keep from crapping when the shit is beginning to flow? As I suggested to Pett, "You just hold it in. Cross your legs, pull your knees under your chin, and with slow, painful control, trickle small blobs of runny crap in your pants. Don't sweat; it will freeze. Just lift your butt so the crap won't splatter and run down your leg."

"Bullshit!"

"No. Human shit."

"Shut up, smart-ass, and get out of my way."

Every POW in Stalag IXB is petrified at the thought of an epidemic. It would wipe out the barracks. We have no resistance to disease, no medicine. We are defenseless.

Pett seems worse every day. The potato slowed the diarrhea, but not his incessant, hacking cough. I provide a small measure of warmth by sleeping close to him at night. The group watches Pett constantly to fight off the sons of bitches who want him to go to the hospital to make more room in the barracks. Someone in the group stays close to him if the others decide to go outside. Leave him and those bastards will carry him off and steal his clothes on the way.

On March 6 I remark, "Well, I wonder what today will bring. The 6th of January we were captured. Last month on this date we were strafed."

Clete replies, "Maybe we'll be liberated today. Rumor has it the end is near. Go outside, away from all the yapping and griping in the barracks. Stand at the top of the hill and listen intently. You can hear the rumble of artillery in the distance."

A sense of liberation permeates Stalag IXB. People talk more rapidly, one or two decibels higher. Often it's just babbling, running at the mouth. "... gonna get new shoes ... love those cowboy movies, especially Tom Mix ... your postman carry his bag on his left or right shoulder? ... I'm gonna eat at every gyro shop in Jersey City ..." and so on.

Prisoners walk with more spring — almost on their toes. Feet don't drag the ground. Shoulders are straighter, as if a heavy weight has been lifted. I hear humming songs now and then, even "... the halls of Montezuma ..." and there aren't any Marines in Stalag IXB. Men begin to trim their beards, brush sticky, stringy hair. The barber's business picks up.

All this hope and expectation helps hide the reality of daily existence. Death, cold and starvation are tangible. The end of the war is an eventuality, indeterminate in time, but good war news is excellent for morale and provides exciting conversation.

It takes willpower and determination — sometimes just plain guts — to get off the floor each morning. Benner's 'gung-ho' demeanor, a result of his training as a Boy Scout leader I suspect, motivates us. He insists everyone go outside every day for exercise, regardless of weather. He preaches a clean body, clean clothes. While outside we pick up all the trash — in Army parlance, police the area. Benner wants everyone to stay active, think positive.

I used to think all this 'gung-ho' stuff was a bunch of crap, but now I admit it is helpful. To survive one must keep a healthy attitude as well as body and clothing. Our group forces Pett to get up and walk around. We refuse to let him die — not if we can prevent it.

→·◄█►·←

Tuesday afternoon, I attend a forum by Benner on job opportunities after the war. On my return to the barracks, a number of us continue the discussion. Those who had sipped from the fountain of academic knowledge plan to continue college. My comment is, "One thing for sure, no more engineering or math stuff. Calculus was my undoing in the Army Specialized Training Program. I'll never forget a question on the final: 'If a cow is on a 15-foot rope tied to a silo 100 feet in circumference, and the cow eats grass as the rope winds around the silo until the rope and cow are against the silo, how much grass did the cow eat?'"

"How much?" Pett asks.

"Hell, if I knew the answer I'd still be in ASTP. I asked for a transfer back to the Air Corp, which was permissible if you resigned from ASTP."

Huckel remarks, "That was smart."

"Yeah, look where it got me."

Clete shrugs his shoulders and scratches his face. "It could be worse. You could have gone to the Pacific and put up with all those gnats and bugs," then smiles as he adds, "But you're from Alabama. You love all that heat and bugs and gnats."

And so it goes. At least the discussions fill idle time, and keep our minds off the miserable conditions in Stalag IXB. Out of respect for the unknown guys, the POWs salute as the funeral procession passes. Someone says, "I wonder if their families will ever learn where they're buried? I wonder if their families will even know they died?"

Pett's shoulders slump as he coughs violently. "I hope we aren't POWs too long. I'm not sure I can last through the spring."

"Oh yes, you can. I haven't told you about all the delicious recipes my Aunt Louise makes. You can't die until I explain all of them."

His black eyebrows arch as he smiles, "In that case, I'll live to be 100 years old!"

Upon our return from Bible study, I suggest we talk about food. I get out a piece of paper and ask everyone to talk slowly so I can write down the good ones. It is agreed that only dishes and recipes will be mentioned, no meals. So many are mentioned I am only able to write a few, such as: Boston baked beans ... franks and brown bread, pork and beans with cheese and bacon and baked in an oven ... fried oysters ... graham cracker pie ... malted milk .... "Wait a minute, there's nothing unusual about malted milk." I stop writing.

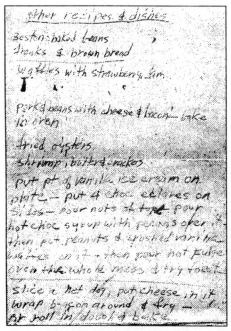

Food, food, food

Tut continues, "It is the way I'm gonna give it to you. Higg, write all this down. What you do is mix a pint of pure whipping cream with butterscotch, lots of malt, scoops of chocolate ice cream, chocolate syrup, a raw egg, and put a marshmallow on top."

"That's sickening," Pett moans, then burps.

Raisin bread, eggnog, French toast, and various kinds of tarts are mentioned. I write quickly. An analytical character asks me for details about upside down cake.

"You put the pineapple, or peaches, or some kind of fruit — pineapple is best — in a pan, then put brown sugar all over the pineapple ...."

"How many pineapple?"

"That depends on the size of the pan. About eight or ten, I think. Anyway, then you put the cake batter on that. It should cook about an hour at 300 degrees ...."

"Centigrade or Fahrenheit?"

"Fahrenheit. Okay. When you remove the cake from the oven, you turn the pan over and out flops the cake — upside down. The pineapple is on top." There were sounds of astonishment.

"I'll be damned . . . no shit . . . just like that?" Clete exclaims.

Pett asks, "Why doesn't it stick to the pan?"

"I don't know, it just doesn't. I never saw it stick. Maybe the heat is the key; it shouldn't be too high. It has to cook slow, too."

"How do you cook it slow?"

I didn't know, nor did anyone else.

There are more and more rumors, repeated so fast it's difficult to digest one before there is another one. I can hear the rumble of artillery, a steady hum rumored to be from Patton's drive to Koblenz.

A walk through Stalag IXB reminds me of a stroll through the midway at the circus. Instead of a concession stand or a barker promoting a sideshow, there are groups of prisoners speculating about the location of the American Army. Everyone is a military strategist.

---

6 March 1945

"Western Front. To the south of Ninth Army, First Army is fighting in Cologne and driving toward Remagen farther south . . . . Farther south still, units of Third Army are making a rapid advance in one section of the front toward the Rhine at Koblenz."

7 March 1945

"Western Front. The leading tanks of III Corps reach the Rhine opposite Remagen and find the Ludendorff Bridge there damaged but still standing . . . . Other Allied units complete the capture of Cologne while XII Corps units from Third Army continue to move forward particularly quickly."

9 March 1945

"Western Front. Bonn and Godesberg are taken by units of U.S. First Army, while others continue to expand the bridgehead beyond the Rhine at Remagen."

[Source: pp 329–330, *World Almanac Book of World War II*, rev. ed., Bison Books Corp., 1986.]

Rumors spark talk about the future, but eventually conversation settles on food. Dreaming and talking about food helps us tolerate the dampness of the barracks, a reduction of the meager ration of soup for dinner and bread for supper. The anticipation of freedom really opens a floodgate of creative juices.

Returning from a pee and crap break (P&C in prison lingo), I note the specks of green on top of the mud and think, Inventing recipes beats lying in the mud and reaching under that hot wire to pick dandelions. I'd rather talk about food.

We regroup and continue to discuss food. Our knowledge of recipes is limited, but not our recall of different foods, real or imagined. We get creative with dishes such as ice cream with Grape Nuts, cold dressing sandwich with cranberry sauce, candy pie, made with cut-up candy bars like Snickers or Mounds, Welsh rarebit flavored with whiskey or beer, pickled herring and pigs' feet. Most dishes are accompanied by some type of bread, like Italian rye, which I've never eaten.

I ask everyone to slow down so I can list the 200 or so dishes and recipes mentioned by the group. Every meal concludes with a dessert, such a mince-meat cookie or brown Betty banana pudding. Sweets top the list of foods and recipes. Every sentence opens with a comment such as, "You ever had ... how 'bout ... here's one for you ... I remember my mother ...."

My aunts are good cooks. I watched them prepare all sorts of delicacies, but mostly candy, cake, or pies. Aunt Louise would be amazed at my knowledge of her multitude of recipes. However, it was her ice box lemon pie that caused the most heated debate and eventual a fight with Lucius Mahoney, a hotheaded Irishman from someplace near Boston.

When there is a break in the conversation, I explain how to make ice box lemon pie. I can hear the sucking sound of mouths retrieving the saliva from chins. "You need Eagle brand evaporated milk."

"Why Eagle? Can't you use some other brand?"

Huckel says, "Shut up, Mahoney, and let him continue."

"Yeah, what difference does it make?" Pett adds.

"My aunt used Eagle. I don't know why. Anyway, you need to grate a bunch of lemons ...."

Again, Mahoney interrupts. "How many in a bunch? One, two, ten? How many?"

"Depends on the size of the pie, I guess. Make it six. Then, roll exactly," and I stare at Mahoney, "two dozen vanilla wavers, or graham crackers. That's the crust. I think you need to separate the whites from the yellows for a lot of eggs."

"How many," Mahoney asks. He is rapidly becoming a pain in the butt.

In a tone of exasperation, I exclaim, "I don't know. Use a dozen." I then explain how the condensed milk, lemon juice and grated lemon rinds are mixed in a gray, eight inch high, Wesson-oil pottery bowl, "one with a blue stripe around the top." I close my eyes and listen to the clanging and rattling of the metal blades of the eggbeater as my aunt rapidly turns the handle.

"After the rolled, or crumbled, wafers are put in a Pyrex dish, the mixture is poured into the dish. The egg whites, which have been whipped to a frenzy in another Wesson-oil container, are poured all over the mixture. Put it in the ice box until cold."

Mahoney, his voice dripping with sarcasm, asks, "What holds the crust together?"

I shrug and say, "I don't know. Nothing. It just does, but when you cut it you get a piece of the crust."

Pett says, "Maybe you mix the crumbs with butter . . . ."

". . . or syrup," opines someone else in the group.

I yell, "No, you don't! Nothing! It just stays together."

Mahoney rises to his knees as he bellows, "You've got to hold the crust together, stupid, or it will run all over the place."

"No!" I scream.

"Yes!"

Then, all hell breaks loose. Nine men argue. Everyone becomes a master chef. Mahoney and I stand toe-to-toe, yelling in each other's face.

Wham! I throw a punch at him and yell, "Don't call me stupid, stupid!"

Whoop! He hits me in the chest. We begin to grab and push each other against the wall, then fall on the floor, where we continue to wrestle.

Someone pulls us apart and says, "Higg, call your aunt when we get home and ask her."

"Yeah, then call me," Mahoney says.

"Don't worry, I will. Give me your phone number." The barracks chief breaks up the food argument with an announcement. "All right, outside to line up. It's lunch time for most of us, dinner for you southerners."

My gosh, we have spent all morning discussing, arguing, and fighting over food! As a parting crack at Mahoney, I whisper, "I'll bet you 10 bucks you don't use anything to hold the crumbled wafers together. By the way, I'm sorry I hit you."

"I'll take that bet. I'm sorry I hit you, too. You pack a wallop for such a small twerp. I just hope someday we can laugh about a fight over pie crust." We hug, laugh, and get in line. Many other meetings are held while in prison camp by the Culinary Concoction Cooks, as we begin to refer to ourselves, but no meeting is as violent as that first morning's session.

While in line for dinner, Benner announces our barracks will be among the POWs to leave Stalag IXB. After we eat watery soup, a messenger from the Commandant arrives. Benner announces that we will not be moving out of Stalag IXB anytime soon. He adds, "The Russian POWs were turned around before they arrived at this camp, and are going north to avoid the American Army. The Americans have bypassed this section of Germany. Bad Orb is in a pocket. Listen, and you can hear the rumble of guns."

The balloon of elation over the announcement that we will not move is punched in mid-afternoon, when Benner says we will move to another barracks. "Why?" I yell. All this indecision and change of plans drives me nuts. The reason for moving was even more devastating. Two men from the barracks who had been taken to the hospital have died of spinal meningitis.

"I hope they got the meningitis *after* they went to the hospital," Pett moaned.

I say, "Me, too, but there is nothing we can do about it. Just try to keep clean." My show of bravery belies the stark fear that is inside me. I can feel the vise of death slowly closing its jaws. My nerves are about gone. My stomach twitches from fear of death and the never-ending yelling, fighting, and complaining.

We do move and there are no complaints. Fear of an epidemic is a great motivator. We gather our belongings and go down the hill to a smaller barracks. I hurry to be one of the first of the 500 from the old barracks to get in the small barracks, pushing and shoving to get up the steps and through the door. I go to the first window and stand by it. I yell, "Hey, Pett, Clete, Huckel, Tut, Mahoney — over here, quick!"

They kick and shove to get near me. Everyone drops their meager possessions and sets up house.

Strubinger immediately reconnoiters the barracks, and returns to announce, "This damn building has two rooms, both about this size. There is only one latrine, between the rooms, and a single faucet and one hole for a crapper. For 500 men, and about half with runny bowels! Lots of luck, fellows. And I didn't see any drain."

I find a place to sit under the window, close my eyes, and wonder how long before we are liberated. Can I stand this existence much longer?

I stay busy Friday and Saturday getting settled in the new barracks. There isn't much to do but it prevents me from thinking about life in this place. Constant talking is a deterrent to sleep. I am restless, so I just walk around the camp and listen to the rumors about the war. Everyone and no one is an expert on the whereabouts of the American troops. I didn't know there could be so much talk by ones who know absolutely nothing. I listen, but do not hear.

I welcome the edict to get up and out of the barracks in the morning and afternoon. Some POWs would literally lie in their own excrement if not forced to get up and out of the barracks. Even Pett, as weak as he is, keeps himself clean and walks outside. "I can't understand how some of these guys can be so filthy," He remarks during one of our walks around the camp. "Even animals clean themselves and their nests."

All we can do is watch life as it stumbles along. I try to dream of a soft bed, good food, warmth, and happy-go-lucky people who laugh, joke, poke, and just kid around, but dare I do so? Dare I look forward to those breast smothering hugs of aunts, the nose-tingling smell of Uncle Leon's roses in Warrington, Florida, the sickening smell of honeysuckle, the hum of honeybees racing from blossom to blossom?

No! No! The joys and sorrows of a chalkboard of youth have been wiped clean. I recall a teacher once said, "We start over at the far left edge of the chalkboard." Start over to what? To where? Each step of prison camp life is a step into an abyss of the unknown. The sequence might change, but not the events. It's all aching feet, filthy bodies, runny bowels, lice, stealing, yelling, fighting.

---

1 March 1945

"Western Front. The British XXX Corps and Canadian II Corps (Canadian First Army) continue to advance in the Kervenheim sector .... Units of the 29th Division (XIX Corps) seize Monchengladbach, the most important town reached by the Allies in Germany so far. The 2d Armored Division advances northward across the Cologne plain ... continuing north to River Ahr, and the units of the 11th Armored Division take Dockweiler, Boxberg, and Kelberg .... In little more than two days, the American Division has advanced 45 miles, taking some 5,000 prisoners, capturing huge amounts of equipment and sowing disorder among the units of the German Seventh Army, dispersed north of the Moselle and west of the Rhine."

8 March 1945

"Western Front. After meticulous preparation, the British 43d and Canadian 2d Divisions ... launch an attack on Xanten, which they take."

[Source: page 661, *2194 Days of War*, Mayflower Books, W. H. Smith Publishers Inc., New York, 1977.]

I pray for liberation, and search the Bible for support. But liberty and all that goes with it is a dimension of existence I can't worry about at this time. I hang on every tidbit, every morsel of news about Allied troop movement thrown in the air. Like a gull behind a ferry I grab each piece of bread thrown in the air, swoop off to swallow it, then return for another bit of sustenance. I grab a piece of a conversation: "... Limeys say Frankfurt was taken ..." and run to tell anyone who will listen, never stopping to note that "Frankfurt" refers to the city near Berlin not Frankfurt am Main, 32 kilometers from Bad Orb. So what? A rumor's a rumor, and the sun and rumble of guns helps fuel the fires of liberation. Sometimes, I think it is great to be alive.

⎯ ⎯

By Sunday, my soul cries for something to calm frayed nerves. I want desperately to sit next to the throne of God, where He will tell me to "calm down, be patient." At the church service, Chaplain Neal speaks of the history and family of the church, but darn if I can remember which church.

I can't keep my eyes off Corporal Weiss. I had seen him slip in the door, and he now stands close to Pett and me. Corporal Weiss is on the staff of the non-English speaking camp Commandant. His attendance reinforces rumors of the capitulation of the German army.

The British report news picked up from a German radio that "... the Yanks aren't bad guys."

The guards are more amicable than usual. Most of us have decided it can't be long before liberation. I look at the ceiling, close my eyes and mumble, "Thanks, God. You did alright. Keep it going."

Chaplain Neal's admonition to participate in church activities allows me to forget the war and reflect on my childhood experiences. I wonder whether going to Sunday School and church is enough to get me upstairs to heaven? If so, I'm in.

The pastor asks for a song. I yell, "In the Garden," but when he asks me to lead it, I mumble that I can't sing. I really don't know the words. Another POW suggests "Onward Christian Soldiers," eliminated when many in the congregation laugh, hoot, and yell, "Onward to what?"

The song "Nearer My God to Thee" is substituted. It is in my Bible. The words make sense, especially the verse that goes, "... yet in my dreams I'll be nearer, my God, to Thee." The services conclude with a long prayer, but no mention is made of seeking deliverance or liberation. That is up to God. If He wants it, we'll get it, so why ask?

As we walk out of the barracks chapel, I recall my favorite poem, "Invictus," by William Ernest Henley.

Pett asks, "What are you mumbling about, Higg?"

"Nothing. Just a poem I remembered."

"Say it out loud."

"Someday I will, but not now."

When I write in my Bible late Sunday, I count seven times I had said the word 'pray' in a week. Did I really pray that many times or is the word just a figure of speech? I may not have actually stopped and looked skyward, but I know silently I asked for deliverance.

The constant rumbling of the distant artillery is a reminder of the war. The sounds of war are an unsettling backdrop to a daily routine of maneuvers to survive.

Chapter 9

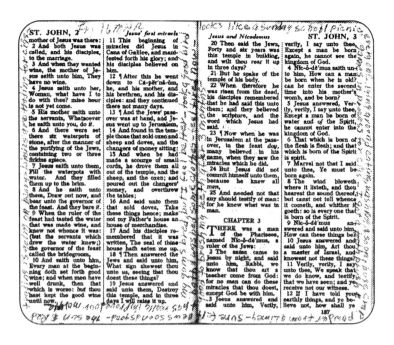

Week Nine

12 March–18 March 1945

━━◆❖◆━━

Monday, 12 March

Red Cross packages came in. We'll get them today or tomorrow. All sorts of good news today; never thought we would get them. The Lord has answered our prayers. I guess we'll get our Red Cross packages tomorrow, as they haven't been brought from Bad Orb yet. Our rations have been cut to rock bottom — seven men to a loaf of bread.

I hear that Patton has crossed the Rhine 25 miles north of Koblenz, so we pray for the best. Some say two weeks. From the cut in rations and news, it seems like a matter of time. This is truly a day for thanksgiving. Everyone has all hope in Patton. He is the main person around here. Of course, some complain just the same. I am on camp detail tomorrow.

Tuesday, 13 March

The Limeys say there are 30,000 prisoners walking the roads in Germany looking for a POW camp; 16,000 left one camp three days before Joe arrived. I am on cesspool detail again. We made our guard mad, so he worked us until 5 P.M. I'm really worried now, as we haven't received our Red Cross packages yet. Our rations have been cut again — eight men to a loaf of bread. I sure pray it won't be long. The artillery has changed to southwest, coming from the drive on Manz, near Frankfurt. The sun came out — it is a pretty day.

Wednesday, 14 March

The sun came up early, and it is a beautiful day. Our guard hasn't come to let us out. I sure want to get in the sun. Trading is going on, all sorts of big deals. We're supposed to get Red Cross packages today. I sure look forward to them. Artillery was loud last night. We got our package — three to a box. I never knew I could be so elated over anything in my life. I'm very thankful. We have quite a problem trying to decide how to eat it. I ate my salmon and marmalade, and I'm full. It really feels good to smoke again; guess I'll be sick, but I don't mind one bit.

Thursday, 15 March

Another sunny day. I stayed outside all day and got a little sunburn. There is a rumor of us moving out. I pray to God it isn't so — I hate to think of walking for 30 days. Two Frenchmen ran away, so we are afraid of anything. One hundred fifty GIs are going out of camp to work. Jerry is carrying on, even though the war is almost kaput. I sure have enjoyed my Red Cross. We are all getting to be old maids in our manner. There sure are some funny food mixtures being made in here.

Friday, 16 March

Trading is going on heavily. Limeys are trading for cigarettes. It looks like a Sunday School picnic — everyone lying around eating, washing, and so on. Huge crap games in process for cigarettes. I got a toothbrush and powder from a Limey. It sure felt good to brush my teeth after three months. My gums bled, but I feel better. I took a good bird bath and washed some clothes; I feel tired now. The news sounds good. The sun and Red Cross packages really improved our morale.

Saturday, 17 March

> *I am miserable. It's a rainy day. I knew the nice weather couldn't continue. It's bad for flu, so I hope we can stay warm and dry. Stealing has started again now that we've had the taste of food. I made some candy last night by mixing up some items; it was very rich and good. The news is at a standstill at the present. I hope that is a good indication of something big. The GI thrives on rumors. I wish I had room to write them all.*

Sunday, 18 March

> *I went to church and enjoyed his sermon a lot. I have felt a lot better lately, probably from the Red Cross package and sun. No artillery for the last two days.*

For the first time since capture, the week starts on a joyful note. I am awake when I see Benner open the door and speak to a guard. He turns and yells, "Rise and shine. Up and at 'em. The Red Cross boxes have arrived. We eat." His voice is vibrant and joyful. He claps his hands and yells, "The Red Cross boxes are in Bad Orb."

The place comes alive. Some POWs praise the Red Cross, probably happy to get American smokes. A few dance the jig, click their boots and warble, "I knew they would come through ... glory be!"

Optimism sweeps through the camp with the cold wind from the mountains. Is it the war news? Is it the announcement the Red Cross packages have arrived in Bad Orb? It doesn't make any difference. Prison life might get better. It can't get worse. For the first time since capture, I feel God raise a hand and pronounce, "Enough! Let them eat!"

I have talked about food, developed recipes for all manner of dishes, and not salivated or doubled up in pain at the mention of food. It is a distant memory like home, childhood, the waves rushing to the shore. There is a total detachment; a far cry from the boxcar days when we fought and screamed 'stop' at the mere mention of food. Now, at least, food is here!

I look with apprehension toward the gate and banter about the contents of the Red Cross boxes. A fellow POW exuberantly says, "I hope I get Lucky Strikes this time. Maybe my box will have chocolate ... yeah, and some good meat ... no more fig bars for me ...."

The talk is noisy. I see POWs back-slapping and arm-waving as I run to the main road to listen for any sound of movement on the road to the camp. All I hear is the distant rumble of guns. Well, I think, liberation is first, food second.

The good war news adds fuel to the fires of happiness as I wait for the Red Cross boxes to arrive. Rumors about Patton near Koblenz pass among the men.

"Where do all these rumors come from?" I remark.

The POW standing next to me shakes his bearded face. "I don't know. I guess somebody just reaches into the air and pulls one down."

The name Patton creates excitement in Stalag IXB. A group of about 15 men gather on the hill behind our barracks and bellow the chorus to the camp theme song as if his troops could hear the off-key singing vibrating among the mountains.

Come and get us, Georgie Patton
Come and get us, Georgie Patton
Come and get us, Georgie Patton
So we can ramble home.

Clete turns to Pett. "Even Higgins is singing, and to the tune of the Battle Hymn of the Republic, too. If the southern boy sings, liberation can't be far away." He puts his arm around me and gives a squeeze.

Elated at his affectionate attitude, I remark, "Don't count your chickens before they hatch. Wait and see."

Everyone put aside all the gripes, complaints, and feeling sorry for themselves. Even the announcement before dinner that rations will be cut is met with a shrug of shoulders and responses like, "So what? We'll get out of here soon."

The Limeys walk through the American compound exclaiming in excited, Cockney voices that POWs are wandering the roads in Germany. These comments, along with the movements of prisoners of war in and out of Stalag IXB, plus talk about the Allied forces closing in, are signs of the end of the war.

I want to believe the end is in sight. I look up at the sky and ask God to wash away my feelings of doubt.

But life goes on. The daily chores must be done, such as cleaning out the cesspools, cutting wood, getting the tea for breakfast and bread for supper. When I say my Aunt Louise always claimed cleaning the house is a daily chore, Clete says, "I wish she was here to take my place." At supper, the names are called for the next day's honey-bucket detail. Everyone in my group is on the list.

Throughout Monday night I feel the closeness of the Allied troops. The "whoom, whoom, whoom" of the artillery gets closer. Flickers of brightness bounce around the dark barracks. I listen intently, just in case the shells begin to drop near the camp. One of them could fall on the barracks.

"Listen. Aren't those sounds coming from the southwest, around Frankfurt am Main?" I say as I rise from the floor and look at my watch. It is 3:30 A.M. I shake Pett and repeat the question.

He listens. "You're right. Frankfurt is only about 40 miles from here. Oh brother, maybe the time is near!"

It is a fretful night. The anticipation of freedom and the noise of the artillery keeps me awake. I just hope and pray a stray shell doesn't hit our barracks. I really don't want to die asleep. Oh, well, maybe that would be better.

⊷ ⊷⊹⊱ ⊶

Tuesday, after the ersatz tea is distributed, the camp detail falls out in front of the barracks. As Huckel, Clete, Mahoney, Tutherow, and I get ready to go, Pett whispers, "Try not to get all shitty. It stinks. I may have to go to the hospital and die just to get away from you guys."

I kick him. "Kiss my butt. You better not die while we're gone. We've risked our lives to keep you alive."

Clete adds, "Yeah. Just guard our stuff. Be a good boy and we'll bring you a big, fat, frozen turd to gnaw."

Tut adds, "And if we're lucky, you'll get one with wheat chaff in it."

Huckel kicks Pett. "For good luck. Hey guys, be sure to give Pett a kick for good luck." One at a time, we line up and kick him. We love Pett. It is a challenge to figure out ways to hide him from a trip to the death house. Affection, companionship, and humor are the few expressions of dignity left in a life of destitution.

Cleaning cesspools is the worst, most humanly degrading camp chore of a POW, and carping can be heard whenever one's name is called. I think they should put the guys who have committed crimes on the honey-bucket detail. Hell, they're already segregated. Let 'em smell each other. The new Man of Confidence, Private Pfannenstiel, and the barracks leaders continue the decision that all details should go from barracks to barracks, without exception. As we leave the barracks, I complain to Benner, "I still think those bastards who have been caught stealing should pull *all* the details. If they die, so what. This democracy stuff doesn't apply to criminals."

The honeybucket is a one-gallon metal container tied to a three-inch diameter pole about six feet long. Its purpose is to lift the contents of the cesspools which are located under each barracks. The four foot diameter cesspool is buried in the ground two feet under a hole cut in the latrine floor about the size of a small dinner plate. The cesspool catches the urine, crap, vomit or anything else that drops through the hole in the floor.

A wooden tank sits on the bed of a four-wheeled wagon. The tank is approximately 15 feet long. It has a large opening on top. The rickety wagon has a 10-foot tongue attached to the font axle. A six-inch plug is located in a hole at the front of the tank.

In theory, the operation of the honey bucket and tank car is simple. The honey bucket is dipped into a cesspool, the contents are lifted out gingerly, and carefully poured into the large opening at the top of the tank. The full tank is pulled outside the camp, the plug is removed, and the contents of the tank rush out onto the ground.

In practice, it doesn't work that way. The first problem is the honey bucket. You must remove only enough of the cesspool contents to prevent dripping on the ground. Secondly, the pole must be tilted upward just enough to keep the liquid from running down the pole onto the arm of the pole-handler. The pole and bucket must be parallel to the ground when retrieved from under the barracks.

The pole must be tilted downward when pouring the liquid into the tank, almost impossible for a small person like me.

The plug is firmly anchored in the hole to prevent premature spillage. It can be loosened and pulled only by tugging with both hands. When the plug is removed, "Swish, gurgle, swish, slush ...." Out comes the runny crap on the hands and body of anything in front of the hole. You gotta be fast to pull the plug and get out of the way.

There is no army manual on the proper operation of the honey bucket. The safe and sanitary methods of honey-bucket operation are passed from group to group — or you learn the hard way.

On an earlier detail, I suggested, as the smallest one in the group, that the tallest prisoner pour the liquid into the tank. No one agreed. The unwritten rule is that everyone takes their turn. For me, that is the worst part of the detail.

Because the tank sits close to the edge of the platform, it is difficult to climb up on the platform. There is nowhere to stand. You get three or four people to hold the wheels to keep them from turning. The one on the platform has to reach down and take the stick with the honey bucket on the end. Deftness and agility are required by two people. When you take into account the bodies stiff from the cold and lack of clothing, it is indeed "hell on wheels."

When the pourer sees the tank is almost full, it is pulled, pushed, and guided out the gate to a place in the woods away from the prison camp.

It is the operation of plug removal that causes the major problem on this day in the ninth week of internment. Our guard is in front of the wagon directing its movement to a spot in the woods. He yells for the men guiding the tongue to "drop it." They do, just as the guard starts to step away from the front of the tank, the plug pops out. "Pop, gurgle, gurgle, gurgle." The runny crap hits the guard in his stomach. He screams in German, then jumps to one side. Out spews the crap. Two other guards run from the back of the wagon, see the crap on the guard, and laugh!

That is a mistake. The smelly, wet guard rages and screams for the other two guards to take over. "Nein, nein," both say, and, shaking their heads, "This is your detail. You are in charge. Better dry off before you get back to the barracks or the Commandant will be all over you. We promise not to say a word." But, they continue to snicker.

The honey-bucket detail usually quits about 3:00 P.M. Not today. We work until dusk. Our shit-covered guard wants to be sure his uniform is dry. He brushes and brushes, and stands in the sun to clean his uniform.

As we pull the last tank out of the camp to the woods, Mahoney whispers, "If it's dark when we get to the woods, I'm leaving. I can make it to the location of that artillery."

Tut says, "Don't be stupid. We'll all be shot. I don't want to be killed over your stupidity. That damn guard couldn't take someone escaping." Mahoney is pushed to the front as lead man to pull the wagon. Tut and I keep an eye on him.

Pett greets our return with the comment, "Rations were cut again, eight men to a loaf." Then, "You guys must have loved that detail, you all stayed out 'til dark!"

Clete snaps, "Aw, shut up, Pett. Wait until you hear what happened."

Sounds from the artillery shake the building. Flashes of light bounce off the dark walls and through the windows. "I hope we don't get hit," I say to Pett.

The artillery continues all night. The building rocks, and dust fills the barracks, caused by the shaking of the boards.

⎯ ⚎ ⎯

Wednesday morning the barracks remain locked long after daylight. Soon, there are shouts from men running up the hill. "The Red Cross boxes are here! We eat, we eat!"

Whoops and yells fill the air when our barracks leader announces, "There are enough boxes so only three men have to share a box. Line up in threes at the door."

Pett, Huckel, and I run to the door and get a box. We hunker in a corner and spread the booty on a blanket. I write the name of each item on a blank page in my Bible as Pett places the items in piles:

box of raisins
5 packs of cigarettes
can of salmon
can of pork and beans
block of butter (really oleo)
block of cheese
box of crackers
2 blocks of chocolate
sugar cubes
can of meat spread
can of coffee — instant
pound of milk (powdered)
2 bars of soap (Swan)
can of marmalade
vitamin tablets
bag of M&Ms

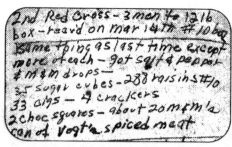

Contents of second Red Cross box

Each one of us takes turns separating the items into three piles. We have a serious discussion whether to select one canned item of meat to divide and eat, or divide the cans first and let each man decide on his own method of preservation. I ask, "Will it rot if we divide it first?"

Huckel says, "Somebody might steal a whole can, but not a portion. I vote to divide everything first."

"I'll go for that. Which one first?" Pett asks.

When no one names a can, Pett says, "The meat has been in a can a long time. It isn't that much anyway. Let's divide it now."

Next, Pett divides the items that can be separated: 35 sugar cubes each, 288 raisins, and the M&M candies. We get four crackers. Pett divides the two chocolate squares carefully into three portions, including the crumbs.

The cigarettes are Chesterfields. Each one gets one pack. We split the other two packs. I get another 13 cigarettes. "What do we do with the one remaining smoke?"

Pett says, "Light it, Sammy-boy, sit back and enjoy our good luck."

The first cigarette in some time. I cough and choke as I inhale.

Pett takes the knife and divides the soap, oleo, and cheese. I instruct Pett, "Cut the soap last. I have enough trouble with diarrhea without eating soap."

After the division of the food, I go outside, sit in the sun behind the barracks, and gobble my food. The salmon is rich. I eat it anyway. After eating the marmalade on the few crackers, I get stomach cramps. I keep eating.

I don't remember if dinner was announced or not. After all, how can a bowl of dirty potato soup compete with this delicious American food? I sit outside until it is dark and begins to turn cold. Inside, everyone is quiet. All I can hear is burps and groans. For the first time this year, I go to sleep on a full stomach. I curl up like a baby, belch, and pass out.

Thursday, I don't know if the tea was ever delivered. Who cares? The sun is warm, so I sit outside and eat once again. Food and rumors combine to make it a day to rejoice. I wash both body and clothes, and listen to the rumors, such as, we will move out in a day or so.

Pett says, "I'm ready. On a full stomach, I can walk across Germany."

Huckel says, "In a pig's eye you can. I doubt you can walk two miles."

"At least I'll die full."

Only the diarrhea keeps me awake. I step over bodies on the way to the latrine about 10 times. I feel miserable. My butt is raw, and I burp putrid tastes.

Friday, the picnic continues as soon as the barracks is unlocked. The English have a field day trading for American cigarettes. I finally manage to trade a few cigarettes for a toothbrush and a cake of peppermint toothpaste. Clean teeth are more important than a smoke. I brush vigorously, then spit blood all afternoon. My gums are still tender, but a clean mouth is worth it.

Men play cards. Huckel says, "Well, I guess when men can play cards and shoot craps, things are looking up. It is better than all the griping. A full stomach does wonders for morale."

Trading, eating, washing clothes, gossiping about the war, more eating, vomiting, crapping, running up and down the streets of the camp, lying around picking lice from body and clothing. Only the sick stay inside. It is a great day to be alive.

Saturday the weather is lousy. It's cold, and there is a slow drizzle. Mahoney looks out the window. "I knew this ecstasy couldn't last. Reminds me of Seattle in the winter — fog, rain, cold. Gad, I was even glad to get back to Camp Adair and Corvallis after a weekend in that city."

The weather compounds my miserable feeling. My stomach is in knots all day as I vomit. I crap. I belch. However, I decide to cook up a concoction of sweets when the stove is not in use. I melt part of a chocolate bar, add powdered milk, oleo, marmalade, and sugar. After stirring it until almost hard, I eat the mess. That night I have the runs, plus vomiting. To kill the sour taste, I smoke two cigarettes and suck on a sugar cube.

Pett looks at me. "Glutton. You look worse than I feel. You just had to eat all those sweets, didn't you? I hope you're happy."

"I'm miserable, but at least I can die full."

Sunday the weather improves. At church, the chaplain thanks God for a good week. I add, "Amen!" He speaks of how the little things in life become paramount and create happiness now. The sun, a bath, clean clothes, a full stomach, the sounds of laughter are all signals that God is with us. The service concludes with the song *Onward Christian Soldiers.*

As I walk around the camp after church, I can see the expressions of joy on faces, the smiles, the laughter. Heads are up, shoulders straight, and those who can walk do so with a slight spring. The rumors lift my spirits, even if they're not true.

---

10 March 1945

"Western Front. The last German forces are withdrawn from the pocket west of the Rhine between Wesel and Xanten. They have lost heavily to the British and Canadian attacks. U.S. First and Third Armies link up near Anernach, completing the Allied hold on the west bank of the Rhine everywhere north of Koblenz."

15 March 1945

"Western Front. The U.S. Seventh Army goes over to the attack once more, especially in the area around Saarbrucken and Bitche. Seventh Army is joining Third Army in the attempt to expel Germans from the area between the Saar, Moselle and Rhine."

18 March 1945

"Western Front. Patton's offensive captures Bingen and Bad Kreuznach as the advance to the southwest continues. To the south, Seventh Army is also beginning to accelerate its progress, most of its forward units having now crossed the Germany border."

[Source: page 330–31, *World Almanac Book of World War II*, rev. ed., Bison Books Corp., 1986.]

The ordeal is almost over. As we walk back to the barracks, I think, The sun and the food, both lift my spirits. The food is real, concrete. The sun is from the hand of God. I turn to Huckel and say, "You know, God sure makes it tough on us. Like a yo-yo. One day up, the next day He slaps us down. I wish He would be consistent."

"That's why you have to keep the faith. You never know when you'll need it."

"I guess so, but damn, it's tough."

"Don't cuss, it's Sunday."

"Aw, shut up, Huckel. Just belch and walk."

Sunday night there is no artillery to rock me to sleep. Where is the American Army? Maybe it's too cold and messy to get out in the weather. They are probably in a warm tent, or even a house. Lucky b .... I remember what Huckel said, so don't finish the word. I thank God for a good week. I pray that I will continue to be thankful for the small things.

Chapter 10

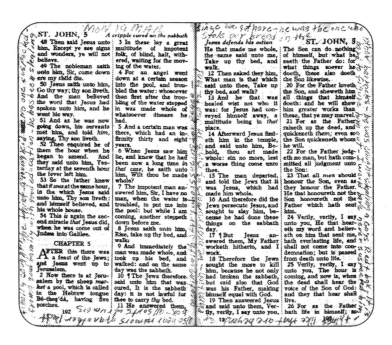

Week Ten

19 March–25 March 1945

——— ·✠· ———

Monday, 19 March

They finally caught the thief, a young kid no one suspected, from a good family, with a good education. He has been stealing since we got here. He was the one who stole our bread in the other barracks. He was caught stealing a boy's Red Cross box. It is hard to figure him out. I would have never suspected him. Things like that are beyond explanation. We hear rumors of the Big Three in Switzerland, meeting with Jerry, who is suing for peace. We also hear rumors of another Red Cross box; all sorts of rumors.

Tuesday, 20 March

Terrific bombing yesterday; it shook the building. I noticed B-29s dropping leaflets for the first time. Six more men have died. The water went off, so we only got a little soup today. I sure hope it comes on tomorrow. All I have left of my Red Cross box is the nicotine stain on my fingers, but I sure enjoyed it while it did last. I feel hungrier today than ever since my capture. I pray my family will never have to experience such hunger. There are rumors of the war ending from 14–20 days; also, more rumors of Red Cross boxes. I never heard so many conflicting rumors.

Wednesday, 21 March

I listened to the birds sing on the first day of spring; it sure made me home-sick to hear them, but I felt a lot better inwardly to know that someone can still enjoy a nice morning. I sure pray we are liberated soon, as I enjoy spring more than any time of the year, and I'd love to be free. A boy from our barracks died; it sure is tough. It seems like quite a few have been dying. The water is still off; there's a short bread ration today. Bread before soup, if we get soup.

Thursday, 22 March

A beautiful day; I spent all my time in the sun. The artillery was closer last night, and has been noticeable all day. B-17s came over in droves all day. I heard that MacArthur has taken all the Philippines and has headquarters in Manila; maybe that war will end before this one. I pray that it's a good indication, as I'm getting despondent in regards to the war again. I feel like I can't stand much more.

Friday, 23 March

The Red Cross representative was here today. I haven't heard his report on conditions. Quite a few men are dying, too many for comfort. Everyone is spending his time in the sun, trying to get rid of the lice. I sure see some ingenious inventions of the GIs; all sorts of cooking devices, as well as forms of clothing. It's funny what a man can do when he has to. I think I've learned the meaning of words like faith, meekness, humbleness, and appreciation since my capture. We are praying harder for the end of the war.

Saturday, 24 March

This weather sure makes one feel more hopeful. The days seem to pass more rapidly, which is good. Another sunny day; I spent a very busy day washing clothes. I feel good now, with all clean clothes on and a clean body. I'm also as weak as a cat. I'm slowing down as I'm using up energy that I

don't have — lots of other men are in the same fix. The news is good;
Patton has nine bridgeheads 31 miles from here. By the first, we hope to be
freed; I sure am praying so.

Sunday, 25 March

Chaplain gave his best sermon today. He is very optimistic about our
speedy liberation. This is a beautiful Psalm Sunday. War news is good; we
can see the strafing plain; artillery is more active. Ludwigshafen is taken,
so we hope to hear of Frankfurt under siege before long. Some, including
myself, pray for liberation this week. The weather is beautiful as one could
ask for. The thought of being freed is a thought one can't describe — I hate
to think about it.

Clete's screaming wakes up everyone in the barracks. I sit up and see him slobbering and wide-eyed. "I got him! I got him!"

His arms are wrapped around Cornelius P. Allison, III, who holds a Red
Cross box in his hands, close to his chest. Allison struggles but another POW
grabs the box from Allison and spits in his face. "Empty your pockets, you
dirty, slimy, stealing son-of-a-bitch. That's my food!"

What a way to start the week.

There are 240 suggestions from the sleepy-eyed POWs about what to do
with the thief. "Kill him ... get him to the latrine first ... don't mess up the
floor with his blood ... shh ... don't alert the guards ... stuff the bastard in the
cesspool head first ... shove him outside naked ... shave his head ...."

Clete: "I caught him red-handed, saw him reach down and take the box. I
was on the way to the latrine." He grabs one of Allison's arms and bends it up
his back until it almost touches his neck. Frankly, I hope the arm will crack.

"And that's my box. See? Here's my initials — T.C.A." pants the livid
owner of the Red Cross box. He adds, "You remember? I won the toss for the
box. It's mine."

Trey, nickname for the third generation New Englander, is pushed and
dragged toward the latrine. Men kick or hit him as he passes. My blood boils as
I see the expression on his face. His eyes, with heavy blond eyebrows closing
the space over his nose, are half-closed. His lips curl into a sneer. The 6 feet
and 3 inches body is ramrod stiff. The long blond hair, neatly arranged around
his ears, reaches the top of his collar.

Pett says, "Now I know why he is so neat and looks so healthy. He's stealing, the no-good bastard. Stealing from his buddies."

Four men pull the prisoner toward the latrine. Secretly, I'm glad I had called him 'Alley,' or 'Alley Cat.' Both names infuriate him, but his superior attitude pisses me off. One of his favorite expressions is, 'you ignorant southerners' when he glares at me as if I was a piece of dirt.

Clete yells, "Your ass is gone, right down the cesspool. Don't let him hold his nose; prop his mouth open with his boot."

My resentment rushes out of my mouth with hurricane force. I jump up and scream, "I have a better idea. Hang the bastard — now, before the guard opens the barracks. He stole the bread we had saved to escape. I . . . I . . . I . . . ."

Tut grabs my arm as I start to swing at the thief. The events that follow are a blur. Pett recaps the episode an hour later, when I finally come back to the present. "Man, you were crazy; kept yelling 'hang him, hang him' and stuff like that. Huckel said we should have a trial. You volunteered to be prosecutor. I was flabbergasted. You, the Bible-reader, the one who's always making me swear on that Bible of yours every time I report something. You, the one who leads us in prayer. Someone suggested we listen to what he had to say, and you screamed, 'No, no, no.' A rope appeared from nowhere. You whipped it around Trey's neck like you were roping a steer."

"What happened then? I almost hate to ask."

Pett continues, "You should hate to ask, 'cause all hell broke loose. You led the chant to hang him. About that time, a bunch of you have the rope up over that small window onto the ground." He stops. "How the hell were you guys going to hang him with the rope outside on the ground?"

"Darned if I know. I guess someone was going to run outside when the barracks were unlocked and tie the rope to one of those brick pillars."

Pett continues. "Well, anyway, the guards throw open the doors, follow all the screaming and yelling to the latrine, grab Trey, and haul him out."

I drop my head between my legs. I wasn't embarrassed, just mad I had allowed myself to sink to the level of an animal. What difference did it make if he stole? We are alive. The fellow in our barracks who died was not deprived of food because of Trey. On the other hand, why should someone get away with stealing? We depend on each other for survival. At least Alley Cat doesn't smell. He keeps himself clean, even if he is a snob and a first-class shit.

I look around, and ask in a quiet voice, "Did I do wrong? Should I have led the charge to hang him?"

Huckel says, "You did right. We were just surprised to see you so violent."

"Not me," interrupts Strubinger. "I remember the time we had the fight over those lousy crumbs."

"You had it coming, buster."

"I think this place is getting to you, Higg," Huckel continues, "and you're the one who always preaches love, cooperation, and humility."

Clete says, "Eye for an eye, I say. Too bad the guards broke it up. Where I come from he would be dead. Never would have gotten to the latrine."

"Wonder what will happen to him?"

Pett says, "Nothing. The Jerries don't care what we do to each other as long as we're no problem to them. They carried him off because you guys made so much noise. It was time to open the barracks, anyway. Best thing we can do is give the bastard the cold shoulder." The incident is forgotten. Just another disturbance to break up the monotony of life in a prison camp.

By the tenth week of captivity, the guards seem to be less noticeable. We are not ordered into the barracks and locked up when American planes fly overhead. We are allowed to stand on the hill, cheer, and wave. The hum of planes is steady, day and night.

— ⚔ —

Sometime Tuesday I look up to see a sky black from horizon to horizon. To the pilots, I guess we look like a bunch of Coney Island sun bathers.

"Must be 10,000 planes! They were over the camp all night, and still coming." The anticipation of freedom changes everybody's mood from futility to happiness.Pett scratches his stomach where the lice are breeding in the seams of his pants.

Tut laughs as he says, "You remind me of my 200 pound aunt when she took off her girdle in the summer. She'd scratch and say how good it felt."

I ask him how he knew.

"'Cause I'd sneak a peek in her room."

Six of us laugh, form a chorus line, scratch our bodies, and sing in falsetto voices, "Oh me, oh my, it feels soooo good."

The lice get into the act and begin to move around in the seams of my clothes. The eggs are yellowish. They attach to the shaft of hair. You can remove them with fingers or a comb. The favorite site for eggs to nest is the hair at the back of the head, but they also lay eggs in clothes. The pointy-head little buggers are almost transparent. Lice suck blood, and itch like a mosquito bite. When you crush one, it goes *pow* or *pop*. A favorite pastime is to sit in the

165

sun, pick the lice, crush them between your nails. Some fellows even keep score of the number discovered and crushed. Like golf, low score wins.

One of the doctors told us during a health lecture that lice spread by contact, especially among people who live in crowded quarters, like us. It is essential to practice safe hygiene. We are lucky that our barracks chief is paranoid and demands that we scrub the floors and air out the barracks and blankets, even in freezing weather.

The American doctors are always reminding us of the signs of typhus — first, a high fever, then the appearance of black spots on the skin and a ringing in the ears. The doctors also told how to distinguish lice from scabies. The former are visible, the latter more difficult to locate. Scabies are caused by a mite that lays eggs under the skin. When hatched they may be harmless, but itch like hell, especially around the butt, armpits and wrists. Another difference is the minuscule dark lines with small red lumps on the skin. Everyone is constantly warned to be careful about scratching. This can cause infection. Getting to the doctor is more critical with scabies than lice.

The prison camp is a maelstrom of activity, card games wherever you find a clean area, bazaars selling or trading clothes, pots, pieces of uniforms, watches, even food and cigarettes. Barkers hawk their wares like a carnival sideshow.

It's a relief to get out of the smelly, dank barracks into the sun. Its warmth makes my skin tingle. The weather affects our dispositions, too. Optimism runs rampant through the camp. I hear the Army expressions more often, "Jesus Christ, man . . . for cripes' sake . . . kiss my butt . . . screw you, Mac . . . . " I often wonder who Mac is. I'm glad that's not my name!

In front of every barracks I see groups debating, arguing, or just talking about the war. Each group has from two to fifteen people; the number depends upon the subject matter or the volume of the participants. Clotheslines are strung between barracks. As he strings up his shirt and jacket, Pett says, "Don't tell my mother you saw me hanging up the wash, or she'll want me to do it all the time. Or sweep, either. My Ma would laugh if she saw me sweeping." Most mothers and wives would be astonished to see their loved ones busy as bees with household chores.

Every barracks has a barber, or at least someone who has a pair of scissors. If all these guys barber after the war, there will be four barbershops on every corner.

The sun loosens the muscles and lifts the spirits of the 4,000 American POWs. Stalag IXB is a promenade. As I walk up and down the hills between the barracks, I pick up snippets of conversation.

"Where you from?"

"What outfit?"

"Where were you captured?"

"How many prison camps you been in?"

"Married?"

Some POWs are loners. A fellow in our barracks does nothing but play solitaire. I tried once to talk to him, but all he would say is that he had spent five years in Greenland and four in Alaska, where "Loneliness is a way of life — the only way to survive." Other POWs spend all day staring out the fence at the mountains.

Fires and grills made of anything metal burn outside every barracks in the American compound. The Mexicans pound corn into a paste on a rock, then fry it on a hot plate on a fire. I ask, "Wonder why they are so intent on making those pancake things?"

Huckel says, "You mean tortillas?"

"Yeah."

"That's the same as bread. Everything made revolves around the tortilla, and beans. You note how they swap for cans of pork and beans?"

Tut says, "Boy, they can have mine. And that black bread, too. Those Russians love that damned bread. I see Mexicans trading their black bread, then swapping what they get for the beans. That's how I got my Russian cap."

Huck adds, "Guess that's what they're used to."

"No worse than those damn grits," Clete says.

Tut says, "Well, they can have my black bread, but not my grits."

Thursday is another beautiful day. I'm happy to get out of the barracks. All night, I had listened to the artillery shells landing in the valleys around the camp. "Boom, boom, boom."

The artillery is intermittently interrupted by the rattle of prayer beads. Thank God the artillery is still about 50 miles away. The B-17s come over in droves on their way to some target in Germany in the morning, back home in the afternoon. The rumor monger comes around to announce MacArthur has taken all the Philippines.

"Hey, to hell with the Pacific. What do you hear about Patton?"

"Yeah, where are the Americans?"

"Tune your radio to another station, buster!"

The English have not reported any radio news for at least a week. Is that good? Bad? Maybe the end is so close it's useless to report news. I hope and pray the war will end soon, but become more despondent as the day progresses. I go up the hill to the fence and look at the mountains.

I try to read the Bible. That doesn't help. I can't understand the verses. Nothing seems to pull me out of my state of depression. Thoughts race through my mind, one after another. How did I get in this place? Why me, God? What did I do wrong to deserve all this misery? I've tried to live a good, clean life. Maybe that's the problem. My life has been so clean and simple, God doesn't have to help me. Well, I'll see if I can correct that when I get home, if I do.

Night finally comes, which is worse. The darkness is fearsome. I don't participate in the division of the bread, but no one cares. We don't council each other. A person is left alone to do whatever he desires ... so long as it isn't stealing, or vomiting or crapping all over someone else.

I can feel the tempo of happiness increase toward the end of the week. No doubt the sunshine improves everyone's temperaments. Conversation is lively, reminiscent of a lunchroom in grammar school. The favorite activity on a sunny day is picking lice. Stalag IXB looks like a monkey colony. We inspect each other's head for the nits that attach to hair shafts.

A number of us continue to make up names for various prisoners of war. The primary contact with the Germans is the Big Dealer. Those who deal only with POWs are wheeler-dealers, traders or swappers. We tagged our group as the Culinary Cooks. I am the Chief Chef because I name so many recipes, real or invented. I name one fellow in our barracks Meow, because he is always meowing like a cat. Another POW I call Whiner because he whines about anything and everything.

Clete says, "Why not Bitcher or Grumbler?"

Pett looks up. "That's what we call you when you aren't around, Strubinger — a bitcher."

I correct Pett, "Naw, Clete is more of a Belly-Acher, always belly-aching over something."

Clete casts his eyes toward me, "Well, I don't fret over everything like you, Higgins. That's what we call you — the Fretter."

"I don't fret. I just want everything in its right place."

Pett says, "I call you Organizer. You organize everything."

Huckel says, "No. I call Higgins Perfectionist."

I switch the talk to the barracks leader. "Benner is the Doer, as in: do this, do that. He reminds me of Sergeant Tibby. I wonder where he and

Holcombe ended up? I bet Tibby has them organized, even if Sergeant Ramos is with him."

Pett pops a lice between his nails. "Since Ramos is a First Sergeant, or was, I guess he still acts like one. I hope he has shaved. If not, all that black hair on his Portuguese body will make him look like a bear. The Jerries might let him run loose for target practice."

Ah, the beauty of spring. God has bestowed good weather on us. The birds sing, the sun shines, my body tingles as the rays penetrate the skin. What more could you ask for? When I mention this while stretched out on the ground, Pett says, "To be liberated. To get out of this hell-hole. To get home."

"Yes, but as long as we're here, we might as well enjoy the bountiful blessings that God has provided."

Tut adds, "Let God provide one more blessing, namely freedom."

"Don't be greedy. Enjoy the simple things in life."

Huckel says, "I have another name for Higgins: Philosopher."

"My friends," I conclude as I stand and stretch out my arm as if bestowing a priestly blessing, "Today's the day, to hell with tomorrow."

I get tired of the idle chatter, so walk around the camp. It is difficult to distinguish nationalities by uniforms because there has been so much trading. Only the language distinguishes the English from the Americans. Why would someone want to wear someone else's clothes? I've never understood that. Even when I was a child, what's mine was mine.

I had eaten and smoked myself sick. All that is left of the Red Cross box I got last week is my nicotine-stained fingers and a growling stomach as the food slowly meanders through my intestines. I gag, then burp. My mouth has a sour taste. I double up in pain, then stretch out on the ground and cross my legs to hold in the runny crap.

Late in the day, after supper, while there is still daylight, I record the events in my Bible and meditate. I ask God to end the war. I wonder if He hears me? I look around and wish I could read what is on each person's mind. Have I learned anything about appreciation while here? I do appreciate even the smallest favor. I know I have faith in God, I have to. There is nothing else. I'm not so sure about meekness, or humility. I suspect that once we're liberated we'll return to whatever approach to life we've known. All of us have short memories.

I lie on my pallet, listen to my bowels rumble, and try to think of family and friends whose faces pass before my tear-filled eyes. I begin to sob, but Pett kicks me and says to shut up.

Saturday is another great day. We sit in the sun and continue our 'tagging people' game. Pett glances down the street to the main road and says, "Hey, here comes the Bobbsey Twins. They look alike — gangly, stringy gray hair, beak noses and eagle eyes, round shoulders. They even sound alike — nasal, singsong voice. The only way to identify them is that one has a goatee and mustache, the other a scraggly beard.

"The one on the right (with the goatee) is the Military Strategist or MS for short. His buddy is Mr. Geography or Mr. G."

I say, "Both are WMs or War Mongers. All they do is spread rumors." The look-a-likes stop close to me. It is difficult not to believe them, especially when bombs shake the buildings and the leaflets fall from the sky.

After the barracks are locked Saturday night it gets scary. I am afraid the artillery, or planes, or both, will hit the camp. I can't sleep. The flashes of light through the windows become more frequent. I silently pray all night.

By Sunday, the rumors fly fast and furious. Everybody has a new tale to relate. I remark to Pett on our way to church, "If I hear one more comment about the location of the Americans, I believe I'll bust somebody's mouth. Don't let the Bobbsey Twins near me."

Just then, they walk within earshot. One of them remarks to a group, "I hear Roosevelt, Churchill, and Uncle Joe Stalin are meeting in Switzerland, and MacArthur has taken the Philippines."

I can't stand it. I run up to one Bobbsey Twin, grab him by the arm, and twirl him around. "So what? I'm half a world away from the Philippines. Just tell me when the Americans are in Bad Orb."

He jerks his arm away and puts it against his face in case I hit him. "Go 'way, nobody was talking to you!" He then yells, "Look over there. That is Ludwigshafen under attack right now. You can see the smoke!"

That's where we got off the boxcar and went in the train station. Maybe those huge railroad yards have been destroyed from the bombs. The city is between 50 and 100 miles from Bad Orb, Stalag IXB, and freedom.

That's where Strubinger and Zion joined us.

Pett says, "I wonder whatever happened to Zion? You remember, he left with the other 350 or so guys."

I recall the first days in Stalag IXB, when Zion was interrogated every day by the Gestapo. They never determined whether or not he was Jewish. He was a quiet, tall man. No one could even recall him except for his owl-like eyes.

Are the rumors true? What is happening? I want to believe liberation will be soon, but the fear of disappointment is almost intolerable. I am sick and tired of disappointments. I can't contemplate a life without pain, cold, or food.

I say to Pett as we walk briskly to church with a spring in our step, "Hell, well probably be given a bath, a meal, a new gun, another division, and sent back into battle."

"And get killed. At least we're safe here, I think."

---

19 March 1945

"Germany, Home Front. Hitler orders a total scorched earth policy to be put into operation on all fronts. Industrial plants, buildings and food are to be completely destroyed . . . ."

"Western Front. General Patch's Seventh Army completes the capture of Saarlouis. Fighting in Saarbrucken and the towns to the east continues. Third Army keeps up its rapid advance east and southeast toward the Rhine. Worms is reached, while to the left and right other units are near Mainz and Kaiserlautern."

20 March 1945

"Western Front. Patch's forces take Saarbrucken and Zweibrucken a little to the east. In the Third Army sector, Ludwigshafen and Kaiserlautern are captured. First Army is still fighting to expand the Remagen bridgehead. It is now almost 30 miles wide and 19 miles deep."

21 March 1945

"Western Front. The main body of the Third Army is now clearing the west bank of the Rhine everywhere north of Mannheim."

22 March 1945

"Western Front. The U.S. 5th Division from Patton's Third Army crosses the Rhine near Nierstein. Other Third Army units are completing the mopping up west of the Rhine."

[Source: page 332, *World Almanac Book of World War II*, rev. ed., Bison Books Corp., 1986.]

I ask Huckel as we enter the church, "Why would the Big Three meet in Switzerland? I doubt Roosevelt would risk coming to Europe."

"I don't know. I wonder if MacArthur is really in Manila. The British just want us to believe the war in the Pacific is over. I like the one about Ludwigshafen. That isn't too far from here, about 50 miles."

As we push into the crowded church, someone reminisces, "I miss the tiny tots walking into the chapel waving the palm fronds, all dressed in white . . ."

". . . and poking each other in the eye, or staring at the congregation."

Easter is next Sunday. I think about the trappings of dyed Easter eggs, everyone dressed in their spring clothing.

The Lambert College preacher opens the sermon with the comment that liberation is close. He parallels our liberation with Jesus' week before His crucifixion. Chaplain Neal speaks of understanding God through Jesus, the living expression of the Father's love, born into the world to manifest God's love for all His creatures. It does help life have some meaning, I decide. Except I don't want to be crucified, and say so to Huckel.

He replies, "I don't think he means we have to be crucified. It just means that Jesus died so we could live."

We sing, "Jesus, Lover of My Soul." I follow the song in my Bible, but don't know the tune.

The concluding song is "Nearer My God to Thee."

Before the light fades away, I record the events of the day. I then read the second verse of the last song.

> *. . . though like the wanderer, the sun gone down,*
> *darkness be over me, my rest a stone . . .*
> *yet in my dreams I'd be,*
> *Near my God to Thee . . . .*

I lean back against the barracks wall, look through the window at the sky. Yes, it has been a wonderful week. Sure, there are deaths. The amount of soup is reduced. The lice begin to drive us nuts, and the bitching continues.

But good things overshadow the bad. The sky is black with American planes. The sun warms both body and spirit. We can move around the camp. The visit of the Red Cross representative is frosting on the cake. He inferred we will be liberated before any action can be taken on our complaints. Deep inside, I believe he is correct. We will be liberated. My portion of the last Red Cross package is gone. Dare I hope that next week will end the misery? No, no, I better not hope.

Today is beautiful, that's enough.

Chapter 11

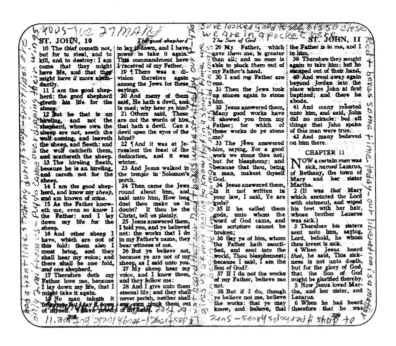

Week Eleven

26 March–1 April 1945

Monday, 26 March

> *Good news; better than any. I'm so elated I can't write. The Second Army*
> *walked into Frankfurt without firing a shot. Jerry army is in complete*
> *route; this came from Corporal Weiss. Also, Red Cross boxes are in. This is*
> *the happiest moment of our prison lives. Weiss says the war will be over*
> *before we are liberated. I wish I could describe this moment!*

Tuesday, 27 March

> *We had a front-line strafing during soup. The front lines are only two miles*
> *from us; P-47s came over, dipping their wings to us. It sure looked good to*
> *see GIs so close. We are in a pocket here. The Red Cross boxes should be*
> *here some time today. Our liberation is a matter of days, and perhaps*

hours. It sure gives us a funny feeling to know that in a short time we can begin to live as humans and not as wild animals. I just heard that our Red Cross boxes were strafed by our P-47s and destroyed. Tough luck, but we'll be free before we get them anyway.

Wednesday, 28 March

We got 11 men on a Red Cross box; just a taste, but it was appreciated. Of course, there are always rumors, that we will be out for Easter. Our loaf of bread today had a .50 caliber slug in it from the strafing; sure was funny! The guards who live nearby can go home, so we are just waiting for the Yanks to move in. Rumors are thick, and everyone is jittery and nervous as we impatiently wait to be freed.

Thursday, 29 March

Got deloused today; sure felt better. It's a rainy, cold day. We are bypassed by 20 miles on one side and 14 on the other, so I guess we'll be freed any day. I'm sure anxious and really sweating it out. Rumors are so thick that I can't remember them. We can hear tank fire, and rumor has it that the Yanks are in Bad Orb. I can't believe that freedom is so close; I can hardly stand the suspense.

Friday, 30 March

No bread, as we are cut off from Bad Orb. We had four potatoes instead. I went to the Good Friday service. Artillery is falling only a couple of miles away; it's shaking the building. The sun came out late this afternoon, so we may have good weather for Easter. It's not as cold as the last two days. I hope the cold spell has broken; men are still dying, and it sure is pitiful to see the bodies go by.

Saturday, 31 March

We got a Red Cross box last night; 20 men to a box. The Jerries told Eddie to clean out the warehouse — we had more food today than in three months. In that Red Cross box was eight containers, each containing two liters of thick soup. We didn't get much in the Red Cross box, but it was a taste of what's to come, not what we're used to. It sure was appreciated. I received two packages of French cigarettes. They're stronger than cigars. I saw my first woman in three months. I went on detail outside the camp to get wood. We didn't even have a guard. I saw civilians evacuating the city.

It was swell to see women and kids again. The fighting is close, so our liberation is a matter of days.

Sunday, 1 April

Rumor says we were officially liberated at 13:00 yesterday. The rumors are so fast and furious that one can't remember them one minute.

It is a clear, windy, cold day, but a nice Easter, even better with the thoughts of freedom in the near future. The rumors have subsided; everyone is tired of them. We are just waiting for official word of liberation. The GIs are running the camp now; our soup has been thick. I'm full from yesterday. The water is off in camp again.

———※———

Sleep is impossible. The anticipation of freedom swirls around in my head. I turn, kick, twist, finally sit up and look around the barracks at the other men. They are on edge, too. All night, men talk and look out the windows at the flashes of light from the distant artillery. The building shakes. The "whoom, whoom, whoom" of the artillery is a backdrop for small arms fire.

Suppose a shell hits the building? Will I die? Maybe. If so, I want to be awake when it hits, see it, feel it, touch my guts when they spew out of my body, taste the warm blood, go with my soul as it lifts up above this place, look down and say: live on, you miserable people. I'm free. I'm outta here. I break out in a cold sweat. I watch men run from one window to another, bang on the walls, doors, windows, yelling, "Let us out. Free us. I wanna run."

Someone yells, "Where to, you fool? You can't escape! Shells are nameless . . . they just hit — wham, you're gone!"

How true that is. I try to forget the bombs. I'll stay here, take my chances. Hell, I won't die. I know it. God isn't ready. I've got more misery, pain, and mental torment to endure. Ashes to ashes, dust to dust. It's the soul that God wants — a soul that's clean, not besmirched with sin. Sin? What kind of sin? Of the flesh? Infidelity? Whore-mongering? Chasing women, men, boys? Or is sin mental? The psyche? The inward fear, cowardice? Not of the flesh, outward. I shake my head to clear away such thinking.

The building rattles. Shells whistle overhead, then fall in the valley beyond the fence. Whew! Close. No need to worry when you can hear the whistle. That means it missed. It's the ones you don't hear that get you.

Whoom! The shell hits the ground. No whistle. That's real. That's now. To hell with all the mental anguish. I gotta live, survive — now!

Pett screams in my ear, "Come on, Higg, dig out of your blanket. Get near the door, it might open!" He jumps up, throws off his blanket, and pushes and shoves to get near the door. I jump up and follow for a few steps, then stop.

"Hey, wait a minute. We're like a bunch of ants that just got stepped on, running here and there, climbing over each other, screaming and yelling."

"I never heard ants scream," Tut says as he pushes me toward the door.

I turn. "You're too darned high and mighty. Your head is too high to look down and . . . ."

Tut says, "Aw, shut up and be happy. Let's go."

Pett, Tut, and I run from one window to the other like a bunch of ants.

Light enters the room through the dirty windows.

No one can sleep. All 200 POWs wander from door to window. I cover my head to hide from the screams within the barracks and the sounds of war outside. Contemplation, fear, helplessness. These feelings are intertwined as I finally settle down and try to sleep while listening to the "whoop, whoop, whoop" of artillery, "thunks" of mortar shells that drop into barrels, the "rat-tat-tat-tat" of machine guns accompanied by sporadic rifle shots. The sounds of war have a rhythmic effect.

I stare at the wall. It is too crowded to turn on my side. I imagine an orchestra conductor. He points his baton at the drums for a few quick beats. The baton whips to the trumpets that blare with staccato quickness. The violins pick up the beat, smooth and soft. I hear Strubinger rattle his beads. I heave and sigh, choke when I try to speak. I close my eyes tightly to stop the trickle of tears.

"Thanks, God, for the good news." We are still behind barbed wire, not free men, so I don't include freedom in my thanks. I'll wait for that.

I am cautiously happy because I am still a prisoner of war. That is obvious even when I walk around Stalag IXB — guards patrol the camp, machine guns point at me from the towers. The Germans carry out their duties with caution, and have more condescending attitudes. They are still soldiers and control our destiny. They'd shoot without hesitation if anyone tries to escape.

Ironically, it is the enemy who announces our prospective freedom. Corporal Weiss arrives, unlocks the door, speaks to the barracks leader, shrugs his shoulder, and shakes his head as if to say, I don't know. He quickly departs.

Benner yells, "No tea today. Water is still off all over the camp. Corporal Weiss just told me 'Allus kaput.' The German army is retreating. We will get another Red Cross ration if the railroad yards in Bad Orb aren't bombed."

There is momentary, silence, as if to say 'it can't be true.' Then, jubilation, followed by the first priority of prison life. "All right! Let's eat. I need a smoke."

I know we're free and the war is pushed aside when food and smokes are foremost on everyone's mind. Men scream, dance, cheer, chatter like a bunch of excited monkeys in the jungle. Others sob in happiness. Some bow their heads in both silent and audible prayers. I do all three.

The action of the Jerries indicates that freedom is near. Our barracks guard comes inside as Corporal Weiss departs. The guard has a Red Cross parcel and traveling pack. A POW yells, "You finally get to eat good food."

Someone else says, "You headed for Boston to find your brother? Can I go with you?"

He is a kind and friendly person. I hate to see him leave, except for the fact he is free. The guard, whose name I never learned, motions for the prisoner who speaks Polish and tells him that those who live in the vicinity will be allowed to go home and change into civilian clothes to prevent capture.

Somebody yells when his comments are translated, "I'll swap my clothes for your guard's uniform."

Others chime in, "Yeah, yeah, me too."

His voice is soft and sad. "I don't think it would be wise at this time to wear my uniform." The barracks becomes quiet when the sentence is translated. There are tears in his eyes. He continues slowly as his words are translated.

"I hope some of my family are still alive. Ask your soldiers to be kind to us peasants." He turns to the translator and smiles, "Look up my brother in Boston. You have his address. Give him my love. Maybe he'll give you a sweet." He hugs the POW, shakes hands with Benner, waves to us, and leaves.

If you strip away the uniform, you find the nakedness of a human being.

We watch through the fence as guards walk down the road. Some pedal on bicycles, others with loaves of black bread tucked under an arm. Huckel turns to me, "I wonder where our guard lives? He never said. I hope he survives the aftermath of this war."

POWs wave at a few of the guards who have been around the camp since our internment. They smile and give a thumbs-up sign. Maybe I'll regain my faith in humans, and not think every German is the enemy. The guards are just doing their jobs. But how do I eliminate cynicism? Not clutch my every possession? What will life be like without suspecting everybody? Not to mention the filth, lack of food, and continuous yelling and gripping.

I reflect on the 11 weeks in prison. Reminds me of riding a horse. Just a series of ups and downs. Rise up in the saddle, then down on your butt when the other leg hits the ground. The upside is the roar of the artillery, the rumble and squeak of tank treads, the intermittent mortar fire, and the pop and crack of rifles. The downside, when your butt hits the saddle, is remembering I am still a prisoner of war, behind the fence. I eat the slop, clean the camp, gather wood, complain.

The battle raging in the forest around the camp is disconcerting, to say the least. A POW says apprehensively, "It would be ironic to get killed by American weapons."

I answer, "Or worse, German guns." I turn to Pett and ask, "You ever see any manuals, procedures, or sets of rules on how to surrender, or be liberated?"

"I guess that type of training is beyond the comprehension of our leaders. Maybe we aren't supposed to get captured."

"Yeah, I guess each step toward liberation is improvised with the situation."

The best rumor is about the area being encircled. The prison camp is in a pocket, which has been bypassed. I can hear the rumble of vehicles, the whoop, whoop of artillery from the mountains and valleys around Stalag IXB. It's possible to identify all of the small arms fire — rifles, mortars, machine guns — that accompany the tanks.

I stay put and do not try to escape. As Pett says, "The Krauts still have the guns, and they're jittery. Don't give them any excuse to shoot. Better to wait and see what happens."

It's an anomaly. The roles of prisoner and guard are reversed. We know freedom is a matter of days. All we have to do is sit tight, behave, and dream of a better day. The guards, on the other hand, have an uncertain future. Will they be shot? Placed in a prison camp? Just like cantering on a horse, we rise in the saddle, they fall.

Tuesday morning P-47s strafe close to the camp, return, and dip their wings. I wave, scream, and jump up and down in front of the barracks.

"Oh, what a glorious feeling!" I yell at the top of my lungs as I cry, hug, dance, shake hands, hit arms and backs, even kiss Pett and Clete. The sight of the planes strafing the front lines reinforces the rumor we heard Monday about the Army walking into Frankfurt. Since it is only about 20 to 30 miles from Stalag IXB, it shouldn't be too long before we are liberated.

Stalag IXB is bedlam. I manage to jot down a few notes in my Bible late in the day. I sit in a corner in the barracks and read a few passages of scripture, recite *Invictus*, and thank God for the deliverance that is sure to come.

Wednesday, the Red Cross boxes arrive, and when divided, there are 11 men to each one. I push and shove in order to get in a group with my friends, or at least with men who do not gripe or try to get more than their share.

I get about five sugar cubes, a handful of raisins, and three cigarettes. The number of M&Ms is piddling so I trade mine for a spoonful of meat. There isn't much concern over the quantities since everyone feels liberation day is just around the corner. Why fuss over a few bites of food? I eat quickly in case we are liberated and to prevent it from being stolen.

The artillery shakes the barracks. If a shell drops on the camp, I'm not sure whether it is safer to be inside or outside. Oh, well, I think, it's exciting to anticipate freedom and not worry about death.

We still get our ration of bread for supper. The Germans are methodical, if nothing else. Won't let a war interfere with their routine.

When Pett cuts the piddling ration of bread, he holds up a shell. "Well, I'll be damned. Here's a .50 caliber bullet."

"It's yours," I say, "since it's in your piece of bread."

"Think I'll put it on a chain and wear it around my neck."

Tut says, "And tell everyone how you stopped a bullet with your teeth. Or someplace else that you can't show them."

It's a great night. The anticipation of freedom keeps me awake, talking to Pett about the anticipation of freedom. The chatter throughout the barracks sounds like a bunch of high school girls at a slumber party. We even have snacks to munch on.

⋯⋯⊷⊶⋯⋯

Thursday is a miserable day. The steady, cold mist doesn't help the sour taste in my mouth, nor the diarrhea. I spend the day belching or running to the latrine, or both simultaneously. I'm sorry I gorged myself all night.

After dinner we get a delousing. As we walk to the building Clete says, "Maybe I can wash off all the shit from my legs. I just wish I had clean clothes. So help me, when I get home, my Ma won't have to tell me to put on clean clothes after a shower."

Even the sickening smell of creosote does not dampen my joy at being clean. I guess the Germans want clean prisoners of war returned to the Americans. I wonder outloud, "How are they going to put meat on my bones, paste it?"

I walk, shivering, back to the barracks when I see the self-appointed military strategist drawing maps in the mud. He is explaining the 'base of fire and flank' maneuver and the approximate location of the American troops. He explains that Patton's advance units are everywhere, capturing towns, chasing the retreating German Army, leaving the rest for the mop-up infantry units to claim, including Bad Orb.

Huckel and I stop to listen. Huckel comments, "I doubt if the Americans are as close as claimed. The artillery could be 20 miles away. The small arms fire is sporadic. It is the tank treads squeaking that really tells us how close we are to liberation. Until that gate is knocked down, we are still in prison."

"Yeah, but ain't it fun to dream, and listen, and hope?"

My stomach growls as I double up in pain. I can feel the wet, slimy crap oozing down my legs.

"Oh, brother, watch out, here it comes. Patton better hurry before I crap myself to death."

I run for the outdoor latrine, holding the cheeks of my butt close together.

The rumors appear more valid, regardless of where the Americans are at this moment.

> 27 March 1945
>
> "Western Front. Third Army has now crossed the Main both west of Frank- furt, where Wiesbaden is attacked, and to the east."
>
> [Source: page 334, *World Almanac Book of World War II*, rev. ed.,Bison Books Corp., 1986.]

When I return, I hear Pett laugh, "Would you listen to Russ? We now have our own military strategist."

Huckel replies, "Hell, I've listened to the rumor mongers so much I'm a strategist, too. I just wish there was someone we could call meteorologist so we'd know about the weather."

Friday it is warmer. The sun comes out about noon. Perhaps in honor of the day Christ was killed. I go to Good Friday services. As a Southern Baptist, I never celebrated this day. A Baptist once said it was because of the Catholics. They celebrated Good Friday, so the Baptists refused to do so.

"Seems silly," I told my childhood friends. "The Episcopalians celebrate today, and get soot on their foreheads, too."

After a dinner of half-rotten potatoes, each one the size of a golf ball, we get another Red Cross box. "Why so soon?" I ask.

Pett coughs as he answers, "Don't look a gift horse in the mouth, just take it."

"I will."

"But if you want to know the reason, I understand the American cook was told to clean out the warehouse."

Everyone lines up outside the barracks and Benner announces that there will be 20 men to a box, including the two-and-a-half liters of soup in each box. The boxes are a new type. I list the contents of the fourth issue of Red Cross rations in my Bible:

2 K-ration cans of ham and eggs

3 K-ration cans of pork loaf

1 box of raisins

2 packages of Camel cigarettes

4 packages of vegetable soybean soup

8 bullion cubes

1 can of grape jam

1 box of sugar cubes

1 box of cocoa

1 box of coffee

3 cans of butter

1 package of processed cheese

1 package of crackers

2 bars of soap

1 can of milk.

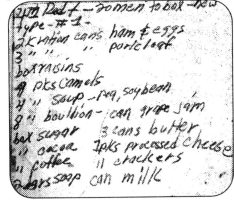

Contents of fourth Red Cross box

We quickly get in groups of 20, appoint someone to get the box, and rush back into the barracks to divide the food. There is no problem in getting in a group. A natural affinity has developed after living in close quarters for three months. It is not based on intellectual, religious, political or geographic preference. The subject of why people will associate with others is not discussed nor debated. It just happens.

The rations are divided. Each group pools everything. All night we wait to get at the stove to cook. Boy, how I eat! It is delicious. POWs unable to keep their food down vomit or crap on the floor in the latrine, or do both at the same time.

I eat, vomit, crap, eat some more, vomit again. In between vomits, I listen to the sounds of war around the camp. The gunfire gets closer.

Saturday the barracks Chief, Benner, asks a few of us to gather wood for the barracks stove. It was all burned last night. "The guards at the gate will not stop you. They don't care if you come back or not. But do come back as we need the wood, and it won't be long anyway before we're free."

I am selected from our group to make up the wood detail.

Pett advises me, "Come back, buddy. I need to cook. And you don't know your way around Germany, anyway."

"You wouldn't be any help, either, with your limited knowledge of German," I laughingly reply as I leave the group and head for the front of the barracks.

The sounds of artillery, mortars, and machine guns vibrate through the hills. Smoke from the weapons filters through the trees into Stalag IXB and onto the road. The seven of us who were selected are apprehensive and constantly look for any signs of troop movement. I have decided if I see Americans, I will hold up my hands and run towards them. Too hell with the wood.

As we leave the camp, I see at least 100 civilians walking up the road, away from Bad Orb. Some pull carts, others carry suitcases or bags. Faces are haggard, and all their clothes are dirty. We run across the road and hide in the woods. We don't want anyone to see us. Darn if I want to be killed by civilians mad at the American Army. The group watches the procession of civilians trudge up the road. The kids stare right and left, eyes wide open, clinging to older folks. The men are old. The younger ones have gone to war. The women glance over their shoulders as if something is snapping at their heels.

My heart aches for the mothers and children. They are the real victims of the ravages of war. At least I will return, hopefully, to a nation of plenty and a family spared the traumatic experience of these people. Safety, health, food, clothing, security. I doubt if any of these are on the horizon for the pitiful creatures hurrying up the road.

I lie in the wet leaves watching these people trying to escape the war. God has some peculiar ideas of justice. Why should these innocent folks suffer for the overbearing actions of a few?

One or two of the POWs in the wood talk escape, but the consensus is: Escape from what? And to what? Where are you going, up or down the road?" At least it is safe in Stalag IXB. Each of us carries an armful of wood as we run out of the woods onto the road, and hurry through the gate and back to the barracks.

Late Saturday night, there is a rumor that Stalag IXB was liberated at just past noon. All hell breaks loose in the barracks. Men scream and yell, beat on the doors and windows, and call for the guards to open the barracks. I turn to Clete, "Those troops must have really moved fast through Bad Orb after we came in from the wood detail. Maybe we should have stayed outside a little longer."

"And get your butt shot, too."

I can hear the crack and whoop of guns on the road from Bad Orb. "Hear the squeaking treads?" I yell at Russ. "Hey, I hear the rapid fire of the BAR. Go, man, go! One shot at a time. Listen, the base of fire is in the woods, just below us."

Huckel cocks his head, holds a hand to his left ear. "And there's the flanker. Listen. Listen. Hear that rifle fire to the left?"

Pett says, "Yeah, man, yeah. Wow! Listen. Listen. Those guys have gone around the camp and up the road."

He runs from window to window, listens, turns, and with joy I haven't heard in months, yells, "It won't be long now. Listen, here comes the half-track. For once, I'm glad to hear those treads."

Clete yells, "Quit saying 'listen.' I can hear."

"Well, listen anyway."

It is impossible to sleep. Every few minutes an artillery shell falls either in Bad Orb or the hills surrounding us. The sky is bright with flashes of light. I can smell the pungent odor of gunpowder. The excitement of the night leaves no time for a quick prayer of thankfulness. I'm sure God knows I'm thankful.

⋅⋅ ▥✦▤ ⋅⋅

Just after daylight Sunday, two Jerry guards open the barracks. Benner, the barracks chief, yells for attention. The screams and shouts stop.

"American POWs are now running the camp."

Secretly, he says, the barracks leader and the Man of Confidence have selected about 50 men, mostly from the 106th Division, to maintain control until the American troops arrive. He says the reason is to prevent all of us POWs from getting shot. The German combat commander has taken over the area from the area commander and decided to fight.

He continues, "Bad Orb and the surrounding area have a couple of hospitals, so the commander of the area has decided not to fight because of the wounded in the hospitals (German troops, I understand), but he was overruled."

All the screaming and yelling last night was justified. We *were* free! Everyone begins to yell at once at Benner, calling him a traitor, or worse.

Benner bellows for quiet. After a long period of time he explains that the American POWs will only guard the main gates, nothing else. "For your own safety, please be calm, stay close to the barracks. Wait for the American troops to arrive. It won't be long. Don't get yourself killed after going through such hell."

When I get outside I can see it is clear, sunny, and still noisy from the firing on the hill overlooking Bad Orb. There is return fire from the Germans. Heads sway back and forth, like a tennis match, following the sounds.

There is no need for any more rumors. It is obvious that freedom is just over the hill, or down the road. I don't want to discuss the war or liberation as I'm tired of the whole mess. As far as I am concerned, it is time to get on with whatever life offers. The fact that the water has been cut off is of no interest. It's too cold to wash, anyway. I don't even bother to get soup for dinner.

Clete returns with his ration. "It's thicker. Guess the Jerries want to clean out the kitchen."

Sunday night, for the first time in many weeks, the sound of artillery and small arms rocks me into a state of lethargic happiness. A prayer of thankfulness begins, then I just listen. God has answered my prayers. From across the room I look through a window and detect a beam of light. Perhaps God's son did rise. I stare to see if it is a star, but see only the light.

God works in mysterious ways. This Easter Sunday certainly proves it.

Chapter 12

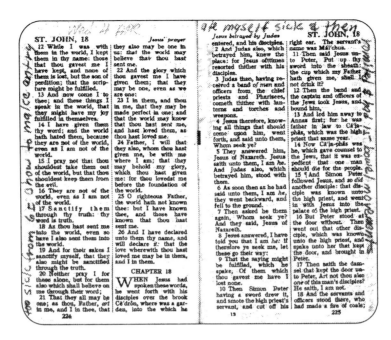

Week Twelve

2 April–8 April 1945

❈

Monday, 2 April

We were liberated at 8 A.M. by 2d Cavalry. I wish I could describe my feeling — the sight of nine Yanks and M-1 rifles is beyond description. Bad Orb fell this morning and the first tank came through the gates at 0800. I can't describe the feeling. For three months, we have been planning how we'd act when liberation came, but it was entirely different. For one thing, we had a scare on the 31st and everyone blew their tops, so when it did come we were calmer. Last night we heard the Yanks fighting on the road below us, and we could distinguish M-1 rifles, BARs, and 75s, so we knew it was only a matter of hours. Men were climbing all over the tanks and jeeps, asking millions of questions, and looking for souvenirs, especially food! We understand the 71st has moved in around us. We are to move out of here in a few days, so the rumor goes. Sure wish I had the use of words so I may describe the joy and actions of the men. This is what we have been praying for, and at last God has freed us. I'm sure all of us will go back to our homes better men and I know we shall appreciate the small things in life — things that we took for granted in our complacent lives of former times. As an example, I went wild with joy when a Yank gave me some Waldorf toilet paper! Of course, our first question was when do we eat; they say GI food is on the way. I had some coffee from a K-ration (which I used to throw away), and didn't know what it was! I got a piece of Wrigley gum — is it good! The 44th is in Bad Orb. We were all given six cigarettes. We are to move out as soon as trucks arrive. They are trying to move us out today, and we may be evacuated by planes — the sooner the better; I like it. Men have been fighting trying to get rations, etc.; I didn't know everyone had such energy left. Some of the Yanks tasted our food and spit it out!

Tuesday, 3 April

Today, we started eating GI chow, and from now on we live as men should live. I have been living for three months to eat my first GI meal, and the joy was greater than my furthest expectation. I had cereal, candy, and some wheat honey — all were delicious. I also got a tropical bar and pack of cigarettes. We shall probably stay here a few more days until available transportation is arranged, but now that our worries are over, who cares!

Still waiting for evacuation; men are running all over the country. We are under guard again. Men are stealing food from the front-line troops. Came back with some food, and it really tasted good. I ate cold ham and eggs for the first time. The D bar was the best yet. I'm living for that first GI meal. We have been given some cigarettes.

Wednesday, 4 April

Too sick from GI chow to make an entry. I ate myself sick and then vomited and had 15 bowel movements.

Thursday, 5 April

I went on sick call for GIs and gas; had some bicarbonate of soda. I still have cramps and am weak; not hungry. The Mobile unit came up, and we got donuts and coffee; they sure were good. I would eat those no matter how I felt. I got to write my first V-mail today; wrote to Aunt Louise and

Charles. It sure felt good to write home. I have more candy, cigarettes, and gum than ever before.

⋯ ▰◆▰ ⋯

"Great gods, listen to the 'whoom' of those mortars . . . . I hear the squeak, squeak, squeak of tank treads . . . listen, listen, listen . . . ."

Pett interrupts me, "I can hear. Quit jumping around."

"Okay, okay, I'm just anxious."

"It will happen when it happens. It shouldn't be too long."

"I don't hear voices."

"Hell, Higg, it's not a Boy Scout trip. You expect whoever is out there to announce their arrival?"

"I wonder which Army will liberate us?"

The barracks shakes from the artillery, mortar, and bazooka shells that fall around the camp. The smell of gunpowder seeps through the windows and cracks in the siding. No one is asleep. I am restless, apprehensive, and scared, but still suspicious. There have been too many disappointments in the past few months. We POWs have been jerked around, experienced broken promises. I don't trust anything or anybody. I don't want to be negative. I want to survive.

A stillness of anticipation settles on the 200 plus men in the barracks. The silence is eerie, broken by the noise of guns in the forest around the camp. I stare through the window on the other side of the barracks as night turns into a grayish-black dawn. My body is tense. I listen. I hear the crunch of a fence, tank treads squeaking over the wire; the 'bang, bang, pop' of rifles. I look at my watch. It is exactly 8 A.M., April 2, 1945.

The barracks erupts. Bedlam reigns. "Here they come! Here they come. Oh, man, I see Americans. At last . . . and tankers, too!" The nightmare is over.

Men climb, kick me to get at my window. I jump up. I see four armored assault vehicles come roaring down the road from the main gate.

When our barracks door is opened — or knocked down, I'm not sure which — I see former POWs are all over the tanks, begging for food, asking a million questions. I rush out of the barracks.

Someone asks what outfit. "Some unit from Patton's 2d Cavalry Division."

"Yeah, might have known it, old Georgie did it." Free! Free! No lock on the barracks door. I run around in circles, like a small kid at recess. The American compound of Stalag IXB is bedlam. We act like a bunch of bees whose hive has been poked with a stick.

Four thousand former American POWs yell, wave their arms, jump up and down. The American vehicles can't move. They are surrounded. Men climb on them. They ask the same questions over and over, "When do we get out of here? Food, food, where is the food? When do we get American chow?"

The American liberators throw boxes of K-rations to the crowd. Each box is about nine inches by four inches. Some get a breakfast box, or a dinner, or the supper. A breakfast K-ration is ripped open. Out falls a small can of meat and eggs, hard biscuits, cereal, a package of sugar, a piece of chewing gum, a pack of four Camel cigarettes and a fruit bar.

I grab the only thing left, the lousy fruit bar.

"Hey, I'll trade my fruit bar for anything. I've got enough problems with the shits now. I don't need any help."

A happy ex-POW says, "Trade it to the Ruskies, or the French."

Another ex-POW gets a dinner K-ration, "Oh, man, never thought I'd be glad to see one of these!"

He rips it open. Starving men crowd around, grabbing for something. "Here, take the biscuits ... you can have the lemonade ... you the four lumps of sugar, and here is one piece of chewing gum ... quit grabbing!"

"Let me have smokes."

"Go to hell ... these are Lucky Strikes ... I'll keep all four of them ... here, take the matches."

I think of my diarrhea, "How about the block of cheese?"

"I'll keep it — maybe it will stop these damn runs. Joe, here is the small candy bar. You take it."

I crowd closer to get something, anything. My small body, already weak, is shoved out of the way. I get nothing. An American soldier from one of the tanks throws another K-ration into the crowd. I almost get it, but, once again, am shoved out of the way.

"Hey, look here — it's a supper K-ration."

"What's it got in it? I never had one of those."

"Lemme see," the lucky fellow says. "Here's a can of beef. Wow! Some bouillon cubes, and crackers and biscuits, and ... and ...."

Someone grabs at the K-ration. The lucky guy continues, "Here's three packs of coffee, and one piece of Beechnut gum."

"What, no chewing tobacco?"

"No, but there is a pack of four Camel cigarettes. You can have them. I don't smoke."

My hands grab for the cigarettes. I hadn't had a good cigarette in weeks, only some weird brand called Chelsea. Again, I lose out. I run to another American tank. A tanker searches in his blouse and retrieves a small pack of toilet paper. He throws it to me.

"Sorry, fellow, that's all I have left. Maybe you can use it."

"Wow! Can I use it? The first toilet paper I've had in three months. Waldorf, too," I exclaim. "I didn't know the Army had anything that good!"

I snatch a piece of chewing gum from a fellow when he opens a pack. I put it in my mouth, taste the sweet flavor, and promptly swallow it.

About that time a voice bellows, "Hell, let's get out of here."

I follow the crowd and run down the road. There are no gates, the fences have been ripped down and no Germans in sight. I stop a moment as I pass through what was the main gate. I look up. "Thanks, God."

Civilians carrying bags of clothes crowd the road. American armored half-tracks rumble up the road swinging its guns back and forth from one side of the road to the other into the forest. Small arms fire vibrates through the trees. Small puffs of smoke rise above the tree tops.

Somebody yells, "Hell, they're still fighting around here."

"So what? Let's get into town." Freedom is paramount to safety. The battle in the woods is ignored. I push past the civilians — carts, kids, old people.

We go into Bad Orb, locate an Army mess tent and rush into it like a bunch of locusts. The soldiers give us tin plates and pile on eggs, bacon, biscuits, butter, and potatoes. I drink the cup of coffee slowly savoring each swallow. I didn't know Army coffee could taste so good.

While we are in the mess tent, an American officer roars up in a jeep and screams, "There is still a war going on around here. Get back up the hill into the camp. We've got enough problems. You guys are in the way."

Combat troops force us the two miles up the road to Stalag IXB.

After everyone is back in the prison camp, the Russians come for their soldiers. The French are just turned loose. The Italians are already free and running around the country. Only the British and Americans POWs will be flown out. I don't know how the other nation's prisoners of war will be sent home.

"Maybe they aren't in any hurry," Tut says. "They may be better off here than in a ripped-up country."

Later when everyone finally quiets down, Benner announces how and when we will leave Stalag IXB, "Twenty-five prisoners an hour — British, then American. Stalag IXB is in the British zone; whatever that means. They have authority over what happens in this area."

Somebody yells, "We were liberated by Americans. I don't see any British troops, except those behind this damn wire fence."

"I don't know," Benner answers in a tone of exasperation. "Just be happy we're free. We'll be out of here before too long."

The grumbling continues all evening and into the night.

As we finally settle down Clete exclaims, "Might know the British would be first."

Tuts replies, "Well, that's the way it goes. Them that's got, gets, and the British have this part of Germany for the mop-up operation."

Clete snaps, "Don't be so damned philosophical. I just wanna get home."

Some people are never happy or satisfied. As my eyes close, I smile and think, it is a good day, this first day of liberty, and it can only get better."

Before daylight, Tuesday, the gates to the camp are repaired and locked. When we arise the American and British soldiers guard the entrance.

"What the hell goes on? Why are we locked up? And by our own troops?" I am incredulous when Clete returns from the latrine with the news.

The complaints begin. I think: back to normal, bitch, bitch, bitch.

Benner yells, "Shut up, you guys, and I'll tell you what happened." The barracks gets quiet. "First, typhus is rampant among the German population. There is concern we might get contaminated, and that is the last thing the Army wants to worry about. Second, we have lice, fleas, and are filthy. Look at those trenches outside the barracks, full of shit and vomit. The Army is afraid we might contaminate the soldiers, so we must be deloused and get clean clothes before we can be returned to American control."

Now, the trading, eating, vomiting, and crapping, begins in ernest and lasts until I leave Stalag IXB six days later. The Russians trade their American rations for black bread, which I quickly trade for five cans of beans and three cans of eggs. Huckel says the Russians won't get sick from eating just black bread, adding, "I don't see any trenches in their area."

Clete says, "Naw, they just don't know good food. I'll take all their C-rations for this lousy black bread."

Pett replies, "If that is all they have ever eaten, why change? I notice none of them are thin. They probably thrive on this prison food. And none of them is sick, either."

The Mexican-American POWs swap for raw potatoes, barley, rye, any kind of meal, even black bread, then pound it with rocks to make a paste and fry it on some type of homemade griddle. Off comes a tortilla. They trade for pork and beans, which is made into a paste.

I watch them cook, then trade a pack of smokes for a tortilla filled with a pasty mixture. "Great gods, this is hot! Where did you get the peppers or whatever makes it hot?"

One of them smiles, "We've been raising them in the barracks in cans." I decide I can vomit and crap without any help from their food.

American troops set up some type of commissary to hand out food. Cartons of K-rations are given to anxious and outstretched hands. Each box has 24 K-rations: three breakfasts, three dinners, and three suppers. Clete takes one box, I take another one for the six in our group.

No one knows anything about eating too much so we eat, and eat, and vomit, and crap, and eat some more. My arms get tired from cramming the food in my mouth. I eat, burp a sour taste, then eat some more. I don't bother to heat water for the six bouillon cubes, just mix and drink the concentrated mixture in a pint tin cup.

The orangeade is better than the lemonade, but I mix both in a can and drink the concoction. I then mix six packs of sugar with the second batch, which makes it sweeter. The confection bar is a one-ounce Hershey Tropical chocolate. I read the label as I gobble it down. It has Vitamin B-1 for go power, cocoa butter, and dry milk.

The Americans give us unlimited cans of C-rations. Each one serves as a meal for one soldier. Most of the time a company mess sergeant mixes a number of cans of the same item as a meal for a company. One C-ration contains eggs, another has meat, either pork or beef, and the third can is cheese. Another large can has a dessert, such as peaches or some kind of cake. There is toilet paper, chewing gum and matches in the packages, but no cigarettes, since packs of 20 are freely given to smokers.

I decide to get creative with the rations. I melt a D-bar, add ten sugar cubes, and a crumbled up honey-wheat bar. The mixture tastes too sweet, so I add two bouillon cubes and a handful of Rice Krispies.

"You gonna eat that mess?" Pett inquires as he stares at my mess kit boiling on the grill.

"Why not? Looks good to me."

"Reminds me of a game we played as kids, called Vomit. We'd mix up everything in the kitchen, then take a mouthful. The last one to vomit is winner."

"Heck, I can vomit here just by eating. I don't need to mix up anything."

I take a sip. "Don't ask for a drink of this, you unimaginative jerks."

Pett looks in horror at the mixture, then pretends to vomit as he says, "Don't worry, you can have it all. And I hope you crap and vomit all night."

Fires for cooking are everywhere and burn all night. Men cook in steel helmets, lids to food cans, tin drinking cups, tops and bottoms of mess kits, anything and everything. I use a German mess kit because it's deep, has a lid and handle, and will hold at least a pint of food.

These are the mess kit and glasses Sam had during his internment

The camp resembles a Mexico City bazaar. Liberated POWs trade, sell, and buy every conceivable uniform, all sorts of trinkets. Makeshift stands, tables, pieces of cloths are set up in front of every barracks. I sit on the hill in front of the barracks and cook, eat, vomit, crap, and watch the different nationalities walk up and down the road.

Pett wonders, "Where did all these guys come from? The Germans must have been fighting the whole world. I never saw so many nationalities and heard so many languages." It is difficult to distinguish POWs of the various nations by their uniforms. Over the years, prisoners of war have traded pieces of their uniforms for food and cigarettes, or warmer clothes.

"Here come some Serbs. You remember them, don't you? Once, they gave us a Red Cross box." I yell at a Serb I recognize. "Hey, comrade." He still wears his pantaloons, a double-breasted tunic, but only one ankle boot. I point to it, make some motions with my hand, and ask, "What happened?"

He runs up to where I sit, jerks me off the ground and smothers me in his huge body, rubs his black beard over me, and jabbers something in broken English like, "Hungry, wanted food," then shrugs his shoulders and laughs.

"Here, you want some of our food?" He grabs his nose, mutters a loud, "Yanks, nein." He laughs as he asks, "Smokes? Yes." Everyone loves the American cigarettes. I hand him a pack of Chesterfields. He hugs me again, backs off a few feet. His right arm makes a salute. He bows. His voice cracks, and with a sad look in his eyes, comments in English, "Good luck, my dear friend." He turns and runs to catch up with his buddies.

My voice chokes as I reply, "Best to you, and thanks for everything." My eyes cloud. I squeeze tightly to hold back the tears. I turn to Pett. "What the heck will happen to them?"

Pett shrugs his shoulders as he replies, "No telling. You know, the Serbs, Czechs, and Yogis are happy, friendly people, and they've been POWs for no-telling how long. I hope they have a good life after the war."

"What is the difference between Yogis, Czechs, and Serbs? They seem to speak the same language and understand each other. Most of them are even in the same compound."

Tut hears my comment. "I think, from what I remember of high school history, there was one country until the war, called Yugoslavia. The country was divided, and now there is a Serb section and a Croatian part. The reason you don't see many *Croaks* is they are close to the Germans. Czechoslovakia is still another country. We just call them Czechs for short."

Clete says, "You're a walking history book. I thought all you rebels learned was the differences between North and South."

I say, "Well, regardless of who is who, they sure saved us. No one else shared their food when we got here."

At least 10,000 of the 14,000 in Stalag IXB wander between the compounds laughing and using sign language to communicate. In every conversation, I hear the wondrous anticipation of life after the war.

"I will . . ., I plan to . . ., I want to . . . ."

I dream and talk of the future as I continue to eat, vomit, eat, crap, or maybe eat and vomit and crap at the same time.

The American doctors don't attempt to control the quality or quantity of food consumed. I guess their role is to stop the diarrhea and severe cramps. Preventive medicine is not the order of the day. I'm not sure anyone will listen anyway. It's too much fun eating and crapping and inventing recipes to try.

The barracks walls are ripped out for firewood. It also makes it more convenient to lean over the floor and vomit and/or crap on the ground. Eventually, a shallow slit-trench is dug along the side of the barracks. That makes it even easier.

I feel lousy. My stomach is doubled up with cramps. My mouth tastes like a sewer. My butt is raw. Each crap feels like ground glass going through sulfuric acid. Just before dark I get some water, wash my underwear and pants, and put them on wet, even though the dampness on the raw cheeks stings my butt. But I never stop eating. My body aches from all the eating, crapping, and vomiting.

Clete, who learned to scrounge in South Philly, returns from the American mess tent with more cans of C-rations, and a few D-bars. These are three inch long, inch-thick chocolate bars given to combat troops to nibble on all day when it is impossible to get a hot meal or a K-ration. Each bar has sufficient protein and other food value to serve as a day's ration.

I have crapped and vomited so many times I decide to keep score to detract from my misery. "Say, men, let's keep a record of the number of times we crap. I'll make a record." Pettingill, Huckel, Strubinger, Tutherow, and Mahoney join in the fun and games. By mid-afternoon the results are tallied. I come in second place with 15 bowel movements.

Pettingill wins with 16. "What's my prize?" he asks.

Between moans and burps I say, "Sleep outside, next to the shit trench."

Later, we debate the difference in trickles and a complete crap. Clete says, "Trickles don't count. You have to crap a stream."

"Yeah, yeah," the others chortle.

Tuesday night I groan, crap, and groan. I want to die, but can't.

I can't make a Bible entry Wednesday — I am too sick. I did keep a record of my bowel movements, but can't get beyond my second place 15 of the day before. I ache all over. Why did I eat all that food? My stomach hurts, and growls like a dog protecting a bone. I half-crawl, half-walk to the edge of the floor, lean over, and vomit. I turn around, drop my pants, and crap until my guts hang out.

Thursday, I jump up early and announce, "I'm off to sick call, men. Watch my stuff."

I return with bicarbonate and advice from the medical man not to eat so much. The Red Cross truck enters the front gate to sounds of loud cheers.

"Finally. Where y'all been? Now you get here, when it's safe. Give me some donuts, Ma'am, I ain't had any since I got over here. You got anything else to eat?"

My mouth is dry. The belches taste like sewer gas, but I turn to Pett. "Gotta have some donuts. Maybe the sweet taste will kill the sour belches." I walk with spread legs to the Red Cross tent and gobble down six glazed donuts and a large cup of coffee. I return to the barracks, legs still apart to prevent the raw cheeks of my butt from touching.

"I'll see you guys," I yell as I close the cheeks of my butt and walk rapidly to the trench.

"So much for the donuts," I moan upon return.

"Dumb-ass, you shouldn't have drunk the coffee," Pett concludes.

"Yeah, but the donuts are so good. Couldn't pass them up."

That afternoon we get paper and envelopes to write letters. While I compose notes to both Aunt Louise and my brother Charles, I continue to eat candy, chew and swallow one piece of gum after another, and chain smoke. I am afraid the bubble will burst, and I'll wake up cold and hungry. Not taking any chances. Get it while I can, I remind myself, while I stuff my face.

I express my thanks in the letters for what I am sure are all the family's and friends' prayers, adding that God has responded.

Benner comments as he collects the letters about our leaving on Monday, April 9, depending on how fast the planes can deliver the cans of gas to the armored units. He confirms the rumor that the Air Corps is flying gas to the front to supply Patton's army. Rather than fly back empty, ex-POWs will fill the bucket seats in the C-47s.

Friday, Saturday, and Sunday are repetitious of the last couple of days. I am exhausted but dream of life after internment.

As the afternoon sun drops behind the mountain late Sunday, I tell Pett, "Well, I guess it's over, ol' buddy. God has done His deed — we are free. I can't ask anything more of Him. I think I'll take a walk to the top of the hill behind the barracks."

At the top, I look beyond the barbed-wire fence to the mountain in the distance. I close my eyes. My mind floats beyond Germany, across France, the Atlantic, the United States, and lands in south Alabama. I squeeze my eyes, smack my lips, draw a deep breath, and cock an ear. I inhale the salt air, listen to the soft splash of the waves. My eyes open to the white sandy beach at Gulf Shores on the Gulf of Mexico, across the bay from Mobile.

The clouds hang over the valley, sitting in solemn judgment on the day. The sun tries one last time to stay above the gray-blue clouds, jagged on the edges but solid in the middle. The rays turn westward and run up and down behind the clouds in an attempt to beam full in a clear sky above the horizon.

My eyes glaze over as I watch the clouds hide from the sun. At each flash of the sun I see forms that look like faces from Baker Company, 275th Infantry. I squint, but cannot identify anybody. One hundred ninety soldiers who came overseas with me struggle up the mountain, bent over with packs, overcoats, shoe-pacs, and rifles. Will I ever see any of them again? Of all the comrades I ate, slept, and fought with, only Pettingill, Huckel, and Strubinger are still here. Tears run down a dirty, bearded cheek.

I shake my head. God, this is no way to think. Give me the strength, the will, the determination to blot out this part of my life, and get on with it. I walk back to the barracks.

Chapter 13

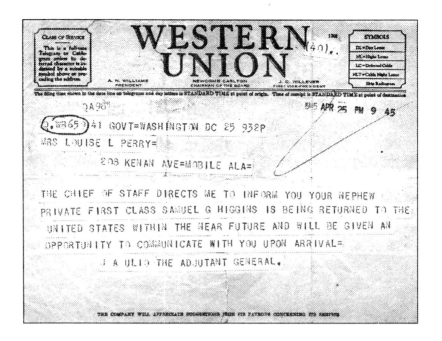

WESTERN UNION

2A98

1945 APR 25 PM 9 45

WB65 41 GOVT=WASHINGTON DC 25 932P

MRS LOUISE L PERRY=

208 KENAN AVE=MOBILE ALA=

THE CHIEF OF STAFF DIRECTS ME TO INFORM YOU YOUR NEPHEW
PRIVATE FIRST CLASS SAMUEL G HIGGINS IS BEING RETURNED TO THE
UNITED STATES WITHIN THE NEAR FUTURE AND WILL BE GIVEN AN
OPPORTUNITY TO COMMUNICATE WITH YOU UPON ARRIVAL=

J A ULIO THE ADJUTANT GENERAL.

Weeks Thirteen to Fifteen

9 April–30 April

Monday, April 9, I am one of 24 selected to leave for the delousing tent. Pett, Huck, Strubinger, Tutherow, and Mahoney are among the group. This eliminates any sad goodbyes. We gather our meager belongings and walk to the main gate.

I am so frail and weak I am pushed and pulled into the covered army truck. My body aches with every move. Cries of anguish and barely audible moans come with every breath. Even the joy of leaving prison camp can't blot out the pain that consumes my body. I don't dare go to the hospital or stay behind, so I don't complain out loud.

I raise my head just enough to glance out the rear of the truck as it turns left onto the road to Bad Orb and Stalag IXB fades from view. My stomach is in cramps. I am wet with sweat. My head is as hot as a pancake griddle. The cheeks of my butt are raw, and bouncing on the wooden seats makes it worse.

No one speaks. There is no jovial bantering, no jokes, no laughs, and certainly no tears (except, perhaps, from pain). The horrors experienced in the past three months fade into the deep recesses of my soul. What would be the effect on me, physically, mentally, psychologically, for however long I might survive? What is my fate? Back into the war? Hospital? I doubt it will be home.

I do not dream of the future. The past few months drop into the bottom of my subconscious. It is over, that's all I know. The pain blocks out any pleasant thoughts about the future. I can't think. I have survived and I want to continue to survive. My soul is at peace, blessed by the unseen God, who taps on my hardened and indifferent spirit to let me know that all is well, and He is with me. There is an indescribable sense of ecstasy.

The 20-mile ride from Stalag IXB to the delousing tent on the outskirts of Bad Orb carries me away from prison camp. The Army truck bounces, twists, and jerks from one side of the road to the other to miss the shell holes. Since my bones are meatless the ride is hell.

First, I sit on my hands. "Ouch!" Next, I lean on one cheek of my butt, then the other one. No relief. I scream. So do the other POWs, "Slow down. Not so damn fast, there's no fat on my bony butt. Whoa, whoa man, whoa!" The driver pays no attention to our moans and groans.

Tears run down my cheeks as I moan, "Oh, my God." Every bone in my body aches. My stomach is in knots from all the vomiting. The ticks and fleas in my mustache and goatee itch. I pick and scratch with one hand, sit on the other one. Tears cloud my eyes. I can't see anyone I know. The truck finally gets to the delousing tent. It is too painful to jump, so I am gingerly assisted to the ground. My cramped legs ache when I walk.

"Throw off those God-damned filthy clothes, then put them in a pile over here so they can be burned, and don't keep the lice with you."

"Ain't it nice to be back in the Army?" a meek voice whispers at the raucous and rasping sound of a three-stripe sergeant.

The warm shower water is black with three or more months of dirt, crap, and other kinds of filth. It is sheer joy to lather my body in a cake of the brown GI soap I had complained about, even shunned, in my prior Army days. The lye in the soap even smells like lavender.

It is tragic to see the bodies around me in the shower — if you want to call them bodies. They're skeletons! No one has an ass. Shriveled flesh hangs loosely from hips to knees like cured, brown tobacco leaves. Wrinkled flesh dangles from arms with bony elbows and enlarged hands. Feet look grotesque attached to the toothpick legs which are covered with hair and skin.

"Is that you, Gleason?" I stare at a head with stringy blonde hair, black pits on each side of a stubby nose. At the end of the tunnels I detect two watery eyes. The twitch of his right eye reveals his identity.

"Yeah, it's me. At least I have my teeth. Look at that poor son of a bitch." I turn to stare into a mouth with a few black teeth and bloody gums. He rattles his head as if clearing it of water. My head drops to avoid the skeletons who were once soldiers.

"Do I look that bad?"

Gleason says, "You won't win a beauty contest."

As I finger the skin drooping from my butt, I smile and think, Well, the famous Higgins butt and piano legs are gone. After the shower, I look at the floor rather than stare at balls hanging loosely between legs. I follow the other skeleton frames into the delousing tent where I am sprayed with a creosote-smelling liquid. As I leave, someone grabs my arm and sticks a needle in it. "My God, it burns! What is it, fire?"

"To prevent typhus. Extra strong, just in case," a medic replies. He hands me a large can, and continues, "Here, dust yourself with this powder. It will kill lice and fleas. Be sure to rub it in your hair, especially around your balls." Boy, am I glad Sergeant Ramos isn't here. With that ape-like hairy body of his, he would use it all. I recognize Pett's voice, and yell to him, "Hey, Pett, where you been? Didn't recognize the clean body. Can you imagine those fleas and lice on Sergeant Ramos? They must have had a real feast."

In another part of the tent I get clean, used Army garments. I notice a big hole over the heart in the field jacket with dried blood around the hole. The patch area once held a triangle, which means the previous owner was a tanker. I ask for another jacket, but get a snide reply, "Be happy you weren't in it when the hole appeared. That's the closest I have to your size. Just take it. This ain't Brooks Brothers, friend." Another friendly supply sergeant. Lazy bastard. He wouldn't look for another jacket if his life depended on it.

With the help of others from the delousing tent, I climb into a truck with about 25 liberated POWs and ride to a landing strip, where we board a C-47.

The flight to Camp Lucky Strike in La Harve, France, is as painful as the truck ride. The metal bucket seats are aligned along the sides of a C-47. The nauseating odor of gas from the cans used to bring fuel to the front permeates the plane. Oh, well, I decide, if that's all I have to put up with to get home, I can stand it.

The plane lands for refueling in Paris. I stretch my legs, get some coffee and donuts from the Red Cross and remark to Pett, "Well, this is as close as I'll get to gay Paree."

We arrive at the airport in La Harve after another butt-shaking flight. Then it's one more cheekbone-to-wood truck ride to Camp Lucky Strike.

I am interrogated by American officers. It takes about ten minutes — name, rank, serial number, unit when and where captured, where interned. Nothing about the squalid conditions in the prison camp. I guess the Army has the information they need or doesn't want to hear any more.

The Army feels safe in giving us twenty dollars pay. An Eisenhower jacket, named for the Allied Commander-in-Chief, is included with the new uniforms we're issued. We are told, "You guys are lucky. These are the first ones to be issued in Europe." For the first time in months, I have a new uniform that fits. The jacket inside breast pocket is great. It prevents a bulge in the hip pants pocket from a wallet. I cram the twenty dollars and pieces of paper with various names and addresses inside the jacket pocket. I put the New Testament diary, the German mess kit, and pieces of paper with recipes in a small duffel bag.

I spend three days at Camp Lucky Strike. Most of the soldiers have been released from hospitals, designated "fit for duty" and await reassignment. The principal topic of conversation among the former prisoners of war is our fate. The war in both Europe and the Pacific is still raging. The rumors remind me of Stalag IXB. Soldiers return from the latrine, the mess hall, every place in Camp Lucky Strike with a new rumor.

"To the Pacific."

"A new Division is to be formed of all cripples and POWs."

"Police duty in Germany as towns are captured."

One day while wandering around the camp, I recognize Sergeants Holcombe and Thibodeaux. The former was my platoon sergeant and the latter my squad leader. Sergeant Thibodeaux's first remark after hugging me was, "Higgins, you better shave off that goatee and mustache. You'll never get off the boat with them."

"Aw, come on, Sarge, give me a break. No orders, please. Anyway, I'm not in your squad now." Over coffee and donuts we relate our prison camp stories. They tell of their experiences after leaving Stalag IXB. Holcombe is still mad over the failure of his one attempt to escape. Three of them put together a makeshift French uniform and nonchalantly walked through the gate of their prison camp.

"We traveled at night, got within earshot of the front lines when it became necessary to go through a town rather than skirt it. We decided to walk through the town as if we owned it. No one stopped us until we got to the last small building in town. Just as we rounded the corner, out stepped a Terry guard. Those damned old civilians with only an Army coat and a rifle think they are hot shit. He pointed his rifle at me and said, 'Allus kaput.' The bastard had trailed us through the city, I guess. Higgins, if the scouts, Fellman and Pettingill, from the first squad had been with us we'd have made it. Back to prison camp we were marched."

I shake my head, laugh, and say, "You're lucky they didn't shoot you, wearing the uniform of another nation."

Holcombe shrugs his shoulders. "Those guys were just civilians in pieces of Army uniforms. They didn't know one enemy from another. Anyway, getting shot would be better than our prison camp." They asked about all the men in the company they had left in Stalag IXB. I told them about Pettingill, Strubinger, Huckel, that Cole, Gleason, Smith, Fellman and Zion left for another camp in February. No one knows what happened to Sergeant Ramos, Company B First Sergeant, Captain Schmied, Company B Commander, nor any of the other officers. None of us mention the men killed in action.

Sergeant Holcombe passes on the rumor we will go to the Riviera for rest and recuperation (R&R) before reassignment. I mention that Dunbar, from our company, claims he has an aunt who lives in Paris, and if we go to the Riviera we can get a pass and visit her. "Yeah," Tibby says, "and then back to the front. Thanks, but no thanks."

"I guess you're right, Sarge. With my luck I'd be back in battle. I don't have enough points to go home. If I get a chance to go back to the States I'll take it."

On 12 April it is announced that the first 500 former prisoners of war will leave for the United States aboard a hospital ship, the John Erickson. All of the former POWs gather in front of a tent to listen to the names called for the first shipment. My head and arms ache. My head drops as I tell Dunbar, "I'm not sure I can make it if my name is called. That second typhus shot yesterday did me in." I lean on Dunbar, so I won't fall. My body is soaked from sweating.

Dunbar says, "Hang in there. If your name is called, go, man, go."

The officer calling out the names says, "Here are the last two names: 'Higgins, Samuel G.' and 'Alphonse, Willie.' The 500 names I just called get over here, ready to go." I can't believe it. I am lucky for the first time in my life. Everyone congratulates me.

Dunbar says he'll send me a card from Paris. "And I'll send you one from Mobile. What is your aunt's address?" He writes the address on a piece of paper, shoves it in the breast pocket of my Eisenhower jacket, then cautions, "Act like you're well, Higgins, or you'll never make it. Your skin is yellow, and with that suntan you got sitting outside the barracks in Stalag IXB picking lice, your face is mustard tan. You look terrible."

I don't complain during the next butt-bouncing ride. We get off the truck and I walk slowly up the gangplank. As I step up on the deck, a voice yells, "Soldier, shave off that mustache and goatee. You have to be clean-shaven when we land in the U.S."

I snap back a smart-mouth answer, "What difference does it make? Is that all you have to worry about?" I go into the latrine after I find a bunk and shave off the mustache. That ought to make Mr. GI Joe happy.

I stay in my bunk during the night. When the ship stops the next morning I kick the bunk above me and ask, "We home already? Damn, that was a fast trip."

The guy above me replies, "We only crossed the English channel. We are docked at Southampton to pick up more wounded."

I hide my duffel bag under the bunk and drop my Eisenhower jacket on the bunk. My legs shake. My body is sweaty and sore, but I am curious as to what is going on topside. As I struggle to the side of the ship I hear a rasping voice. "It's you again, soldier. I told you when you got on board to shave off that goatee or you don't get off the ship. You heard me, shave it off. Where are you bunked?"

"Aw, come on, sir. I shaved off the mustache. Let me keep the goatee."

"No way. Off it comes. I ask you again, soldier, where are you bunked?" I lie. Oh, hell, I think, of all the people on this ship, why did I have to run into him?

I struggle down the steps to my bunk. My mouth falls open. My Eisenhower jacket is gone! With all those addresses — and my wallet, too. I look under the bunk and find the duffel bag, but no jacket. I ask the soldier above me if he has seen anyone. He replies, "You should've had better sense than to leave anything lying around. Didn't you learn that in prison camp?"

I lie in my bunk, too sick to eat or even move. As soon as I am confident the ship is at sea, I report to the sick bay. The ship sways from side to side in the rough sea. Waves splash on the deck. I hold onto a rope to keep from washing overboard and finally get down the steps to the sick bay. The medical officer looks at me. "Get this soldier into bed. He is yellow. I believe he has yellow jaundice."

I complain bitterly about my missing jacket with all the papers in the pocket. As I struggle to stay conscious, I hear the announcement on the ship's intercom asking for the return of the jacket and papers. Nothing is ever returned.

The semi-hospital ship tosses in the North Sea like a toy boat. It is a semi-hospital ship because it is armed, even though it has Red Cross emblems all over the sides and deck. I wonder if the German subs can see these in the fog? I sure hope so. The announcement is made that President Roosevelt died the day before the ship left Southampton. I am too sick to attend the services on deck.

It takes about two weeks to cross the Atlantic. Two days before we land in New York I get out of the hospital. When I return to my bunk, I find my duffel bag under the bunk, but no sign of the jacket or all those names and addresses. I go up on deck to bemoan my loss.

I can see a convoy spread out over the entire surface of the sea. I am fascinated with the destroyer escorts that dart between the ships. I look at the soldiers on deck but do not recognize one person from Stalag IXB. Everyone has eaten so much they are bloated beyond recognition. Thank goodness, while in the sick bay, I have been too weak to eat.

Then, that loud, obnoxious voice that bellows like a horse in heat. I freeze in my tracks. "Soldier, I thought I told you to shave off that goatee. Now, come with me and I'll watch you shave it off." Who the hell is this guy? Has he been waiting for me to get out of sick bay?

"Okay, sir, I'll shave it off."

"You bet your ass you will, because I'm going to follow you to the head and watch." I wonder if this character has ever been in prison camp. I doubt it. Otherwise, he would not insist on such a trivial matter.

On 28 April 1945, the *John Erickson* lands in New York. The seats are softer on the bus to Camp Kilmer, New Jersey. The place crawls with print and radio reporters and newsreel cameras.

"Hey, man, we're heroes, the first POWs to return home. Wow! Ain't it great to be greeted with open arms. Where are the girls?" It didn't take long for someone to think of sex, with a full belly and good night's sleep.

After assignment to a barracks, we get to call home. My first question to Aunt Louise in Mobile after all the greetings: "What holds the vanilla wafers together when you make a lemon ice-box pie?"

She thinks I've lost it. "What?"

I repeat the question and say it is important.

She replies, "Nothing. It just does. The juice from the mixture makes the crust stick when you brown it in the oven."

"Ha! I thought so!"

After discussions about the whereabouts of everyone, I hang up and head for the next barracks to find Mahoney. He walks toward me with a dejected look. "Here's your ten bucks. I just talked to my mom, and she agrees with you. She says I am crazy asking such a dumb question." In a barely audible voice he adds, "She should have been there."

We wish each other good luck, hug, and depart.

As I wander around Camp Kilmer I hear about a fellow broadcasting on the radio from one of the barracks. It is the Blue network of NBC. My brother Charles works for that network, so I ask the announcer if he knows him. The guy nearly jumps out of his skin. "Yes, I know Charlie. Stand right there. Let me see if I can locate him."

He finds Charlie at home. I hear the announcer say something like, "And now, folks, we will listen to a conversation between a former prisoner of war as he talks to his brother in New York." He hands me the mike. "Talk."

With emotion at both ends of the line, we forget the broadcast and just talk. Charles, ever the older brother, gives me advice. "As soon as you get home, write down all those experiences before you forget them. I can get it published. That is hot news right now. And for God's sake, spell *cannot, can't* and not *cain't*." A tried and true public relations man.

Chapter 14

WESTERN UNION

THE SECRETARY OF WAR DESIRES ME TO EXPRESS HIS PLEASURE THAT
YOUR NEPHEW PFC HIGGINS SAMUEL G RETURNED TO MILITARY CONTROL
02 APR 45=
J A ULIO THE ADJUTANT GENERAL.

Week Sixteen

1 May–7 May

On 1 May 1945, those of us who live in the south board trains for Fort McPherson in Atlanta, Georgia. We arrive after two days, full of soot from the coal-fired engine that came through the open window of the day coach.

The motley group stumbles along in the hot, humid May weather to a large room. The soldier in charge announces, "I have the orders that gives each of you a 60-day furlough. The white soldiers will report to Miami Beach on July third. The two Negro soldiers, Higgins and Alphonse, will report to Atlantic City."

Well, kiss my butt! So that is why I was last on the list to leave Camp Lucky Strike! The combination of yellow jaundice and suntan gave my skin a tan, Hershey-chocolate appearance. I yell, "I'm not a Negro, and I'm not going to Atlantic City."

RESTRICTED

HEADQUARTERS RECEPTION STATION #15
Fort McPherson, Georgia

JCW/hd

SPECIAL ORDERS

1 MAY 45

NUMBER 121

EXTRACT

8. Fol EM (male) having ret US and rptd this Hq in compliance auth appearing first below name reld from dy this sta and trfd in gr Redistribution Sta indicated for processing and reasgmt. Delay enroute and tvl time indicated atzd. EM will rpt new sta on or before date indicated (all dates 1945). In accordance AR 35-4520 FD will pay in advance prescribed monetary alws in lieu rat for tvl a/r $1.00 per meal per man number meals indicated. TCB PCS TDN FSA. 501-31 P 431-02 212/50425. Auth WD Ltr file AG 370.5 Subj PW 16 Aug 44 and WD Lt AG 383.6 (5 Apr 45) OB-S-A-SPGAN Subj POW 21 Apr 45.

					DAYS TVL	DAYS DELAY	RPTG DATE	
NAME	ASN	GRADE	BR.	MEALS				ADDRESS
LIBERATED POW (PROJECT R) (W male) AGSF MIAMI BEACH FLA								
Robinson, Warren C	34245039	Pfc	INF	4	2	63	5 July	Box 2 Jesup Ga
Raulerson, James	34790814	Pfc	INF	4	2	63	5 July	RFD 1 Bushnell Fla
Rearden, Paul G	34945701	Pfc	INF	4	2	63	5 July	RFD 3 West Point Ga
McPherson, Charles H	34446466	Pfc	TD	4	2	62	4 July	RFD 1 Acworth Ga
Miller, John W	34546488	Pfc	INF	4	2	63	4 July	Bell Fla
Leggett, Robert L	34195250	Pvt	FA	4	2	62	4 July	Rt 4 Eatonton Ga
House, Peter	34546785	Pfc	FA	4	2	62	4 July	1661 Pershing Rd Jacksonville 5 Fla
Ivey, Thomas E	34263609	Pfc	INF	4	2	62	4 July	210 Houston St Hawkinsville Ga
Karpin, Herman D	34972677	Pfc	INF	4	2	62	4 July	Rt 2 Box 39 Brooksville Fla
Roberson, Walter M	34973109	Pvt	INF	7	3	63	5 July	4837 Court R Birmingham Ala
Napnier, Leo V	34390778	Sgt	INF	7	3	61	4 July	Rt 1 Valley Head Al-
Pogue, Clyde L	34500552	Tec 5	MD	7	3	61	4 July	813 Swansea Ct Harriman Tenn
Lee, Herman E	26903111	Pvt	INF	7	3	61	4 July	Rt 2 Dexter Tenn
Mason, Talton E	34974372	Pvt	INF	7	3	61	4 July	Lee Ave Florence Al
Jones, BHBryan W	36657705	Pvt	INF	7	3	61	4 July	Bristol Tenn
Lane, John H	70041135	Pfc	INF	7	3	61	4 July	1412 Eslava Mobile
Harper, James A	34738644	Pvt	INF	7	3	61	4 July	3203 Lincoln Ave Nashville Tenn
Harrell, James R	34973054	Pvt	INF	7	3	61	4 July	Rt 5 Box 177 Troy A
Helton, John C	34903400	Pvt	INF	7	3	61	4 July	RFD 3 Shelbyville T
Hoagland, Raymond L Jr	34971181	Pfc	INF	7	3	61	4 July	26 Audubon Pl Mobile
Hamilton, Ruddie M	34010945	Pvt	INF	7	3	61	4 July	Rt 2 Scottsboro Ala
Hampton, Bynum G Jr	6972007	Tec 4	MD	7	3	61	4 July	1704 S Greenwood Ave Chattanooga Tenn
Harper, Clyde N	34143684	Pvt	MD	7	3	61	4 July	1813 14th Ave N Nashville Tenn
LIBERATED POW (PROJECT R) (N male) AGSF ATLANTIC CITY NJ								A:
Higgins, Samuel C	14150151	Pfc	INF	7	3	60	3 July	203 Kenand Ave Mobil
Alphonse, Willie R	34654500	Tec 5	FA	7	3	60	3 July	Rt 1 Box 102 Daphne

(1st Ind ASF NYPE Camp Kilner NJ NJ 28 Apr 45 to Ltr Subj MO RO Gp B426-15 Hq Normandy Base Section Comm Z ETO APO 562 USA 12 Apr 45)
EM referred to in par above last ratione to include noon meal 1 May 45 and will lv this sta 1400 1 May 45 by rail and/or bus. TR was not furnished at this sta.

BY ORDER OF MAJOR DE WEES:

OFFICIAL:

JOHN L. BAKER

Assignments of white and black soldiers

He bangs on his head. "Well, I'll be damned. You are white. Oh, brother, I just got busted from Sergeant. See where the stripes were?" He points to his sleeve. "Now, another mistake. Well, they can't bust me any lower than a private." He continues, "You go on home. I will be sure you get another set of orders making you white and sending you to Miami Beach."

I make out like a bandit on this color deal. Alabama only sells liquor in state-owned stores. Soldiers on leave can purchase one bottle per set of orders, which are punched to prevent additional purchases. Since I have 60 sets of orders, I can buy 60 bottles of liquor!

Atlantic City orders revoked

```
                         R E S T R I C T E D

                HEADQUARTERS RECEPTION STATION #15              JCW/jfm
                      Fort McPherson, Georgia

SPECIAL ORDERS                                                  2 MAY 45

    NUMBER   1 2 2                  E X T R A C T

         1. So much of par 8 SO 121 this Hq cs insofar as it pertains to Pfc Samuel
    G Higgins 14150151 is deleted.

         2. Fol EM (W male) having ret US and rptd this Hq in compliance auth
    appearing first below name reld from dy this sta and trfd in gr Redistribution
    Sta indicated for processing and reasgmt. Delay enroute and tyl time indicated
    atzd. EM will rpt new sta on or before date indicated (all dates 1945). In
    accordance AR 35-4520 FD will pay in advance prescribed monetary alws in lieu
    rat for tyl a/r $1.00 per meal per man number meals indicated. TCP PCS TDN FSA.
    501-31 P 431-02 212/50425. Auth WD Ltr file AG 370.5 16 Aug 44 Subj PRI. and WD Ltr
    AG 383.6 (6 Apr 45) OP-C-A-SPAA Subj sept Apr 45. EDCMR 5 May 45.
                                             DAYS DAYS  RPTG
    NAME                ASN     GRADE BR. MEALS TYL DELAY DATE        ADDRESS
                                   AGSF R S MIAMI BEACH FLA
    LIBERATED PRISONER OF WAR (PROJECT "R")                                      Ala
    Higgins, Samuel G  14150151 Pfc   INF   7   3    62  5 Jul 208 Kenand Ave Mobile/
       (1st Ind ASF NYPE Camp Kilmer NB NJ 28 Apr 45 to Ltr Subj MO RO Gp E426-15 Hq
       Normandy Base Section Comm Z ETO APO 562 USA 12 Apr 45)
    (EM left this sta 1 May 45.)

         3. Par 26 SO 120 this Hq cs as reads "EDCMR" is amended to read "EDCMR 3 May
    45".


         4. Fol Off (W male) atchd TDY this Hq per auth appearing first below
    name WP address indicated. Upon arrival Off granted TD number days indicated
    for recuperation. Tyl time indicated atzd. Off will ret this sta on or before
    18 Jun 45. Provisions WD Cir 280 apply period tyl. TCT TDN FSA. 501-1 P 432-02
    212/50425. Auth WD Ltr file AG 370.5 16 Aug 44 as amended.

                                          DAYS DAYS
    NAME                ASN     GRADE BR TYL  TD      ADDRESS
    WHEELER, WALTER B  0588364  CAPT  BI  2   45     Rt 2 Maplewood Dr Rome Ga
       (1st Ind Hq ASF NYPE Fort Hamilton Brooklyn NY 25 Apr 45 to Ltr Subj Tyl Orders
       Hq Iceland Base Command APO 860 %PM New York NY 11 Apr 45)

    EM referred to above last rat this sta noon meal and left this sta 1400 1 May 45 by
    rail and/or bus. TR was not furn at this sta.


               BY ORDER OF MAJOR DE WEES:


    OFFICIAL:                                              JOHN L. BAKER
                                                           1st Lt AGD
                                                           Adj.
    J. C. WILLIS
    Capt INF
    Asst. Adj.

                         R E S T R I C T E D
```

Reassignment orders for Miami Beach

Eventually, I get a letter from Atlantic City. It rescinds the prior orders and instructions to report to Miami Beach 5 July 1945. But the real treat is another 60 copies of my orders. No one in my family drinks, so my 120 orders provide all my friends and their friends, sufficient liquor for parties galore. The liquor store employees are suspicious of me, but after reading the orders they just smile. "Better you than some draft-dodger."

Since butter and meat are rationed, I trade the liquor for chits to buy meat, butter, and cheese. Being tagged a Negro sure paid off.

My aunt gives me the letters I sent from prison camp. The telegram from the Army listing me as "missing in action" is dated 1 February, 1945; the one returning me to military control was 24 April 1945. Then on 25 April 1945, my aunt receives notice I am on the way back to the United States I call her on 28 April 1945. She is angry at the rapid turn of events, but adds, "At least you are home; skinny, but safe. I can put meat on those bones. God has answered our prayers."

The phone call from the newspaper for an interview embarrasses me. I don't want to have an interview, but relent under pressure from my aunt. I do not consider myself a hero. I only feel guilt and shame at being captured in my first battle. There are others from Mobile who had been POWs for two or three years, and some lost limbs or life. Reluctantly, I consent to an interview. My comments to the reporter are factual. The skimpy menu, general living conditions, chopping wood. How do you describe sadness or remorse over friends killed in battle? Or death from starvation or disease in prison camp? Can words describe the filth, the weakness, the hollow-eyed expressions on bodies that smelled and had festering sores? Or how the mere mention of meningitis or another possible epidemic struck fear in our hearts?

Would a reporter understand the four-inch diameter black spots on both my hips from sleeping on the floor? I doubt it. I even lied about the weight loss. I weighed 90 pounds, fully clothed, at the delousing tent, and that was after a week of gorging myself. My weight when captured was 155. No one, except a caged animal, can understand or appreciate existing, not living, behind electrified wire. Sure, a person will say "Tsk, tsk; how horrible," but will these experiences be burned on their soul? I doubt it, so I keep quiet.

Mobile Like Heaven To Ex-Nazi Prisoner

Samuel Higgins, Liberated By Patton At Bad Orb, Returns Home After Ordeal Of Three Months

Pfc. Samuel Higgins, after practically three months of privation at the hands of the Nazi war machine, is back in Mobile looking fine despite the loss of about 30 or 40 pounds. He is visiting his aunt and uncle, Mr. and Mrs. U. L. Perry, at 208 Kenan St. A prisoner-of-war at Bad Orb Prison Camp in Germany, Pvt. Higgins was among those freed when the camp was captured by Patton's Third Army on April 2. There were about 12,000 prisoners including 4000 Americans, at the camp.

"I am really glad to be back home. I didn't realize what a wonderful place Mobile was until I was at Bad Orb," Higgins said.

Tea, Soup and Bread

The daily menu at Bad Orb consisted of a cup of "tea," a bowl of soup and a piece of bread. In the morning each man received a cup of tea, which was actually nothing more than warm water.

"We couldn't drink the tea, so we put it to use by shaving in it," Higgins remarked with a grin.

"At noon we were given about a canteen cupful of soup—usually potato soup with peelings and all. After a while even that began to taste good. At night we each received a piece of soggy bread. Those of us who were sick had to have our bread toasted. There wasn't much left after that. Each man received a certain amount of grams per day.

Jammed Together

"We were jammed so close together in our quarters that we had to sleep on our backs in rows. We couldn't move, much less turn over, without knocking the other fellow in the face. The rooms were infested with lice."

"We were allowed only a few blankets for cover. The more fortunate of us slep on mattresses made of straw. I was one of the unlucky ones and slept on the floor. It was freezing cold and snow was always on the ground."

Old Men In Charge

The work performed by the inmates at the Nazi camp was made up chiefly of sawing wood and chopping down trees. Due to the lack of food, the men were not strong enough to perform heavier or more strenuous tasks.

"The men didn't torture us. Most of those in charge of the camp were old men."

When Bad Orb was liberated, Pvt. Higgins was among the first boatload of Americans to come to the States. Arriving in New York, he reached Mobile about a week ago and will be here for 60 days. He will report to Miami in July.

Going overseas in December, the soldier was reported missing in action on Jan. 8. His family received word of his capture by the Germans only after the camp was liberated.

Chapter 15

Journey's End

⊷ ▣◆▣ ⊶

After a few days at home, I hitchhike to my beloved Gulf of Mexico. I don't have a car. It's easy to catch a ride, especially when in uniform.

I walk on the white sand in front of the Gulf Shore Pavilion, recall my high school days when a cousin and her husband operated it. I sit on the sand and watch the jellyfish float in a quiet, soft surf. Even the seaweed looks good. The sand fleas scamper at the speed of light, dig into the sand when the water rushes back from the beach to the surf, afraid to be caught naked, I guess. These inch-long crustaceans live in a rough-and-tumble world where the waves meet the beach. Sort of like life. You gotta stay on the run to keep out of the way, to survive. I recall how I used a metal tea strainer to catch the fleas before they could escape the waves.

The vastness of the water beyond the foam that gently washes ashore reminds me of the omnipresence of God.

The early May sun warms my body. I wiggle my toes in the cool, wet sand, push my feet below the surface. My eyes blur and moisten as I watch each wave form in the distance, rise gently, and reveal the face of a B Company soldier I knew in Stalag IXB.

Robert Zion was tall and red-headed, with the dour eyes of an owl. Dark-haired Homer Smith was from Dothan, Alabama. I wonder if he got home? He left prison camp with the non-coms, even though he wasn't one. I pick up a handful of sand, let it fall through my fingers, and wonder if he was luckier than the rest of us.

Here comes Melvin Pray, with his thin, long black hair and serious eyes. I didn't see my ammunition bearer after we got to Stalag IXB, even though he was in the next barracks.

A wave forms out in the Gulf. I watch as it picks up speed. Hey, there is the face of Fred Gleason, the quick-witted, happy-go-lucky Irishman from Boston. He left prison camp in late February along with Hugh Cole. I shake my head as the sharp-nosed face of Hugh appears beside Fred. His mouth forms that Virginia accent of 'ought' and 'about.' Will we have the meal Fred, Pett, and I swore we would have?

Down the beach I see a wave form off shore. As it comes by me on my right on its way to the beach, I see the flash of sunlight reveal the steel glasses of the six-foot, red-headed body of Russell Huckel. He cocks his head sideways and winks. Behind him is the helmetless head of Don Pettingill. Further back I see the head of Norm Fellman, and the smile that cracks the corner of his mouth as he says, "How the hell did a small twerp like you get home so fast?"

I missed Norm's jovial bantering since the days at Fort Leonard Wood. I hated to see him leave Stalag IXB. He was in a group of 300 that included Robert Zion and a few others from our barracks. Norm was segregated before he left prison camp, because he was Jewish. Zion said he was not Jewish and stayed with our group until he left with the 300. I wonder what happened to him and whether or not he was Jewish?

The sun is warm. I lie on the sand, cover my eyes, and think about others in my Company. Capt. William Schmied, shot before we were captured, and carried away in a Jeep by the Jerries, with 1st Sgt. Carlos Ramos holding his head, tears in his eyes. I didn't realize first sergeants had compassion. There is Lt. Edward Groffie, Executive Officer; and Lt. Francis Buttrick my platoon leader; platoon sergeant Tom Holcombe; squad leader Walton Thibodeaux, and Joseph Albert, platoon sniper. I recall Paul Gartenmann, and how lucky he was to leave the company to be an interpreter for the battalion commander before we got captured. And just because he could speak German.

Company B, 275th Infantry, 70th Division, was a happy-go-lucky group of soldiers, a well-oiled machine. In one day, the realism of life rolled over us like an avalanche from Pikes Peak. All the thoughts, dreams, aspirations, and big talk of our youth were shattered and scattered to the winds. Were we lucky? Would any of us have lived through the war if we hadn't been captured? Who is alive now?

Only God knows, and He ain't telling.

I sit up and take the envelope, found on a table in my home, from my pocket. In the distinct handwriting of Uncle Leon, I read:

We of the younger generation look steadfastly to a world future when the crescendo of screaming shells shall have ended, a future when this nightmare of blood, sweat, and tears shall pass, and to the dawning of a more beautiful day when we may again practice the pursuit of a peaceful living, and resume the quest for happiness. End.

How beautiful, and prophetic. I didn't realize he was sentimental, much less poetic. Did he copy this quote? It is analogous to Churchill's "blood, sweat, toil and tears" speech. So what? It's still poetic.

For me, a new day has arrived. I am home. I am free. My quest for happiness? I'm not sure about that. For now, I'm happy just walking and sitting on the beach. I look at the blue sky and watch the puffs of white clouds drift eastward. To find what is beautiful in life, to think and act happy, is to me the essence of serenity.

No use thinking about the past. It is over, just as a wave becomes foam when it hits the beach. The beach is swept clean and the noises of humanity have not yet begun. My days in Stalag IXB are over. The past is gone, or at least buried in my psyche.

A glance seaward reminds me that each day is a new beginning, a new chapter in the pageant of life. My stomach growls. I recall a letter I sent home from Stalag IXB in which I wrote that when liberated I would appreciate the small things in life.

I belch as my stomach continues to growl. I smack my lips. I taste lemon. There is one piece of lemon pie left in the refrigerator.

Right now, that is the future. That will make me happy.

About the Author

Sam Higgins left his hometown of Mobile, Alabama, at the age of nineteen to join the Army, serving in the Air Force and Infantry. In 1944 during intense battles against the Germans in the Vosges Mountain Campaign portion of the Battle of the Bulge, Sam, a Browning Automatic Rifleman found himself surrounded and destined to become a prisoner of war. During his internment at Bad Orb, Germany, Sam secretly kept notes of his experiences in his pocket-sized, Army issue Bible. Fifty years later, these entries would serve as the basis of *Survival: Diary of an American POW in World War II.*

After his release, Higgins returned to the United States and attended the University of Alabama. He received his J.D. in 1949 and his M.B.A. in Labor Economics in 1950. He worked in the textile industry for E. I. duPont de Nemours & Co., Inc. and Rockwell International. Higgins wrote and published over 300 promotional and direct mail brochures, newsletters, and advertisements, such as the definitive, "duPont Fibers for Industry" in 1956.

After a few years, Higgins returned to college to pursue a second career in education. In 1972, he received an M.Ed. in Education from West Chester

State College (now West Chester University). In 1982, he received his Ph.D. in Philosophy with a Major in Education Administration from Florida State University. Higgins taught elementary to graduate school levels and worked as an industrial training specialist in South Carolina and Florida. His extensive experience, which includes conducting motivational workshops, public speaking, and producing and hosting faculty educational television programs, bears witness to his love for educating and writing.

It was not until he joined the Lafayette Park Writers Group in Tallahassee, Florida that Sam begin to explore the story of his capture during the war. The memories of Stalag IXB, its brutal conditions and interrogations, are remembered in *Survival: Diary of an American POW in World War II.*

Sam is currently writing about his experiences during the war prior to and including his capture, with the hope that lessons can be learned from them. Sam lives with his wife and most valued critic, Bernice, in Quincy, Florida.

K-9 SOLDIERS
Vietnam and After
by Paul B. Morgan

ISBN: 1-55571-495-1
Paperback: 13.95

A retired US Army officer, former Green Beret, Customs K-9 and Security Specialist, Paul B. Morgan has written *K-9 Soldiers*. In his book, Morgan relates twenty-four brave stories from his lifetime of working with man's best friend in combat and on the streets. They are the stories of dogs and their handlers who work behind the scenes when a disaster strikes, a child is lost or some bad guy tries to outrun the cops.

AFTER THE STORM
A Vietnam Veteran's Reflection
by Paul Drew

ISBN: 1-55571-500-1
Paperback: 14.95

Even after twenty-five years, the scars of the Vietnam War are still felt by those who were involved. *After the Storm: A Vietnam Veteran's Reflection* is more than a war story. Although it contains episodes of combat, it does not dwell on them. It concerns itself more on the mood of the nation during the war years, and covers the author's intellectual and psychological evolution as he questions the political and military decisions that resulted in nearly 60,000 American deaths.

GREEN HELL
The Battle for Guadalcanal
by William J. Owens

ISBN: 1-55571-498-6
Paperback: 18.95

This is the story of thousands of Melanesian, Australian, New Zealand, Japanese, and American men who fought for a poor insignificant island is a faraway corner of the South Pacific Ocean. For the men who participated, the real battle was of man against jungle. This is the account of land, sea and air units covering the entire six-month battle. Stories of ordinary privates and seamen, admirals and generals who survive to claim the victory that was the turning point of the Pacific War.

OH, WHAT A LOVELY WAR
A Soldier's Memoir
by Stanley Swift

ISBN: 1-55571-502-8
Paperback: 14.95

This book tells you what history books do not. It is war with a human face. It is the unforgettable memoir of British soldier Gunner Stanley Swift through five years of war. Intensely personal and moving, it documents the innermost thoughts and feelings of a young man as he moves from civilian to battle-hardened warrior under the duress of fire.

THROUGH MY EYES
91st Infantry Division, Italian Campaign 1942-1945
by Leon Weckstein

ISBN: 1-55571-497-8
Paperback: 14.95

Through My Eyes is the true account of an Average Joe's infantry days before, during and shortly after the furiously fought battle for Italy. The author's front row seat allows him to report the shocking account of casualties and the rest-time shenanigans during the six weeks of the occupation of the city of Trieste. He also recounts in detail his personal roll in saving the historic Leaning Tower of Pisa.

GULF WAR DEBRIEFING BOOK

An After Action Report
by Andrew Leyden

ISBN: 1-55571-396-3
Paperback: 18.95

Whereas most books on the Persian Gulf War tell an "inside story" based on someone else's opinion, this book lets you draw your own conclusions by providing you with a meticulous review of events and documentation all at your fingertips. Includes lists of all military units deployed, a detailed account of the primary weapons used during the war, and a look at the people and politics behind the military maneuvering.

FROM HIROSHIMA WITH LOVE

by Raymond A. Higgins

ISBN: 1-55571-404-8
Paperback: 18.95

This remarkable story is written from actual detailed notes and diary entries kept by Lieutenant Commander Wallace Higgins. Because of his industrial experience back in the United States and with the reserve commission in the Navy, he was an excellent choice for military governor of Hiroshima. Higgins was responsible for helping rebuild a ravaged nation of war. He developed an unforeseen respect for the Japanese, the culture, and one special woman.

NIGHT LANDING

A Short History of West Coast Smuggling
by David W. Heron

ISBN: 1-55571-449-8
Paperback: 13.95

Night Landing reveals the true stories of smuggling off the shores of California from the early 1800s to the present. It is a provocative account of the many attempts to illegally trade items such as freon, drugs, sea otters, and diamonds. This unusual chronicle also profiles each of these ingenious, but over-optimistic criminals and their eventual apprehension.

ORDER OF BATTLE

Allied Ground Forces of Operation Desert Storm
by Thomas D. Dinackus

ISBN: 1-55571-493-5
Paperback: 17.95

Based on extensive research, and containing information not previously available to the public, *Order of Battle* is a detailed study of the Allied ground combat units that served in Operation Desert Storm. In addition to showing unit assignments, it includes the insignia and equipment used by the various units in one of the largest military operations since the end of WWII.

PILOTS, MAN YOUR PLANES!

A History of Naval Aviation
by Wilbur H. Morrison

ISBN: 1-55571- 466-8
Hardbound: 33.95

An account of naval aviation from Kitty Hawk to the Gulf War, *Pilots, Man Your Planes! — A History of Naval Aviation* tells the story of naval air growth from a time when planes were launched from battleships to the major strategic element of naval warfare it is today. Full of detailed maps and photographs. Great for anyone with an interest in aviation.